Howard W. French

Everything Under the Heavens

Howard W. French wrote from Africa for *The Washington Post* and at *The New York Times* was bureau chief in Central America and the Caribbean, West and Central Africa, Japan, and China. He is the recipient of two Overseas Press Club awards and a two-time Pulitzer Prize nominee. He is the author of *A Continent for the Taking: The Tragedy and Hope of Africa* and *China's Second Continent: How a Million Migrants Are Building a New Empire in Africa*; he has written for *The Atlantic*, *The New York Review of Books*, *The New York Times Magazine*, and *Rolling Stone*, among other national publications. He is on the faculty of the Columbia University Graduate School of Journalism.

www.howardwfrench.com

Everything
Under the
Heavens

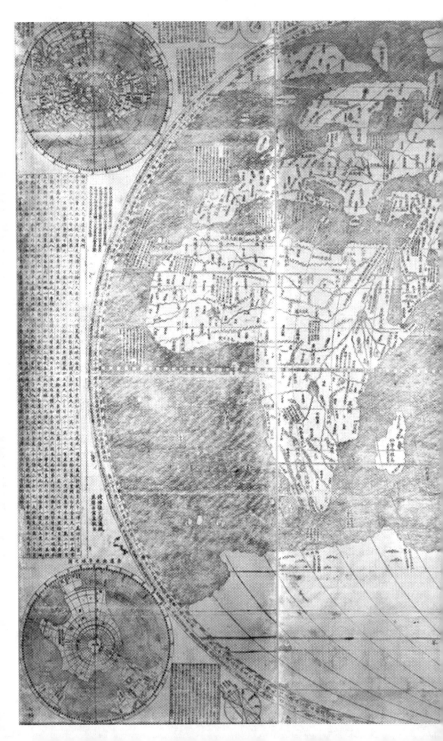

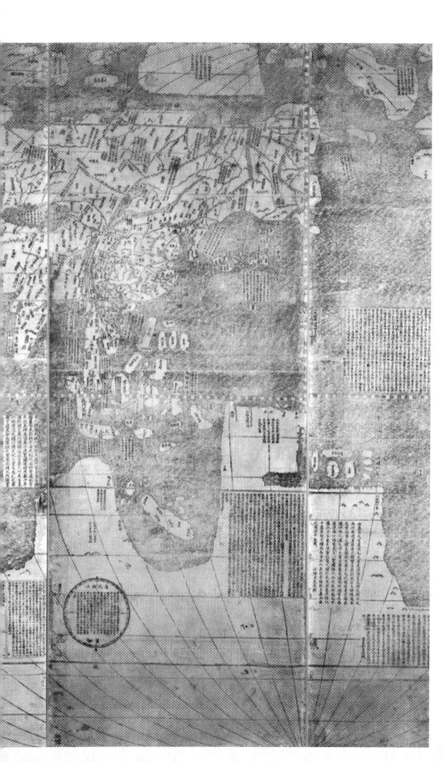

Everything Under the Heavens

HOW
THE PAST
HELPS SHAPE
CHINA'S PUSH
FOR GLOBAL POWER

Howard W. French

VINTAGE BOOKS
A Division of Penguin Random House LLC
New York

For those whom you love,

words can never suffice.

FIRST VINTAGE BOOKS EDITION, FEBRUARY 2018

Copyright © 2017, 2018 by Howard W. French

All rights reserved. Published in the United States by Vintage Books, a division of Penguin Random House LLC, New York, and distributed in Canada by Random House of Canada, a division of Penguin Random House Canada Limited, Toronto. Originally published in hardcover in the United States by Alfred A. Knopf, a division of Penguin Random House LLC, New York, in 2017.

Vintage and colophon are registered trademarks of Penguin Random House LLC.

The Library of Congress has cataloged the Knopf edition as follows:
Names: French, Howard W., author.
Title: Everything under the heavens : how the past helps shape China's push for global power / Howard W. French.
Description: First edition. | New York : Alfred A. Knopf, [2017] | Includes bibliographical references and index.
Identifiers: LCCN 2016021957
Subjects: LCSH: China—Foreign relations—21st century. | China—Foreign relations—Asia. | Asia—Foreign relations—China. | Strategic culture—China. | Geopolitics—Asia.
Classification: LCC JZ1734 .F74 2017 | DDC 327.51—dc23
LC record available at https://lccn.loc.gov/2016021957

Vintage Books Trade Paperback ISBN: 978-0-8041-7245-5
eBook ISBN: 978-0-385-35333-5

Author photograph © Stuart Isett
Cloud illustrations © Peratek/Shutterstock.com
Border illustrations on pages xiii & xiv © poppindx/Shutterstock.com
Frontispiece: 1602 map of the world presented to the Ming dynasty
by the Jesuit priest Matteo Ricci
"Map of National Shame": Dongfang Yudi Xueshe
All other maps by Mapping Specialists, Ltd
Book design by Betty Lew

www.vintagebooks.com

147468846

Everywhere under vast Heaven
There is no land that is not the king's.
To the borders of those lands
There are none who are not the king's servants.

—from *The Book of Odes,*
Zhou dynasty (1046–256 BCE)

If those who are distant do not submit, one must cultivate patterns and virtue to attract them.

—Confucius (551–479 BCE)

The fact of the matter is that our China must be regarded as the root of all other countries.

—Li Ruzhen, 1827

A naval empire has always given the peoples who possessed it a natural pride, because, feeling themselves able to insult others everywhere, they believe that their power is as boundless as the ocean.

—Charles de Montesquieu, from
The Spirit of the Laws, 1748

Let the House recollect that our empire in the East was founded on the force of opinion; and if we submitted to the degrading insults of China, the time would not be far distant when our political ascendancy . . . would be at an end.

—Sir Thomas Staunton, speech to the
British House of Commons, 1840

Contents

TIMELINE OF CHINESE DYNASTIES AND OTHER KEY EVENTS

ca. 2100–1600 BCE	Xia (Hsia) dynasty	
ca. 1600–1046 BCE	Shang dynasty	Capitals: near present-day Zhengzhou and Anyang
ca. 1046–256 BCE	Zhou (Chou) dynasty	Capitals: Hao (near present-day Xi'an) and Luoyang
	Western Zhou (ca. 1046–771 BCE)	
	Eastern Zhou (ca. 771–256 BCE)	Spring and Autumn Period (770–ca. 475 BCE)
		Confucius (ca. 551–479 BCE)
		Warring States Period (ca. 475–221 BCE)
221–206 BCE	Qin (Ch'in) dynasty	Capital: Chang'an, present-day Xi'an
		Qin Shihuang dies, 210 BCE
206 BCE–220 CE	Han dynasty	
	Western/Former Han (206 BCE–9 CE)	Capital: Chang'an
		Confucianism officially established as basis for Chinese state by Han Wudi (r. 141–86 BCE) Luoyang
220–589 CE	Six Dynasties period	Period of disunity and instability following the fall of the Han; Buddhism introduced to China
	Three Kingdoms (220–65 CE)	Cao Wei, Shu Han, Dong Wu
	Period of the Northern and Southern Dynasties (386–589 CE)	
581–618 CE	Sui dynasty	Capital: Chang'an
618–907 CE	Tang (T'ang) dynasty	Capitals: Chang'an and Luoyang
907–60 CE	Five Dynasties period	
960–1279	Song (Sung) dynasty	
1271–1368	Yuan dynasty Reign of the Mongol empire	Capital: Dadu (present-day Beijing)

TIMELINE OF CHINESE DYNASTIES AND OTHER KEY EVENTS

1368–1644	Ming dynasty	Reestablishment of rule by Han ruling house; Capitals: Nanjing and Beijing
1644–1912	Qing (Ch'ing) dynasty Reign of the Manchus	Capital: Beijing
1912–49	Republican period	Capitals: Beijing, Wuhan and Nanjing
1949–present	People's Republic of China	Capital: Beijing

Everything
Under the
Heavens

Introduction

There was once a country at the very center of the world, whose position was recognized as such by peoples both far and wide. Today, we call that country China.

Using the very word "country" is actually deceptive. The nation that we now instantly identify on the map as China hasn't existed long. Throughout most of its history this dynastically ruled land would not even have recognized itself as a country, let alone seen its neighbors as such. It was an empire, and a largely borderless one, both in its geographical form and in what it considered to be the relevance or applicability—what the French would call the *rayonnement*—of its ideas. One could argue that there has never been a more universal conception of rule. Practically speaking, for the emperors of the Central Kingdom, this place we call China, the world could be roughly divided into two broad and simple categories, civilization and non-civilization, meaning the peoples who accepted the supremacy of its ruler, the Son of Heaven, and the principle of his celestial virtue, and those who didn't—those who were beyond the pale.*

For the better part of two millennia, the norm for China, from its own perspective, was a natural dominion over everything under

---

*As the Yale political scientist James C. Scott explains in his book *The Art of Not Being Governed,* at least since the twelfth century the Chinese have made a further distinction among the "uncivilized," dividing this world into two categories, "raw" and "cooked," with the latter meaning amenable to assimilation.

heaven, a concept known in the Chinese language as *tian xia.*[*] It is not a term to be taken too literally. From very early times, China had an awareness of faraway places, including other great empires, like Rome, but contact with such distant regions of the world was tenuous at best and hence both economically and politically marginal.

In the geopolitics of Chinese empire, what was most vital to the Central Kingdom under *tian xia*, sometimes interpreted as the "known world" in this context, was a vast and familiar swath of geography that consisted of nearby Central Asia, Southeast Asia and East Asia. Among these regions, Central Asia constituted a near-constant challenge to Chinese power, and quite often an outright threat. The dimensions of the Central Kingdom ebbed and flowed, mostly as a function of the shifting balance of power between Han (Chinese) and the peoples to the west and northwest, be they Turkic, Mongol, Manchurian, Tibetan or others. (China itself would come to be ruled by invaders from two of these cultures, the Mongols, from 1271 to 1368, and the Manchus, from 1644 to 1912, at the very end of the dynastic era.)

In geographical terms, we usually think of oceans as barriers that effectively separate countries, regions and continents, and in the faraway past nearly sealed them off from one another. But the littoral of East Asia, which runs in a gently articulated crescent from the Korean Peninsula south to the Strait of Malacca, has more typically served as

---

[*] *Tian xia* is customarily translated as "all under heaven," though I prefer the slightly modified form "everything under the heavens." In his book *Ancient Chinese Thought, Modern Chinese Power,* the prominent Chinese political scientist Yan Xuetong cited the ancient classic *The Book of Odes* to explain these terms: "The term all under heaven was virtually synonymous with the world. The title Son of Heaven referred to the person who ruled over all people on the earth as the representative of Heaven. The emperors of China's feudal times called themselves Son of Heaven, which shows that they thought of themselves as rulers of the world. The idea that 'under heaven's canopy there is nowhere that is not the king's land; up to the sea's shores, there are none who are not the king's servants' illustrates that the contention for the power of Son of Heaven was, from another point of view, a contention for world-leadership."

a transmission belt for Chinese culture and prestige, Chinese commerce, and ultimately for Chinese power, although only occasionally hard power. From at least the Tang dynasty (618–907) nearly to the chaotic end of dynastic rule in China in 1912, to one extent or another, the peoples of this sea-bound region often found ways to defer to China, acknowledging its centrality and loosely following its lead.

Functioning in this way, Chinese power came to underpin one of the most remarkable international systems that human civilization has ever seen—a unique form of what has sometimes been described as an extremely loose and distant brand of indirect rule by China over a very considerable slice of humanity. This description is inadequate in part because there were important variations in China's relations with its eastern neighbors, including degrees of intensity of both contact and obeisance. But at the foundation of this remarkably resilient Pax Sinica lay a basic proposition that was reasonably consistent: Accept our superiority and we will confer upon you political legitimacy, develop a trade partnership and provide a range of what are known in the language of modern international affairs as public goods. These included policing the maritime commons, mediating disputes and granting access to China's would-be universal system of learning, broadly based on Confucianism. In the core states of this region—Korea, Vietnam and, albeit with growing ambivalence, Japan—Chinese values, Chinese culture, the Chinese language, Chinese philosophy and Chinese religion were all regarded for long stretches of history as essential references, and even universal standards.

The "system" referred to here has long been known in the West (and yet never among Chinese themselves) as China's tribute system. Throughout this period, beginning as far back as the Han dynasty (206 BCE–220 CE), peoples in China's imperial orbit regularly dispatched "embassies" to perform ritual submission before the Chinese emperor. The granting of trade rights by the imperial court by way of reward represented a tremendous boon that served as a powerful lubricant in bilateral relations. When the Chinese spoke of this system, their language was often full of euphemism and self-regard, frequently referring to the task of what would today be called in foreign policy "barbarian management."

"To control the barbarians the sage rulers punished and resisted them when they came [to invade China], and prepared and guarded against them when they left," reads one nineteenth-century account. "If attracted by China's civilization, they came to offer tribute, they would be treated with courtesy, and kept under loose rein without severing the relationship, so that the blame of being crooked would always be on them."

Within this system, foreign leaders often owed their very titles to the grant of recognition via patents of appointment bestowed by the Chinese emperor. Even as they sat on their thrones, new rulers in compliant tributary states had to content themselves with the title of heir apparent until they could receive their letters of investiture from the Celestial Emperor, for fear of infringing protocol.

Just how seriously this business was taken is vividly conveyed by a story from second-century BCE Vietnam, when a local king got it into his head to proclaim himself emperor in his own land. The response of the Han dynasty emperor Wen-Di was swift and unequivocal. "When two emperors appear simultaneously, one must be destroyed . . . struggling and not yielding is not the way of a person endowed with humanity," he wrote to scold the Vietnamese ruler, whose response was one of abject submission. "I hear that two heroes cannot appear together, that two sages cannot exist in the same generation," he stated in a public proclamation. "The Han emperor is the sagacious Son of Heaven. Henceforth, I shall suppress my own imperial edicts." This pushback from China operated at two levels. Most explicitly, it was a direct statement that in its home region, the Han emperor would not countenance any would-be peers. Beyond that, China was signaling its determination to intervene anywhere in the world where it felt its central role or its vital interests might be challenged. In 1979, more than two thousand years later, as we shall see, China would mount an invasion of Vietnam aimed at making these precise points.

In fact, China would invade Vietnam numerous times during the succeeding centuries, which still resonates powerfully in their relationship today. But using violence to get its way was far from the ideal. As the Japanese scholar Takeshi Hamashita has written, "Like any hegemonic order [the tribute system] was backed by military force, but when the system functioned well, principles of reciprocity involving politics and economics permitted long periods of peaceful interaction."

It has often been argued that the tribute system cost China more in trade concessions and in the constant hosting of visiting foreign delegations than any economic benefit it might have derived from commerce with an assortment of much smaller neighboring societies. But this is to ignore the domestic political value of the system for China's emperors. As important as it was for neighboring rulers to enjoy the recognition of the Central Kingdom, it was equally important for the authority of a succession of Chinese emperors to have symbolically obeisant foreigners bowing regularly to their moral prestige and power. In other words, the willing subservience of others to prostrate themselves before the emperor provided domestic proof of his unassailable moral authority, of his possession of, in the well-worn phrase, the mandate of heaven. This was as true near the end of China's imperial era as it was during early dynasties, such as the Han. When Britain, approaching the apogee of its global power in the late eighteenth century, sent a mission to China to try to establish relations on an equal footing with the Qing dynasty, Emperor Qianlong exceptionally granted permission for the envoy of King George III to visit Beijing, on the basis that it would "contribute to the Emperor's glory." Finally arriving in China after a nine-month sea voyage, the British were disconcerted to find that all along the route to the capital were hung banners written in large characters proclaiming that the European delegation was led by an "envoy paying tribute to the Great Emperor." Indeed, Qianlong's court had informed the public that the head of the foreign delegation, the Irishman George Macartney, was a member of the British royal family who had traversed the oceans in order to "contemplate Civilization."

"Most dynasties collapsed under the twin blows of 'inside disorder and outside calamity' (nei-luan wai-huan), that is, domestic rebellion and foreign invasion," wrote John King Fairbank, the eminent Harvard scholar of the tribute system. "Every regime was therefore under pressure to make the facts of its foreign relations fit the theory and so confirm its claim to rule China."

The essence of this thought survives even in contemporary Chinese political thought. As Wang Jisi, dean of the School of International Studies at Peking University, wrote in 2015, "Ever since the founding of 'New China' in 1949, China's foreign and domestic policies have both served the same goal: to maintain internal political stability under the leadership of the Communist Party."

It is scarcely appreciated in the West today that the "international system" we so readily take for granted is actually a recent creation. It took shape between the middle of the nineteenth and the middle of the twentieth centuries, and started to be cobbled together at the precise moment that China was being subjugated by others and the world order it had sustained, and that had in turn sustained it for so long, was being replaced.

As our modern world was being born, China was plummeting toward a historical nadir in its relative regional power and influence. The norm for it had long been an unshakable conviction in the enduring universality of its values and ethics, its own culture, and its unquestioned centrality. The new, Western form of global universality was based not on a presumed natural hierarchy in the world, with China at the apex, but rather on the presumed equality (at least legally and theoretically) of clearly defined nations, on a raft of Judeo-Christian ideas and institutions, on spreading principles of electoral democracy, on open trade instead of managed tributary exchanges, and finally on a fast-emerging regime of international law. Underwriting all of these fine-sounding notions was, of course, Western and, in the twentieth century above all, American power.

China's experience of its own successful and long-lasting international system, and of its long and mostly unchallenged status as the standard-setter of civilization itself by right, would have necessarily made a shift to almost anything new a difficult downgrade.

But to an extent that is underappreciated in the West, the brutal circumstances of the transition to what is our now familiar world, coming at a moment of unprecedented Chinese weakness, feeds an unusually deep-seated ambivalence toward contemporary norms, which is becoming more and more apparent with each passing year of increasing Chinese power.

Fairbank wrote with considerable understatement nearly fifty years ago, when China was ruled in largely autarkic fashion by Mao Zedong in near-permanent, revolutionary tension with the postwar system, "Modern China's difficulty of adjustment to the international order of nation-states in the nineteenth and twentieth centuries has come partly from the great tradition of the Chinese world order. This tradition is of more than historical interest and bears upon Chinese thinking today."

In its most familiar form, the narrative of the demise of the Chinese world order is the story of rampaging Western imperialism's triumphant march into East Asia. In its textbooks and in its nationalist propaganda, China itself has styled the one-hundred-year period during which the modern world was built as its Century of Humiliation, with Britain's Opium Wars and the sack of Beijing by both Britain and France accorded pride of place. Although the aggressive expansion of Western powers into the China-centered world of East Asia was a critical fact of that period, it seems more likely that what the West achieved was in reality the early transformation of the old Chinese world that would soon lead to even more dramatic changes. Principally these would be wrought not by Westerners but rather by historically subsidiary nations in East Asia, as the yawning discrepancy between China's self-image and geopolitical reality became unsustainable.

Although there were many actors in Asia seeking their own separate accommodations with the nascent international order, the main driver of the change that definitively closed the curtains on the two-millennia-old Sinocentric order in the region was without doubt imperial Japan. It defeated its much larger neighbor in 1895 in the Sino-Japanese War, and thereafter surged ahead of it according to almost every measure of national power over the next half century, only to be driven out of China and defeated in World War II, mostly as a result of reckless military overreach. But even in the decades following its ultimate defeat by the United States, Japan has remained well ahead of China in numerous ways, most obviously in per capita wealth and quality of life, but also, even if the lead here is shrinking, in things like technological advancement and global cultural influence. If nothing else, Japan's grab for great power, coming very largely at China's expense, proved the enduring relevance of the previously quoted maxim "When two emperors appear simultaneously, one must be destroyed." Indeed, up until the present day, East Asia has never proven large enough for two great powers to coexist peacefully, and the question of whether this will be possible in the future looms darkly over the region and frames many of the questions to be explored in these pages.

Seen from this angle, the lingering place of the tribute system in the Chinese psyche takes on a new importance. It was one thing for China to be humiliated by the West; Chinese thinkers have taken comfort in the idea that barbarians from afar could never have been expected to accept the Central Kingdom's virtue and cultural superiority. But the defeats administered beginning in the late nineteenth century by an upstart Japan, for the Chinese an intrinsically inferior nation whose very origins lay in immense cultural debt to China in everything from writing systems and literature to religion and governance, were a different matter, and the energies unleashed by this history are still profoundly at work in the world today. The towering early-twentieth-century Chinese intellectual and seminal figure in the birth of the country's modern nationalism, Liang Qichao, wrote that China's loss in the Sino-Japanese War "awakened my country from the long dream of four thousand years."

During most of the second half of the twentieth century, including most of the Maoist era, Beijing took a relatively relaxed attitude toward Japan, eagerly absorbing its technology and increasingly massive investments and studying its successes once China's so-called reform and opening period got under way in the early 1980s. As it did so, Beijing mostly deemphasized the divisive past. China similarly took a largely accepting view of American military primacy in

East Asia in the post-Mao era. In hindsight, with both of these positions recently having changed dramatically in the space of less than
a decade marked by sharp national ascent, one is tempted to say that
China simply made a pragmatic calculation that it was too weak to
do anything about either of these situations and should therefore
concentrate on quietly building its strength. This it has certainly
done, and today, as China's self-regard has swollen, along with its
newfound power, Japan has returned to the center of the Chinese
gaze in the form of a bull's-eye; the focus of Beijing's approach to
the country (and indeed to the entire sea-bound region that once
defined the tribute system, and especially Vietnam and the Philippines) is to restore what from the perspective of the Central Kingdom
is considered the natural order. This, it must be said, is not merely the
preoccupation of the Chinese state, though. It has also increasingly
become a consuming obsession of rising populist nationalism. Success or failure in this grand pursuit, therefore, will go far in determin-
ing the legitimacy of China's leaders, from the assertive incumbent
president, Xi Jinping, onward, and indeed could well decide the survival or failure of the Chinese Communist Party.

China's ultimate goal, however, is not merely to restore a sem-
blance of the region's old order, an updated kind of tributary system
in which the nations of Southeast Asia or even a wealthy and customarily diffident Japan will have no choice but to hitch their fortunes
to it and bow to Beijing's authority. A larger, more ambitious goal is
already edging into view. This ambition, evident from behavior even
if still not fully avowed, involves supplanting American power and
influence in the region as an irreplaceable stepping-stone along the
way to becoming a true global power in the twenty-first century. Shi
Yinhong, one of China's most prominent foreign policy realist thinkers, has written that Xi's goal is "to give [China] a dominant role in
Asia and the Western Pacific—at the cost of the U.S.'s ascendancy."
In a conversation with me, he added, "The West shouldn't think so
much about integrating China into the Western liberal order, but
rather try to accommodate China." This, he said, would ultimately
mean having the United States accept military parity with China in
the Pacific, the ceding of what he called a "narrow but substantial

span of strategic space" for China in the nearby seas, and a loosening of America's alliance structure in the region.

Even though he is a respected insider, Shi's vision is provisional and anything but official. It points us nonetheless toward perhaps the most important question there is in this era's realm of international relations: What kind of power is China likely to become? What follows is an extended reading of the country's long past undertaken in order to comprehend how it has conceived of and used its power historically. I do not believe in what is sometimes referred to as cultural DNA. With their infinite contingencies, China, and indeed the world, is far too complicated for anything so simple as that. And yet in drawing on these traditions and exploring a number of historical Chinese reflexes, I believe we may better inform our sense of how China might exercise its growing national power in the decades ahead.

CHAPTER ONE

National Humiliation

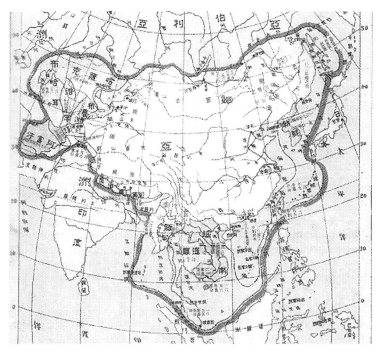

"Map of National Shame"

To travel the twelve hundred miles southwest from Tokyo to Yonaguni, a tiny island at the farthest end of the Ryukyu chain, in a single day requires setting out early and flying on one of the two days of the week when the connections match up in Naha, the capital of Okinawa Prefecture.

During the postwar era, Japan has enjoyed a reputation as perhaps the most peaceful major country in the world. But in Okinawa, even from the air there is no escaping how incomplete, or even deceptive, this widely accepted picture is. Upon our final approach before landing in Naha, three of Japan's white Self-Defense Force (SDF) fighters, spooling contrails in their wake, darted parallel to us in formation. Down below, both at dock and at sea, were SDF coast guard cutters and other smaller ships whose white hulls stood out against the placid-looking blue carpet of the Pacific.

Okinawa is the island where American-led Allied forces famously launched their ferocious invasion of Japan in early April 1945, losing 14,000 personnel while killing at least five times as many Japanese soldiers, along with between 42,000 and 150,000 civilians. Okinawa was captured in order to serve as the springboard for what would have been a far more challenging assault on Japan's so-called home islands, aimed at capturing Tokyo or forcing surrender. As it happened, the war was brought to an end by the dropping of atomic bombs on Hiroshima and Nagasaki that August. This hardly meant the end of the American story on Okinawa.

The Americans never left. Over the next seven decades the island became the most important anchor of American power in the Western Pacific, enabling the United States to hedge, or balance, seemingly indefinitely against China, whose mainland lay a mere four hundred miles to the west. From the perspective of the locals, that has made it the unhappy home of about 63 percent of the roughly twenty-five thousand American troops who are permanently stationed in Japan, despite the fact that Okinawa makes up less than 1 percent of Japan's total landmass.

On the connecting flight to Yonaguni, we strung our way along a necklace of tiny islands that drooped off to the southwest from Okinawa, first past Miyako, then Iriomote and then an assemblage of smaller others—some flat as pancakes and patterned in the green geometric fields of commercial agriculture, others darkly mountainous, their coral approaches ringed by encroaching circular tides. Most of the visitors who come this way are drawn by great surfing or diving or the prospect of a rustic nature retreat, all of which these islands offer in abundance. The specks of land below are of greater interest, however, because they have served as interstitial tissue in the ebb and flow of empires, and today are the focus of an enormous geopolitical contest that has recently resumed in this part of East Asia. It was here, in this watery realm, that China, drawing on a combination of newfound wealth and power and some impatience, was girding for a showdown with Japan, the neighbor that had most persistently defied it over the past thirteen centuries.

For hundreds of years this string of islands, often collectively referred to simply as Okinawa, a name that fittingly means "a rope in the offing," had been the quasi-independent kingdom of Ryukyu. Throughout much of that time, for China, this tiny monarchy had mostly served as a reminder of the nuisances of the tribute system, because the hospitality costs associated with hosting frequent visits by embassies from such a small vassal state were far out of proportion to the value of bilateral trade, so much so that Beijing made little noise about its loss when Japan annexed the islands in 1879. At altitude on a cloudless day, though, it is easy to understand how important an impediment the Ryukyus may now seem to be for the global aspirations of a rising power that sees itself as increasingly entitled.

In its entirety, Japan takes the shape of an elongated archipelago, a gently curved scythe stretching all the way from the icy ports of Russia south to the doorstep of semitropical fringes of the South China Sea. For the purposes of maritime navigation, the archipelago serves as an immense picket fence that looms off of China's shores, restricting access to the open waters of the Pacific to a handful of easily guarded choke points. At its southern end, at Yonaguni, the westernmost point of Japan, it also comes within eyesight of Taiwan, just sixty-two miles distant. For this reason, and for reasons of history as well, the Ryukyus have come to powerfully concentrate China's attention. It is here that this fence is at once its most fragile and strategic, sitting astride critical sea lanes connecting southern China and the vast blue waters of the Pacific Ocean.

During China's nearly four decades of recent resurgence, Japan has represented many things to Beijing. Early in China's opening-up period, it was, as noted, an important source of investment, especially during the 1980s. For the second time in its modern history, China saw Japan as a country that it could study and learn from economically and copy selectively as it modernized. Shortly thereafter, as an accelerating China began to pile up successes, Japan became a benchmark to be overtaken in order to affirm that China's destiny had been redeemed and its true potential was being realized. Although China remains far poorer on a per capita basis, an important milestone was crossed along this path in 2009, when it displaced its neighbor to become the world's second-largest economy.

But in modern times economics has represented only one dimension of the deeply competitive dynamic between the two countries. Despite its unique "peace constitution," a legacy of its World War II defeat and American occupation, Japan is inescapably seen by Beijing as a major military rival supported by a sixty-year-old alliance with the United States, and it must be overcome if China is to recover the status it regards as its due in the region. This was stated with striking baldness even for a frequently bombastic Beijing-based newspaper, the nationalist *Global Times*. In a September 2014 editorial, it declared, "We should try to gain overwhelming advantages over Japan in major areas. Tokyo only shows respect to countries that have once heavily struck it or possess much greater strategic ability." And since the early years of this century, a campaign to demonstrate this greater capability has been under way, with China sending coast guard, fishing patrol vessels, and even naval ships into the surrounding waters of the Ryukyu chain, as well as aircraft into the skies overhead, both to challenge its neighbor's claims to sovereignty over the islands and to wear Japan down.

Had it been a theatrical production, this resumed contest between Japan and China could have been titled "The Revenge of History." Its chief protagonist was a revitalized China, as energized and motivated as an aggrieved legal plaintiff in a liability case freshly recovered from a severe injury caused by the other party's willful misconduct. And the interim award for damages that it seeks to recover consists of a group of five small islands and three barren rocks, collectively known as the Senkaku Islands, which are adjacent to but geologically distinct from the Ryukyus. Japan has controlled this uninhabited real estate since it annexed the Senkakus in 1895, which may seem like a long time by the standards of the familiar international system that governs our world, but is of course a mere blink of the eye in China's long history. Chinese imperial records mention the islands as a well-known navigational marker on the seafarers' route to the Ryukyu kingdom as early as the fifteenth century. But even more important to an aggrieved China is the timing of Japan's annexation of the islands following its defeat of China, accelerating the collapse of the age-old Sinocentric world.

Yonaguni measures a bare eleven square miles, and its only real town is Sonai. Outside Sonai, one could go for hours without encountering another person. When I visited the island I made a brief stop at a horse farm to ask for directions. There, I struck up a conversation with a worker, who eagerly briefed me on what for him was clearly rare big news. The Japanese government had made a locally unpopular decision to build a radar station on Yonaguni, along with a billet for its newly constituted marines, he said. He pointed to a dramatic escarpment in the near distance where the station was to be built. "Most people here don't want a base on this island," he said. "But for quick deployment there is surely no better location."*

Actually, I had already read items in the Japanese press saying that tiny Yonaguni was being put into play in a major way in an intensifying renewal of a competition between Tokyo and Beijing whose origins lay fourteen hundred years in the past. At that time, a Japanese empress named Suiko sent an "embassy" to the Sui dynasty capital, Chang'an, led by a diplomat bearing a letter informing the Chinese court, in effect, that in protocol terms Japan would no longer be content to play the role of an ordinary vassal and considered itself to be on equal footing with the Central Kingdom.

---

*The radar station was inaugurated in March 2016, and Japan has announced that it will boost its Self-Defense Force presence in the Ryukyus by 20 percent over the next five years, as well as install new missile batteries.

One way to understand the Japanese move to build an early warning station and rapid response base on Yonaguni is simply to regard it as the latest reenactment of this flintiness; a firm and very public statement that Tokyo would not be intimidated by China's size, its might or its bluster. But unlike in the past, when flintiness was cushioned by the two countries' coexistence as neighbors with limited contact, now they lived edgily in almost promiscuous closeness.

Another way to view it, however, is simply as prudence. A few months after my visit to Yonaguni, another confirmation of its special place in the looming struggle between Japan and China was delivered by James Fanell, director of intelligence for the U.S. Pacific Fleet. Speaking at a Navy conference in San Diego, Fanell made a surprisingly blunt pronouncement about Beijing's designs on the area, citing its large-scale military exercises in 2013 to claim that China was preparing for a "short, sharp war to destroy Japanese forces in the East China Sea, following with what can only be an expected seizure of the Senkakus."

Captain Fanell's comments were immediately criticized by many in the foreign policy community for their alarmism, and a few months later he was quietly forced into early retirement. But looking at Beijing's actions in the waters of the East China Sea, it is difficult to escape the conclusion that either China is preparing to do just as Fanell said, or it wishes to instill fear in the minds of the Japanese, and most likely of the Americans too, of such an eventuality.

Since 2010, the narrow seas between the two countries have seen a severe ratcheting up of pressure on Japan as Beijing has used a range of steadily more assertive tactics. In January 2013, a Chinese frigate locked its firing radar on a Japanese destroyer, an action that is customarily taken as a threat of imminent use of force, especially in an encounter between unfriendly countries in contested territory. Under circumstances like these, it is not hard to imagine how a conflict between the two nations could easily break out by accident, as when two fighter aircraft or opposing coast guard vessels collide, with a loss of life.

There are precedents for such dangerous mishaps. The United States and China were plunged into a major bilateral crisis under circumstances like this in 2001, when a Chinese fighter pilot died in a crash after bumping a U.S. Navy EP-3E surveillance aircraft gathering signals intelligence just off the Chinese coast, seventy miles from Hainan Island. The very large power differential between China and the United States at the time prevented military retaliation by Beijing, confining the damage to diplomatic relations.

The gap in power between China and Japan in the contested seas that separate them, however, is much narrower, with Japan widely presumed to hold a tenuous and increasingly vulnerable lead. Practically, this means that even if China has not chosen this as quite the right moment for a direct confrontation, it could prove very hard or indeed impossible for it to back down after a fatal accident, particularly one in which it came off as the initial loser. The main reason for this is history—past history as well as the making of a new and future one.

After taking power in November 2012, Xi Jinping wasted little time setting the tone for his expected ten-year tenure in office. His first trip outside of the capital was to visit troops in the Guangzhou Military Region, telling them that "being able to fight and win wars is the soul of a strong army." A few months later, just before it began operations, he toured China's first aircraft carrier, the *Liaoning,* which had been purchased from Ukraine and refurbished. None of this early military signaling by Xi would have been remarkable had it not been accompanied by an increasingly full-throated state campaign of vengeful nationalism.

As anniversaries go, seventy-seven doesn't have a very special ring, not in China nor in any other culture. But in July 2014, that didn't discourage Xi from presiding over the largest ever commemoration of what is officially known as the War of Resistance Against Japan, which China says began with the Marco Polo Bridge incident, a showdown with Japanese troops just outside Beijing on July 7, 1937, hence the elevation of 7-7 as an anniversary as a way of exploiting anti-Japanese feelings. In his speech, Xi denounced Japanese whitewashing of the past, and vowed that the "Chinese people who have sacrificed . . . will unswervingly protect, with blood and life, the history and the facts." At the conclusion of his remarks, the crowds of Chinese youth gathered for the event gave it a Maoist hue, collectively chanting, "Never forget national humiliation! Realize the Chinese dream!"

"The Chinese dream of great national rejuvenation" was how Xi often put it. It is the kind of watchword or slogan that Chinese leaders since Mao have adopted, drawing on an imperial tradition of reign slogans. But where most of Mao's successors have waited several years, even until the second of what is traditionally a mandate of two five-year terms, before announcing the organizing thought behind their presidency, Xi proclaimed his from the very start. The Marco Polo commemoration was by no means a one-off, either. Under Xi, a spate of other propaganda initiatives have been regularly orchestrated with the aim of reviving and channeling popular ire toward Japan.

In January 2014, the northeastern city of Harbin opened a memorial hall for the Korean independence activist Ahn Jung-geun, who assassinated Japan's first prime minister, Hirobumi Ito, in 1909. The following month, two new national holidays were introduced, both of them focused on Japan: the "War Against Japanese Aggression Victory Day" and the "Nanjing Massacre Memorial Day." For good measure, the government commissioned the $6 million construction of a full-size replica of an eighty-meter-long warship sunk by Japan during the Sino-Japanese War, intended as a reminder to the Chinese people of their country's defeat in that conflict.

Xi was by no means the first Chinese leader to seize upon hardline nationalism as an instrument of power. A nationalist education drive has been in force since the 1990s, with the aim of centering history education on the so-called Century of Humiliation. Previous leaders had usually been subtler on this score than Xi, though. I was working in China in 2008, for example, when the country's leaders discreetly let the Marco Polo anniversary pass without commemoration in order to facilitate negotiations with Japan over the joint development of undersea gas fields in the East China Sea. Likewise, whenever it seemed expedient, China's past leaders had also been willing to acknowledge Japanese efforts over the years to acknowledge and make amends for their country's past aggression and atrocities.

Today, however, it is hard to overstate how far China's leadership has moved away from such suppleness, or to overemphasize how little effort is spared to ensure that revanchist messaging is not lost on the Chinese people. In marking Japan's defeat in World War II, Xi took the unusual step of turning out with all seven members of the Politburo's Standing Committee, the highest-ranked members of the Communist Party. Two days after his "blood and life" speech, a major Chinese newspaper, the *Chongqing Youth Daily,* ran a full-page map of Japan with mushroom clouds hovering over Hiroshima and Nagasaki, in taunting celebration of those cities' destruction.

Meanwhile, to turn on the television in China is to be inundated with war-themed movies, which overwhelmingly focus on Japanese villainy. More than two hundred anti-Japanese films were produced in 2012 alone, with one scholar estimating that 70 percent of Chinese TV dramas involve Japan-related war plots. "Only anti-Japanese themes aren't limited," Zhu Dake, a culture critic at Shanghai's Tongji University, told Reuters. "The people who make TV think that only through anti-Japanese themes will they be applauded by the narrow-minded patriots who like it." The real question is whether the narrow-minded patriots he refers to include not just members of the general public but also—and it clearly wouldn't do for a Chinese academic to say so—members of the country's top leadership. In a 2014 interview, though, a prominent Chinese foreign policy thinker who has had extensive contact with the country's leadership told me, "In meetings since Xi has been in power you can feel the hatred. Everything is about punishing Japan. Punishing this damned Abe"—a reference to the deeply conservative Japanese prime minister, Shinzo Abe. China's leaders are all of an age to have grown up hearing vivid stories from their parents and grandparents about war with Japan.

Beyond hatred and purposes like propaganda and mobilization for the mounting contest between the two neighbors, there is yet another powerful motive for antagonism toward Japan: It buttresses a rickety political system that is bereft of any modern ideological underpinning and has failed to reform itself even remotely in pace with the economic transformation that has swept the country in the last generation. In the current post-Marxist, quasi-capitalist, and yet still stodgily restrictive Communist Party–governed era, the country's system reposes unsteadily on a two-legged stool. Its legitimacy is sustained mostly by fast economic growth, but also by nationalism.

As with the United States in the financial crisis that began in 2008, or Japan, whose extraordinary rise gave way to an era of contraction and then minuscule growth that has continued since the 1980s, the Chinese economy, like any other, could suffer a major reversal at any moment. The Chinese stock market crash of July 2015, in which the Shanghai Composite Index lost about a third of its value in the space of three weeks, after a dizzying run-up during the preceding year, laid bare the political anxiety of the hitherto ultra-confident government of Xi Jinping. Panicking at the prospect that the market collapse could shatter the Communist Party's legitimacy, the state halted trading in about half of all equities, suspended the issuance of new IPOs, banned short selling and threatened to use law enforcement to go after shadowy operatives who were said to be deliberately undermining the market. On top of all of these exceptional measures, Beijing ordered a group of big state banks to spend the equivalent of $209 billion to prop up stocks and end their rout. Another sharp market sell-off followed in January 2016, deepening a sense of doubt about the soundness of the country's economic model and the ability of the Xi government to enact overdue reforms.

As China enters into a period of long-term structural adjustment, involving a necessary and long-delayed departure from dependence on exports and on investments in heavy industry and infrastructure, and implicitly bringing about much slower rates of economic growth, stoking the fires of territorial and historical revanchism and of anti-Japanese passion born of nationalism becomes all the more necessary and urgent to keep ruling groups in power. As Zhang Yunling, director of international studies at the Chinese Academy of Social Sciences in Beijing, told me flatly, "Of course we must reinforce patriotism. Patriotism is very important for a rising power."

The day when China is prepared to mount a preordained frontal challenge to Japan over the ownership of the Senkakus may not be upon us quite yet, but it is clearly approaching. The popular mood in China is not just unforgiving toward Japan, but also often seems increasingly impatient toward the Chinese government, a gathering storm of nationalism that reflects a yearning for some kind of action, a show of force. Additionally, a number of the most sober analysts of foreign policy and international affairs in Beijing say they fear the government is steadily becoming a prisoner of its own rhetoric.

"There is a kind of view that if we only assert ourselves, we can overcome Japan," one highly respected scholar told me in 2014. "Nowadays the idea of fighting easily comes to mind. In 2010 there were big anti-Japanese demonstrations and yet nobody talked about fighting Japan back then. But starting just two or three years later, everybody talks about war. You hear Chinese people saying that during the many weak years under Hu Jintao [Xi's bland and consensual predecessor from 2002 to 2012], China did not protect its own interests. Now they say we are able to, because we have grown much stronger. Therefore we must. You even get the sense that Xi sincerely believes this, but he also feels that this is an easy way to be seen as great. And who does not want to be great?"

If anything, comments like these are relatively mild in the spectrum of expert opinion in Beijing. "China has decided to be a maritime power," another leading international relations thinker told me. "This means that there is no chance of these disputes [with Japan] being resolved. . . . We will have to settle it by arms, or at least with arms being taken into account."

"The Chinese government cannot change its position [on maritime issues]," said Shi Yinhong, a prominent scholar at Renmin University. "It is unrealistic to believe that this confrontation will pass over."

What follows here is an extended exploration of the history of China's conceptualization of power and of its place in this region and a view as to how this face-off and the associated contest with the United States for primacy and influence in the world could play out.

Among other things, an attack on the Senkakus would represent a wager by the Chinese Communist Party that, vis-à-vis its public opinion at home, the country cannot continue to grow richer and stronger without making demonstrative use of its newfound strength against its most recalcitrant regional rival. For an already insecure system, to defer confrontation would be to squander domestic legitimacy, just as surely as incurring defeat at the hands of Japan would constitute a disaster that would be difficult for the party to recover from. Shi Yinhong reached back to the French Revolution to explain the stakes, saying that Tocqueville's description of the cause of France's eighteenth-century convulsion, which focused on how rising elements in the society had outgrown feudal institutions, was mistaken and that what actually spurred revolution in that country was the loss of a seven-year war with Prussia. "We can see the same pattern in China," he told me. "Anytime a regime has lost a major war, this was followed by radical reform or collapse. Right now, I'm afraid our foreign policy depends a bit on providence."

What this suggests is that the world should prepare itself for the playing out of a large and immensely consequential gamble in the seas that separate Japan and China. The most readily imaginable scenario revolves around a struggle for control of the Senkakus, and one that, moreover, hews closely to the predictions of the cashiered captain, James Fanell. Perhaps it would roll out this way: First, there is a violent, "accidental" collision between Chinese and Japanese ships, a jousting between coast guard vessels that quickly escalates, drawing in naval vessels, after one side, especially if it is the Chinese, suffers the loss of a ship or an aircraft. Then there is an inevitable flurry of intense, high-level diplomatic activity to arrest the crisis, but events are moving too fast and temperatures running too high. Public opinion in China in particular sizzles, with the Internet over-run with bloodcurdling calls for revenge, which the government is fearful of suppressing. The censors lose control. The Japanese, now collectively reduced to pirates, dwarfs and devils, all ancient epithets directed at them, must be taught a lesson. The Chinese people will not countenance humiliation.

The political leadership in Beijing feels backed into a corner. There is no other choice but to make a show of strength. Chinese divers or parachutists then take advantage of the element of surprise to establish a position on the Senkakus, finally acting on Chinese claims. For the first time in history, the Chinese flag is raised on these rocks. This gesture temporarily rallies the public and slakes the nationalist thirst, but there is an inevitable Japanese response. A beachhead position that consists of a small number of Chinese is easily overcome. This delivers to Beijing a disastrous setback following upon empty symbolism. This is Shi Yinhong's lesson from the French Revolution writ large.

It is therefore unlikely that, as in the above scenario, China would try to move men into position before it is able to do so in number, but the day when just such a capability exists is also rapidly approaching. In May 2013, Beijing took delivery of the first of an order of four Ukrainian-built hovercraft known as the Zubr, or bison, which can carry about five hundred troops and fly men and materiel at 66 miles per hour. With four of these craft, Richard D. Fisher, an expert on Chinese military modernization at the International Assessment and Strategy Center, estimated that the People's Liberation Army Navy could put "2,000 troops or up to 600 tons of weapons and materiel on the Senkakus in about four to five hours." There are few missions this hovercraft seems more suited to than a Chinese bid to assert control over the undefended Senkakus, and indeed when the first ships were delivered, one Chinese television broadcaster enthusiastically proclaimed that they would enable China to "win the war even before any battle had taken place."

For the foreseeable future, Japan's best deterrent consists of the controversial American base deployment in Okinawa. Long-standing local opposition to the presence of U.S. troops, fueled by complaints of aviation noise, overcrowding on the island, environmental damage and the repeated rape of Japanese women, forced the U.S. and Japanese governments in 1996 to devise a plan that would "return" the most important base, the Marine Corps Air Station Futenma, to Okinawan control. The "solution" they came up with, however, was to eventually relocate Futenma to a new 160-hectare base to be built on reclaimed land in Henoko Bay, one of the most biologically diverse and sublime maritime settings in all of Japan. Although this project, which was approved in 2006, was supposed to be completed within five to seven years, nonviolent Okinawan resistance, in the form of legal challenges and resolutions passed in local government councils, has so far prevented any construction.

While Tokyo's creation of a small outpost on Yonaguni for Japanese marines and to provide early warning may help, presently the only thing that can preempt a Chinese takeover force swooping in on the wings of a fleet of Zubrs is a forward-positioned fleet of twenty-four American MV-22 Ospreys, unusual airplanes capable of vertical takeoff because of their twisting rotors, that can fly at 280 miles an hour. In a clear pitch to blunt opposition to the U.S. Marine base at Futenma, in September 2013 the commander there, Lieutenant General John Wissler, told the local press in Okinawa that the Osprey "has the ability to reach the Senkakus, should we need to support any sort of Japan-U.S. security treaty." A few months later, during a visit to Japan in April 2014, President Obama publicly confirmed that although the United States took no position on the merits of China's and Japan's rival claims to the islands, the United States would defend Japan's long-standing control of them if it came under attack, under the Treaty of Mutual Cooperation and Security between the United States and Japan, which was first signed in 1952. Privately, the two countries had been making contingency plans for just such a situation since 2012. In fact, in a full-out tilt, it has been estimated that the American Osprey fleet at Futenma could place five hundred troops on the Senkakus in an hour. If a future American president received a telephone call in the night informing him that Chinese Zubrs were en route to the disputed islands, one can readily imagine the rapid narrowing of choices: Call his Chinese counterpart and demand that there be no further Chinese deployment to the islands, or order that American Ospreys beat the Zubrs to the Senkakus, possibly fighting their way onto the islands in the face of hostile fire from the advance team of Chinese frogmen.

The choices would necessarily narrow in the space of a late-night phone call or two, because an American refusal to take action would poison the United States' treaty relationship with Japan, and quite likely threaten the entire American security architecture in the western Pacific. The world would be left to ponder the question of how to describe the United States under the resultant new status quo—a superpower that could not or would not honor one of its most important and long-standing overseas commitments. Immediately, voices would rise in Japan calling for that country to bow to the inevitability of Chinese supremacy in the region and make its peace with Beijing. South Korea, which has hewed a middle path, carefully balancing its security ties with the United States against increasing economic integration with China, would tilt similarly toward Beijing. One after another, other countries in East Asia—Vietnam, the Philippines, Singapore—would feel great pressure to accommodate China.

There is scarce comfort, though, in knowing that the United States could prevail in such a logistical footrace, perhaps preempting a major crisis between Japan and China three or five years down the road. For one thing, Beijing will continue to expand its rapid airlift capacity by adding more Zubrs, both building them under license and developing new and improved homemade derivatives. As its economy continues to outpace those of its neighbors, further fueling its determination to become a full-fledged superpower, China will also eventually begin to bring other powerful new assets to bear. Beijing is already working hard, for example, to develop a twist-rotor aircraft of its own design, known as the Blue Whale, that would be faster and substantially more advanced than the Osprey, and capable of carrying more than three times the load, whether troops or materiel. Successful development and deployment of this system, a model of which has already appeared at Chinese air shows, would ultimately lay bare the inherent limitations faced by a remote offshore power like the United States, no matter how muscle-bound, and hence the limited utility of its alliance in protecting Japan. Demonstrating this would seem to be at least as important to China as the simple fact of possession of the otherwise forgettable barren rocks of the Senkakus.

Japan, in the meantime, has embarked on the swiftest, steepest demographic decline that the modern world has ever seen in a large nation thus far, and the country can be expected to shrink 30 percent in size by 2050 from its peak in the mid-2000s. Demographers project that in the twenty years beginning in 2010, when its population was 128 million, Japan will face a net loss on average of an astounding

660,000 people a year. To put this in historical perspective, this represents the equivalent of the country's entire combatant death toll in World War II roughly once every three and a half years. Already, the male population eligible to join the military (the Japan Self-Defense Force) has shrunk from 9 million to 6 million since 1994. This has forced the SDF to open up more and more jobs, including roles like fighter pilot, to women, who presently make up 5.7 percent of the Japanese military, or roughly 13,000 troops and staff. Even with this evolutionary change, though, planners have warned politicians that at this rate in ten years they will be unable to staff the military with enough recruits to sustain present force levels. Meanwhile, the country is also aging faster than any other. According to the Ministry of Health, Labor and Welfare, there were 153 centenarians in Japan in 1963. There were 58,820 in 2014, the *Wall Street Journal* reported, with 4,423 joining this demographic in the last year alone.

In the early summer of 2013, seven months after Abe took office, I met an affable former high-level Japanese diplomat, Kiyotaka Akasaka, over lunch in Tokyo's downtown Chiyoda district, a neat and impressively ordered world of parks and anonymous office buildings. Akasaka wasted no time before launching in anxiously about his country's future, speaking as if tormented by ulcers. "By 2050, Japan's economy will be one-sixth that of China's and the United States', as measured by PPP [purchasing power parity]," he told me.

"This is according to a recent study by Keidanren [the main Japanese business association]. The U.S. and China will each be about $24 trillion. Japan is going to be smaller; much smaller. What is more shocking is a projection of the *Economist,* which said that by 2050 Japan's GDP per capita will be 0.58, if the United States' GDP per capita is taken as 1, as an index. Korea's will be 1.05. Chinese people will be at about the same level as Japanese. This has really surprised people here. . . . If things go this way, the weight of Japan in international affairs will decrease drastically. This is worrying politicians here, and it is the basis of a lot of the Abe policies. How do we preserve our place? How do we energize our young people? I know it is not possible to regain our place, but we must do something.

"Certainly the emergence of China as a great military and economic power has woken up a lot of people," he added after a pause. "The Japanese are not prepared to see China become the regional hegemon."

The Keidanren report that Akasaka cited began with this bleak assessment: "Japan is falling into a 'no-growth economy' where nominal GDP has stopped at approximately the level of 20 years ago. National government debts have reached 200% of GDP, and public finance and social security are facing a crisis." As for demographics, the business association, whose historic role has been that of a resolute booster, spent 107 pages painstakingly arguing that Japan is condemned to a fading population and to minuscule economic growth at best. This is the Japan that will eventually have to somehow summon the resources and will to hold off a Chinese challenge over the Senkakus substantially on its own, which is how the frenzied diplomacy and sudden security assertiveness of Abe must be understood. Failing that, it must simply resign itself to peacefully giving up the islands and reaching an accommodation with China based on subordination.

A day or two later, I lunched at the exclusive Ark Hills Club in the Roppongi district, which had been a center of American military life in the city during the U.S. occupation of Japan, and then a seedy nightlife quarter. In recent years, Roppongi had been extensively redeveloped and is now home to some of the most expensive residential high-rises in the city, along with some of its toniest shopping malls. There, at an elegant restaurant on the thirty-seventh floor of a newish tower, amid sweeping views of the city, I was received by Yoichi Funabashi, a prominent former foreign affairs columnist and later senior editor at the *Asahi Shimbun,* Japan's largest liberal daily, who now runs a foundation aimed at reviving Japan.

Funabashi, a leading public intellectual in his country, wasted little time in setting the tone of the conversation. "What we are witnessing here is the beginning of tectonic change [in East Asia], and the contours are not really understood by most of the people here yet." Because of its long shared history with China, marked like now by periods of intense rivalry, Japan was becoming a linchpin for the entire region: Either it would find a way to hold the line as a sig-

nificant, autonomous power, or it would buckle, thereby removing
the last rampart constraining Chinese power throughout East Asia.
"Hundreds of smaller societies have been absorbed by China over the
last two thousand years," he said. "The remaining ones, whether Vietnam, or Mongolia or, say, the Uighurs, whatever, have somehow managed to survive what has been an endless ordeal. Now China seems
to believe it is its time again. They are pursuing their dream, which
means expansion and consolidation. They have always been a land
power, but now they are reasserting themselves as a great maritime
power. The problem for us is that China believes in a tributary system; that is the normal order of things to them. They are determined
to change the status quo, and their ultimate goal is expelling the U.S.
as a regional power and to take control within the First Island Chain."

On a muggy midsummer Tokyo afternoon, I made my way to the
campus of Waseda, the country's second oldest private university,
founded by a samurai scholar and former prime minister, Okuma
Shigenobu, in 1882. Okuma didn't interest me per se, but the era in
which he had left his mark on Japanese education did. I had made
an appointment at the university's rare documents collection to see
some papers dating from the late 1870s that were not only rare but
unique.

I was shown to a seat at a shiny wooden table inside a hushed
and brightly lit special viewing room. A prim library staffer appeared
before me and opened a brown box containing an orange-and-
sienna-colored binder. She politely asked me to confirm that these
were the documents I had come to see, and once I had issued an
affirmative nod and a thank-you, she silently disappeared. I unfolded
the delicate and musty-smelling parchment on which was correspondence between highly cultivated men of Japan and China. On
the very first page, three different hands jumped out at me. One
was tight and edgy—stylized Chinese characters, all tightly angular,
with sharp points, written in what I imagined to be a showily self-
conscious style of the time. There on the page alongside of it was
someone else's brush writing. Its characters were open and loopy, a

flowing effect that for me conjured a drunken poet. And next to it was the third person's penmanship, unremarkable for the most part, like the product of endless classroom repetition. On the next page came drawings that seemed to match the hand of the man with the sensual flow. In one of them I found the scribbled figure of a monk, wandering through an abstract countryside, following alongside a river or a stream that poured down from a mountainside. He carried a walking stick hoisted over his left shoulder. Was this a scene from some well-known tale from the classics? Was it an artifact of the shared culture between Japan and China? More hands appeared on subsequent pages.

Over the years, I had acquired a reasonable ability to read Japanese and a better one to read Chinese, but handwriting, let alone the heavily stylized brush writing like this, had always stumped me, and I could make little sense of the text that appeared on the bound pages. From previous research, however, I knew that these pages were a kind of sign language practiced between alien cultures that would not have been able to understand each other via the spoken word and yet could communicate well enough in writing to reveal each other to not be so alien.

The Japanese participants were intellectually curious members of the samurai class, which had just been set adrift by the Meiji Restoration of 1868. The restoration had ended seven centuries of feudal rule in the country at the conclusion of an intense civil war, and under the slogan "Civilization and Enlightenment," or *Bunmei Kaika*, men of purpose (*shishi*), mostly from outer domains, far from the capital, had launched Japan on the path toward constitutional government inspired by contact with the West, involving, inter alia, Western learning of all kinds, including industrialization and military modernization. This so-called restoration was ill-named, not because it failed to place the emperor at the center of Japanese life but because this placement itself was based on a false premise. Japan had had emperors at least since the sixth century, but they had reigned rather than ruled.

Ōkōchi Teruna, a former feudal lord from mountainous Gunma Prefecture, living in forced retirement at his Tokyo estate when these documents were produced, had convened a smart set of elite friends, mostly conservative educators and officials, to meet with Chinese newcomers to the country who were members of the first embassy that China established in Japan to function according to the patterns of Western diplomatic tradition.

By 1870, Japan had already deeply imbibed a range of Western ideas and mores, and was giving every appearance of hoping that the more ostentatiously it embraced these appurtenances of "civilization," the more respect and perhaps immunity from the violent Western expansionism—well under way throughout the region, and indeed around the world—it would be granted. That year, in this spirit, it requested a treaty of trade and friendship with China. The Meiji government envoy dispatched for this purpose, Yanagiwara Sakimitsu, was refused entry to Beijing and was received instead in the nearby port city of Tianjin, where he delivered a letter that managed somehow to be both prescient and in part even poetic, stating that "recent changes in Civilization had unfolded in great measure," and that "paths to international communications were multiplying daily, so that near and far ceased to be." This was the Japanese official's delicate way of saying that the West's arrival in force in East Asia was quickly rendering the region's Sinocentric system and its old rules obsolete.

But rather than receiving a prompt green light, the treaty request was lengthily debated in Beijing, initially engendering contemptuous dismissals from opponents in the orbit of the imperial court. The Chinese sometimes used particular insults reserved for their maritime neighbors in speaking of the Japanese. For China, given both its hierarchical view of the world and its sense of itself as the sole source of all knowledge and culture, the Japanese request posed a host of intellectual and political challenges as old as the tribute system itself. In his book *The Mind of Empire*, Christopher Ford relates the attitudes of the Han dynasty around 200 BCE when it was faced by a rising threat from the Xiongnu, a formidable Turko-Mongol steppes-based confederation, whose power had risen to such an extent that it could only be held at bay through onerous payoffs. The powerful Xiongnu sent a representative to the Han court to "request the ratification of peaceful relations" with China, but rather than accept the equality this implied between the two sides—an affront to the very concept of *tian xia*—the emperor repudiated all notions of a truce and launched a fierce preemptive war. "There was no tradition of states with differing cultures coexisting on a theoretical basis of equality," Ford writes, and all other peoples in diplomatic contact with China must necessarily be "in some way tributary to the Chinese state."

In the late nineteenth century, however, as the last dynasty to rule China plunged into advanced decay, Japan posed a unique challenge to the imperial ego that even went beyond such considerations: Its demand for diplomatic parity had come on the heels of similar demands from the West. For China, it was one thing to have recently been obliged by Western powers to engage in diplomatic relations according to their terms, given that the Europeans had arrived from afar eagerly demonstrating clearly superior naval force, and could not be expected to have any real appreciation of Chinese civilization, which, one must remember, from the Chinese perspective meant Civilization period. But for opponents of Japan's request within the Chinese court, any notion of accepting Tokyo's treaty proposal would have been far more odious. This meant implicit acceptance of the idea that Japan, which was customarily viewed as a culturally derivative, subsidiary nation on the margins of their celestial empire, deserved an equal footing with it. Put another way, this meant the end of hierarchy at home, in the known world; even from the perspective of an already tottering Central Kingdom, for many it was totally inadmissible.

The treaty's adoption was delayed further by Beijing's displeasure over a Japanese military intervention in Taiwan in 1874 to punish local pirates there who had attacked fishermen from the Ryukyus who had strayed into Taiwanese waters, and then, once again, by a pause in affairs of state brought on by an imperial succession in China, when the emperor Guangxu took the throne. Finally, in 1876, diplomatic ties were opened between the two countries, with He

Ruzhang arriving in Tokyo as the first ambassador late the following year. This represented the two countries' first formal contact in
nearly one and a half centuries.

This was mostly attributable to the fact that under Japan's last
feudal regime, the Tokugawa shogunate, the country had practiced
sakoku, a policy of official seclusion from the outside world. It was
also a reflection of the fact that Qing China considered its sole neighbor to the east to be difficult to access across the rough waters of the
East China Sea and practically irrelevant in terms of Chinese wealth
and material power. Hence it was deemed best left alone.

Gathering with his elite Japanese friends in teahouses and sometimes over alcohol, Ōkōchi, the retired samurai, became the privileged host to members of the new Chinese diplomatic mission, and
eventually to its ambassador, He, who had been tasked with making
sense for Beijing of a Japan that was changing rapidly and in unusual
ways. With the Meiji Restoration well under way, by name and
appearance the country had just returned to rule by an emperor, with
all of the punctilious and colorful court ritual that this implied, and
yet at the same time it was clearly, and for the Chinese dismayingly,
coming under the influence of the Westerners who were intruding
deeply into Asia. For all of this, in the crucial opening years of these
exchanges, the Chinese could not see past their own abiding sense
of superiority. Instead of getting quickly down to the task of understanding Japan's ongoing transformation, the Chinese were absorbed
above all in the ultimately self-flattering pursuit of information that
might confirm traditional Chinese views of the origins of the Japanese race. According to ancient Chinese myth, the original Japanese
were descendants of a lost tribe led by a man named Xu Fu, who
was dispatched by China's first emperor, Qin Shihuang, in the second
century BCE, in the company of three thousand youths. Xu Fu's mission was to search for Yingzhou, one of three supposed "Mountains
of the Immortals," but Chinese histories say that he never returned
from the second of two attempted voyages.

"The Qing envoys . . . were not favorably disposed toward Japan
from the outset," writes the Japanese historian Shinichi Kitaoka per-

ceptively about the He embassy. "He Ruzhang would eventually gain an accurate understanding of Japan's development, but at first he held Japan in contempt and had an inflated estimation of his own country. Seeing Japan outside the Confucian and Chinese cognitive paradigm was not easy, and before he could do so, one problem after another emerged in Japan-Sino relations."

Almost all the members of the early Chinese mission to Tokyo became preoccupied with the legend of the Xu Fu mission in one way or another, starting with He. In his 1878 book *Concise Account of the Eastern Embassy,* the ambassador wrote with utter conviction about the Chinese origins of the Japanese people and of their institutions as well, claiming that many of the names for Japanese offices had been adopted directly from the ancient Zhou and Qin dynasties. One of He's principal assistants, (Counselor) Huang Zunxian, who figures in the dialogue below, and whose rendering of his experiences in Japan later helped establish him in China as a poet of some renown, lamented that Japanese histories of recent centuries had excised all mention of the legendary Xu Fu. "Although Japan desires to cease being our dependency," he wrote, "they need not deceive themselves with this falsification."

Because of the aforementioned lack of a shared spoken language, the conversations were conducted in writing, with ink brushwork and paper, hence the name "brushtalking" given in the invaluable account of these encounters by D. R. Howland, from which I have drawn substantially here. With a little work, the Japanese who were party to this correspondence could manage written Chinese. It was not the characters that would have posed a major obstacle. This strange intercourse was largely staged in the classical idiom, which Japanese gentlemen of a certain standing had learned since the ninth century, and which still served widely as a benchmark of one's culture and cultivation in the country. What would have challenged the hosts most were the little stories, the countless parables and allusions that the Chinese deployed, a bit mischievously, drawing on the bottomless wealth of their classic Confucian literature and five thousand years of culture to test their "little" Japanese brothers. And it was child's play for a well-bred Chinese to blend familiar sops with enough truly recherché references from ancient poetry or theater to leave even reasonably well-educated Japanese scratching their heads.

A brushtalk drawn from Howland dated May 30, 1878, which begins with the Japanese discussing their Chinese acquaintances' interest in finding grounds for a new embassy and is quoted here at length, gives a flavor not just of the style of banter between the two sides but of important underlying cultural dynamics, especially Chinese (Qing) condescension and Japanese gameness.

> Ōkōchi: I'll ask everyone who would be concerned. As for the size of the property, how much would be needed?
>
> Counselor Huang: About three or four thousand *ping* [approximately three acres] would be best, on solid ground and in fresh air, and one or two *li* [two-thirds of a mile] from Tokyo.
>
> Ōkōchi: Perhaps the ambassadors could ask Mr. Wei Li to look into the matter with our representatives; since he's most accustomed to this sort of thing, it might be as easy as a turn of the hand.
>
> Counselor Huang: I'm aware of that, but I'll take your advice—to the word.
>
> In a poetry game of ours recently, Meishi composed the riddle: "Man-made wagtail mating technique; I am Prince Unmixed-Feathers." It uses expressions from your nation's history—do you know the meaning?
>
> Ōkōchi: I know not the first line, and blush red as a skirt; I know not the second, and am shamed to the light of my soul. Whenever I ascend the [Manchu] Banner Pavillion, I've no one to accompany me; I guess that you, sir, are a handsome man—would their maidens be safe from your surprise attacks? Should I invite you on another day, I certainly won't accept a refusal; and even if you decline, I'll force your carriage forward.
>
> Counselor Huang: I couldn't dare disagree.

Ōkōchi: I often take Wang Qiyuan and Wang Qinxian to the Rijogo for conversation; it's like discussing family affairs with my wife at my own home—their words are respectful and chosen with care; they bow their heads at my command. But when I go to the Gakkain with Huang, Liao and Shen, it's like coming upon famous beauties in the sultry world of smoke and flowers. Words are graceful and show charm and character; listening to the talk, I'm lost in love and unwilling to leave. Do you have such feeling for us Easterners?

Attaché Liao: With conversation, each follows its inspiration. When there's romance, it's romantic; when there's talk of economy, it's economics. There's no difference between Chinese and Japanese. You're an intelligent man, surely you understand this point.

What was it that the Chinese were missing? All along, the notion of superiority had been central to the Chinese tribute system. This meant the maintenance of several ultimately costly pretenses. The first of these involved trade, which the Central Kingdom routinely feigned was of little consequence to it; instead, commerce was spoken of almost as a favor of Chinese beneficence granted to an array of less fortunate others. The most famous illustration of this posture, touched upon in the introduction to this book, came in an audience granted in 1793 by the Qing emperor Qianlong to Lord Macartney, the envoy of the British monarch, George III.

Macartney had arrived aboard a sixty-four-gun man-of-war on a special mission aimed at opening trade and diplomatic relations with China. He represented a country of 8 million subjects that was rapidly developing a trading system to span the globe and had recently become convinced of its status as the most powerful nation on earth. Qing China, a country of 350 million people, or more than the entire population of Europe, however, "was the largest, wealthiest, and most populous contiguous political entity anywhere in the world," in the words of the historian James L. Hevia, and could not conceive of parity with any nation. In the account of Stephen R. Platt, another expert in the period, the English envoy plied his host with six hundred crates full of gifts, all carefully chosen to impress. Befitting a fast-industrializing nation, these included some of the finest examples of British manufacturing and technology, including "cutting-edge scientific instruments, a room-sized planetarium, giant lenses, a hot-air balloon, a diving bell and modern weaponry." In his sole audience with the emperor, however, Macartney had declined to perform the "full" kowtow while presenting himself before the Chinese throne, meaning kneeling three times and prostrating oneself nine times, taking care to touch the forehead to the ground each time, according to the standard of ritualized submission demanded by Chinese protocol under *tian xia*. (Contemporaneous Chinese accounts make no mention of Macartney's grave breach of protocol, which was papered over by Qianlong's son and successor, Jiaqing, who wrote that the Briton "was so overcome with awe and nervousness" in his father's presence "that his legs gave way under him so that he groveled abjectly on the ground, thus to all intents and purposes performing an involuntary kowtow.") When Macartney departed he carried with him a letter from Qianlong meant for George III:

> You, O King, from afar have yearned after the blessings of our civilization and in your eagerness to come into touch with our converting influence have sent an Embassy across the sea bearing a memorial [memorandum]. I have already taken note of your respectful spirit of submission, have treated your mission with extreme favor and loaded it with gifts, besides issuing a mandate to you, O King, and honoring you at the bestowal of valuable presents. Thus has my indulgence been manifested.
>
> Yesterday your Ambassador petitioned my Ministers to memorialize me regarding your trade with China, but his proposal is not consistent with our dynastic usage and cannot be entertained. Hitherto, all European nations, including your own country's barbarian merchants, have carried on their trade with our Celestial Empire at Canton. Such has been the procedure for many years, although our Celestial Empire

possesses all things in prolific abundance and lacks no product within its own borders. There was therefore no need to import the manufactures of outside barbarians in exchange for our own produce. But as the tea, silk and porcelain which the Celestial Empire produces are absolute necessities to European nations and to yourselves, we have permitted, as a signal mark of favor, that foreign hongs [groups of merchants] should be established at Canton, so that your wants might be supplied and your country thus participate in our beneficence. But your Ambassador has now put forward new requests, which completely fail to recognize the Throne's principle to "treat strangers from afar with indulgence," and to exercise a pacifying control over barbarian tribes, the world over. Moreover, our dynasty, swaying the myriad races of the globe, extends the same benevolence towards all. Your England is not the only nation trading at Canton. If other nations, following your bad example, wrongfully importune my ear with further impossible requests, how will it be possible for me to treat them with easy indulgence? Nevertheless, I do not forget the lonely remoteness of your island, cut off from the world by intervening wastes of sea, nor do I overlook your excusable ignorance of the usages of our Celestial Empire. I have consequently commanded my Ministers to enlighten your Ambassador on the subject, and have ordered the departure of the mission. But I have doubts that, after your Envoy's return, he may fail to acquaint you with my view in detail or that he may be lacking in lucidity, so that I shall now proceed . . . to issue my mandate on each question separately. In this way you will, I trust, comprehend my meaning. . . .

It may be, O King, that the above proposals have been wantonly made by your Ambassador on his own responsibility, or per adventure you yourself are ignorant of our dynastic regulations and had no intention of transgressing them when you expressed these wild ideas and hopes. . . . If, after the receipt of this explicit decree, you lightly give ear to the representations of your subordinates and allow your barbarian merchants to proceed to Chêkiang and Tientsin [a southern province and a nearby Chinese port city, respectively], with the object of landing and trading there, the ordinances of my Celestial Empire are strict in the extreme, and the local officials, both civil and military, are bound reverently to obey the law of the land. Should your vessels touch the shore, your merchants will assuredly never be permitted to land or to reside there, but will be subject to instant expulsion. In that event your barbarian merchants will have had a long journey for nothing. Do not say that you were not warned in due time! Tremblingly obey and show no negligence! A special mandate!

Far more important to the Chinese than trade in goods was the question of ideas, and the cost of maintaining the appearance of Chinese superiority in all manner of knowledge was the need to adopt a posture toward foreigners that approached sheer incuriosity. "It was firmly held that all non-Chinese had much to learn from China; China had little or nothing to learn from them," writes the historian Alain Peyrefitte in his account of the Macartney embassy, *The Immobile Empire.* Worse, officials in the imperial court sometimes took pride in flaunting their ignorance of foreign customs and institutions; such was the arrogance that came with believing oneself at the center of the universe.*

Reading brushtalks like these for the first time, I was reminded of the work of some Western correspondents who arrived in Japan in

---

*Early in his mission to open relations with the Qing, Macartney presented a gift of eight cannons. Highly advanced for their day, they could fire seven shots per minute, but officials of the Chinese court responded with smugness, saying they were nothing new. Months later, as he was leaving the country, his mission a failure, Macartney received a final rebuff when he offered to have his military guard drill with flintlock rifles as a demonstration of European innovation. The Qing second minister scoffed at the idea that the guns could represent anything new. This drew a remark from Macartney that he had never seen anything more advanced than a more primitive matchlock during his months in China, and as Peyrefitte wrote in *The Immobile Empire,* "That would still be true half a century later, during the Opium War."

the late 1950s and early 1960s. I had surveyed it four decades later, as I prepared to take up an assignment there. Some of them were so busy writing clichéd stories about geishas, Japanese men with bad haircuts dressed in bad Western-style suits, and a range of what they regarded as quaint cultural practices that they missed the country's economic takeoff, which remains as impressive as any the world has seen. The Chinese visitors of the 1870s had a similar fixation on empty clichés. Their accounts heavily favored images of rickshaws, cherry blossoms and teahouses, along with erotic fantasies about the supposed sexual adventurousness of Japanese women. China would begin to ramp up its knowledge of Japan toward the end of the decade, several years after the creation of the brushtalks I had sat in the library to examine.

By the time the Chinese emerged from their fog of self-absorbed condescension it was too late for them to get out of the way of the train that was speeding headlong in their direction, much as the United States was largely taken aback by Japan's dramatic if brief economic ascendancy in the 1980s. A hundred years earlier, Japan had leaped ahead of China in ways that would soon prove lastingly fateful for its larger neighbor, even before the geopolitics of the region were transformed by Japanese victories in repeated wars of aggression. China's sudden realization that its ideas were no longer held in high esteem and its model no longer worthy of emulation came as a profound psychological shock.

Ironically, Ambassador He's first critical order of diplomatic business had been the question of the Ryukyus. Tokyo had commanded the Ryukyu king, Shō Tai, to stop paying tribute to China in 1875. But Beijing didn't fully comprehend what was transpiring there until 1876 when the Ryukyu king secretly dispatched a messenger to the Chinese city of Fuzhou, via the Senkaku Islands, to alert the imperial authorities there about Japan's power play. At Shō Tai's behest, the envoy requested that Beijing intervene so as to allow the Ryukyu kingdom to remain a Chinese tributary, that is, within Civilization.

He advised Beijing to confront Japan, arguing that Japan's navy could be handily defeated, or even scared off with a mere show of force. With China facing larger challenges holding its faltering empire together, namely from Europe and Russia, though, other, stronger voices, notably Li Hongzhang, the general and influential diplomat of the late Qing dynasty who had led the case for opening a new era of ties with Japan via the exchange of ambassadors and the signing of the friendship treaty, prevailed. More realistic and somehow better informed than his own ambassador, Li warned that Japanese warships were iron-plated to a thickness of twelve centimeters, and were not to be underestimated. After visiting both Japan and China shortly thereafter, former U.S. president Ulysses S. Grant declared that China's military capacity was no match for Japan's. In March 1879 this all became moot, though, when Japan unilaterally abolished the Ryukyu kingdom and incorporated Okinawa into Japan as a prefecture before China ever got around to marshaling a strategy.

One must go back in time, beginning a decade earlier, to events unfolding in Ryukyu to gain a fuller appreciation of the fog that China was laboring under—substantially a fog of its own smugness and self-esteem—as the peerless international system it had built and sustained in Asia over a long string of centuries began unraveling in this unlikely place. During the Qing dynasty (1644–1912), there were eight royal successions in the Ryukyu kingdom, each of which occasioned the dispatch of an imperial investiture mission from China, whose purpose it was to preside over the enfeoffment of a local leader, a ceremony in which he accepted his role as a vassal, without which, according to the rules of the tribute system, he could not officially call himself king. But since 1609, like a man who secretly sustains two households, Ryukyu kings had in fact been living a strange and elaborately concealed double life. Culturally they had continued to display their habitual reverence for China, to which they had willingly paid tribute, even though the cost of this practice was often onerous for such a small and resource-poor society. But beginning with its invasion that year by the Satsuma daimyo, which ruled over part of the southern Japanese island of Kyushu, Ryukyu formally became a vassal of feudal Japan as well.

For the next two and a half centuries, under close Japanese supervision, the Ryukyu kingdom managed to maintain a deliberate and carefully staged deception, appearing to the Chinese to be a loyal tributary. Under this arrangement, the Satsuma clan actually vetted and approved the choice of each Ryukyu king, but allowed the Chinese to carry on ritually investing them. Satsuma kept agents on hand in Ryukyu to carefully keep watch over the kingdom, but whenever Chinese visitors came calling, and especially when the moment arrived for each new investiture mission, the Japanese deliberately stayed well out of sight. Japanese objects that might attract attention were hidden away. Satsuma officials coached Ryukyu traders and ambassadors to China, with the help of a special handbook, on how they should answer questions from the Chinese should the matter of relations with Japan arise. The goal was to sustain plausible deniability of any political influence. This went so far as obliging Okinawans who had contact with the Chinese to feign ignorance of the Japanese language, despite their speaking it fluently.

The stark difference in Ryukyuan attitudes toward their two overlords is reflected in a traditional local saying from that time, "Intercourse with China and service to Japan," as well as in a statement attributed to Shō Tai, the last Ryukyu leader, that if the kingdom offended China it could explain things away, but if it offended Japan, it would be punished.

This charade rose to a new height in 1663 when the first Qing dynasty investiture mission arrived in the islands. China's new Qing rulers were not members of the country's Han ethnic supermajority, but rather Manchus, who had conquered China from the north, spoke their own language, and had their own distinctive customs, including the wearing of hair by males in a topknot. Early on, the Manchu takeover of China at the end of the preceding Ming dynasty engendered both confusion and dismay among China's most faithful tributary states, for example, Korea and Ryukyu itself, which saw the Qing as uncultured usurpers. Fearful that the Qing investiture mission would impose Manchu dress and topknots on the Ryukyu elite, the island leaders asked their Satsuma overlords what they should do in such an event. The Japanese ordered them to simply comply, fearing that to resist the new imperial ways would draw unwelcome attention to Ryukyu from Qing China. (In the end, this concern was for naught. The Qing envoys allowed the Ryukyuans to wear whatever they pleased.)

Ryukyu had begun to garner serious attention from Japan in the previous century, under Japan's megalomaniacal feudal ruler, Toyotomi Hideyoshi. In the 1590s, Hideyoshi conceived of a plan to essentially take over all of Asia, beginning with the conquest of China, a country twenty-five times larger than Japan, a disparity in size as great as that between the earth and the moon.

"Letters were prepared calling upon the 'King of India' to submit," writes George H. Kerr in *Okinawa: The History of an Island People*:

> A mission was dispatched to Formosa (Taiwan) to demand the surrender of the island; and a representative of minor rank carried orders to the haughty Spanish governor-general in the Philippines directing him to acknowledge Japan's claims or risk punishment. The letters did not reach India, and no government could be found on Formosa to which the demands might be presented. The Spanish ignored the summons but increased outpost garrisons in northern Luzon and in time constructed two forts and a mission on the northern tip of Formosa.

Hideyoshi ordered Ryukyu to contribute troops for his scheme to invade China, but the kingdom demurred. Subsequently, it also failed to provide material supplies, as ordered, to support the Japanese invasion, which proceeded via the Korean Peninsula and ended there in stalemate. Moreover, it informed on its powerful neighbor, warning China of Hideyoshi's invasion plans. After his death in 1598, Hideyoshi's successor, Tokugawa Ieyasu, briefly entertained thoughts of establishing formal relations with China, but rejected the idea once he understood clearly that this could not be done without submitting to the rules of the tribute system. Among other things, this would have meant calling himself a subject of the Ming emperor and adopting the Ming calendar for official correspondence.

"With the severing of diplomatic ties with Ming China, the

Tokugawa bakufu [government] created its own ideological centrality and attempted to establish [a] *Nihon gata kai-i chitsujo* [Japan-
centered civilization] in East Asia," writes Seo-Hyun Park in the book
Negotiating Asymmetry. "The Tokugawa *bakufu*'s most potent self-
legitimation tactic was the manipulation of relations with Korea (via
Tsushima, a small island that lies between the two countries) and the
Ryukyus." Ieyasu ordered that Ryukyu be placed under Japanese control, authorizing its takeover and administration by Satsuma. From
the perspective of the Japanese capital at Edo (modern-day Tokyo),
the takeover of the islands represented the first, still stealthy step by
Japan to hoist itself up toward equality with China. It had long had
an emperor, and now, finally, it had at least a miniature empire, all
of which came at China's expense, even if China for the time being
was unaware. In some sense, 1609, the year of Satsuma's takeover of
Ryukyu, was a dress rehearsal for 1879, when Japan would annex the
kingdom outright and unilaterally. In addition to the repositioning
vis-à-vis China, the 1609 takeover of Ryukyu demonstrated great sit-
uational awareness by the Japanese, who sought to use the islands as
a defensive lookout and early warning outpost against the encroachments of increasingly aggressive Western powers into the region,
including Spain, Portugal, Holland and England.

Although Ryukyu has played a key and largely underappreciated
role in East Asian history, Japan's posture of diffidence toward China
was a long-evolving thing, a trend that had kicked off in earnest three
centuries before Hideyoshi, when the Yuan dynasty, under its Mongol leadership, had attempted a gigantic conquest. The Yuan leader,
Kublai Khan, was taken with rumors that Japan possessed immense
stores of gold and sent a series of missions demanding that it submit and begin paying tribute. By that time, most of Asia had already
fallen before the redoubtable Mongol armies of Genghis Khan and
his heirs, and when the Japanese refused, the Yuan dynasty twice
mounted maritime invasions of the country, both of which failed.
Before the second attempt, in 1281, Kublai twice sent envoys to Japan
to demand its submission, and twice the envoys were beheaded, their
skulls put on display in Kamakura, the capital of the shogunate. The
emissaries had been forbidden to return home to China without

achieving success. Had they been allowed to do so, they might have informed the Yuan court that the Japanese by now believed firmly in their own divine origins and therefore could not conceive of submission to any foreign emperor.

The Mongols responded to Japan's defiance by assembling an army of forty thousand troops who sailed to Japan aboard nine hundred ships. Though badly outnumbered, a Japanese samurai army defeated the attackers by mounting effective defensive maneuvers from strategically positioned coastal fortifications. The Japanese were critically aided by a fierce two-day-long typhoon, subsequently known as *kamikaze,* or divine wind, that destroyed much of the Mongol fleet. The defeat of the invaders "fed the growing sense of self-confidence that Japan was in no way inferior to its mainland neighbor," writes Joshua A. Fogel in his book *Articulating the Sinosphere: Sino-Japanese Relations in Space and Time.* It was a feeling that would take root and grow over the centuries, placing the countries in a situation resembling galaxies locked in each other's gravitational fields, destined to collide repeatedly only to sail past each other after wreaking their damage.

Sitting outside of China's tributary realm, and officially closed off from the rest of the world since the 1630s, Japan limited its trade with China to the flow of tightly regulated shipping that was permitted to make call at Nagasaki. By allowing Ryukyu to continue paying tribute to China, Satsuma was able to quietly keep a profitable commercial channel open for luxury and prestige goods from there. In doing so, writes George H. Kerr, it disloyally ran the Ryukyus "as a private income-bearing property, not a part of the political fabric of Japan."

Under *sakoku,* which translates literally as "chained country," Japan would remain officially sealed off from the outside world until it was forcibly opened in 1853 with the arrival of Commodore Matthew Perry and his modern, steam-powered and cannon-bearing Black Ships. This meant that with rare exceptions, such as the Nagasaki trade, no foreigners were allowed to enter Japan, and no Japanese subjects were allowed to leave the country, on penalty of death. By the 1840s, however, there were already powerful premonitory signs in the maritime fringes of the Chinese empire of seismic changes that were about to make themselves felt. The French arrived in the Ryukyus in 1844, followed very shortly thereafter by the British, who established a medical mission there. In 1854, Perry obligated the kingdom to sign a treaty guaranteeing good treatment for American vessels, officially titled the "Compact Between the United States and the Kingdom of Lew Chew." Perry even urged his government to place the islands "under surveillance," meaning a loose form of "protection"—one of the many modes of imperialist takeover that were being experimented with by the West in that era.

"The department [of the navy] will be surprised to learn that this royal dependency of Japan . . . is in such a state of political vassalage and thralldom, that it would be a merit to extend over it the vivifying influence and protection of a government like our own," he wrote. Then, in a passage that prefigures the establishment of American hegemony in the Western Pacific by a century, even hinting at the eventual deployment of the Marines and Navy on Okinawa, Perry continued, "It is self-evident that the course of coming events will before long make it necessary for the United States to extend its territorial jurisdiction beyond the limits of the western continent, and I assume the responsibility of urging the expediency of establishing a foothold in this quarter of the globe, as a measure of positive necessity to the sustainment of our maritime rights in the east."

President Franklin Pierce rejected Perry's idea, though, writing, "If in future, resistance should be offered and threatened, it would also be rather mortifying to surrender the island, if once seized, and rather inconvenient and expensive to maintain a force there to retain it." With the Civil War looming, American attention to Okinawa dissipated, and practical moves toward expansion in Asia were put off until the end of the nineteenth century and the takeover of the Philippines.

Despite American reticence, Perry's era had already been one of steady encroachments by outsiders into the region, and the Ryukyu kingdom, fearful of what the new jockeying meant for it, asked for China's help in forcing the Westerners to withdraw. Beijing took a passive attitude, complacently assuming that the foreigners' interest in Ryukyu was mostly aimed at establishing a stepping-stone to Japan. Although not altogether incorrect, seen from the perspective of the present this now looks like a major historic miscalculation on the part of China. For the West, Japan was always at best a sideshow in comparison to the Central Kingdom, which James L. Hevia described in an apt phrase as "that most superlative object of European expansionist fantasies from the fifteenth century to the present." The islands, as noted earlier, are geographically situated as guardians of the eastern sea lanes for any Pacific approach to China. This remains their major strategic value.

By 1866, the pace of change in both China and Japan had quickened dramatically. Japan was locked in political turmoil, as the authority of the Tokugawa shogunate came under serious challenge by regional lords who were outraged that Tokyo was opening the country to Westerners. That same year, a Chinese envoy arrived in the Ryukyu Islands for what would prove to be the very last imperial investiture mission in the five-century history of this ritual. No one, of course, could have known this yet, but the Chinese emissary, Chao Hsin, completely missed the extent of the transformation sweeping this ordinarily quiescent little tributary, along with all the ominous implications this held for *tian xia*. Of the seven written records that survive from Qing investiture missions to Ryukyu, historians say his was the most cursory.

In his essay for Fairbank's *Chinese World Order*, Ta-Tuan Ch'en writes that some previous Chinese envoys had seen through some of the deceptive measures taken by the Ryukyuans to conceal their contacts with Japan, but had no knowledge of the formal state of subordination to Satsuma:

> Some did note the Satsuma invasion (of 1609) in their journals, with details, but they recorded it as a historical event and made no mention of Satsuma's continued control. They realized the Ryukyuans were hiding something. There is no evidence that they ever bothered to make a deeper inquiry, much less an issue of the matter. They demanded no explanation and never reported Shuri's [the name of the castle

that was headquarters of the Ryukyu kingdom] deceptions to the Chinese court. They rested content with the loyalty shown the Ryukyuan government, pleased with all the Sinicized forms they witnessed in Shuri and Naha. The evidence of all the mission journals written in the Qing era indicates that the Chinese envoys—and also the Qing court—remained indifferent toward Ryukyu-Japanese relations. Not until 1875, when Japan ordered Ryukyu to stop sending tribute to China and Ryukyu petitioned China for help, did the Chinese court realize that Ryukyu had actually been a vassal of Satsuma ever since 1609. During the ensuing Sino-Japanese negotiations over the Ryukyu problem, the Chinese court displayed an appalling lack of information about the situation in Ryukyu.

This was knowledge that even Perry's mission had possessed more than a decade earlier. While still on his way to Okinawa, he wrote from Madeira to the secretary of the navy explaining his choice of Ryukyu as a temporary base:

> The islands called the Lew Chew group are said to be dependencies of Japan, as conquered by that power centuries ago, but their actual sovereignty is disputed by the government of China. These islands come within the jurisdiction of the prince of Satsuma.

China's negligence toward the Ryukyus was of a piece with its hauteur and self-absorption during the early days of the He embassy to Tokyo. At this late date, evincing little sense of how sharply the tables had turned on their country, Chinese officials and intellectuals were still struggling to somehow contain Japan, at least conceptually, to keep it shoehorned within its would-be universal Civilization by foraging for anecdotes about the supposedly Chinese origins of the Japanese people, a matter of pure fantasy. But by that time, Japan had already closely observed China's spectacular nineteenth-century setbacks and repeated indignities, including the Opium Wars, a spate of subsequent "unequal treaties" it was forced to sign with Western nations, and perhaps especially the sacking of Beijing by Britain and France in 1860. In the space of a few decades, for the Japanese China had gone from being a model to emulate, at least selectively, to a cautionary tale of the steep costs to be paid in lost sovereignty and control over one's own destiny for failing to learn from the West and to embrace change. "By mid-century," writes Fogel in *Articulating the Sinosphere*, ". . . the best that the Chinese could hope for on the part of the Japanese was pity or perhaps pan-Asian resentment. The worst was much worse." And to be sure, far worse was to come.

A mere decade and a half after the brushtalks, Japan would defeat China in the First Sino-Japanese War. The victory would propel the country to take on Russia in 1904 over competing interests on the Korean Peninsula and in nearby Manchuria, and its victory the following year—the first ever by a "colored" race against whites in a major conflict—would embolden Japan to annex Korea in 1910, and eventually to invade all of China and take over much of Southeast Asia. It also led, of course, to Japan's fateful decision to take on the United States, beginning with the attack on Pearl Harbor, a catastrophic case of *fuite en avant* by the militarists who had taken over the country.

But what ended at Hiroshima and Nagasaki was much more than a four-year course of recklessness. On the contrary, Japan's defeat was the culmination of what had been over the course of four centuries, for the most part, a measured and gradual campaign to constitute a new Japanese-centered order in East Asia and eventually to replace imperial China and its disintegrating *tian xia* at the region's apex. This entire momentous train of events had begun in Ryukyu, when Japan began demanding tribute in the opening years of the seventeenth century. And it gathered further pace with the annexation of the islands, just three years after the teahouse brushtalks. In the Japanese reading of history, ever since the arrival of Europeans in the region in the sixteenth century, maintaining independence required of them two things: tolerating no proximate rivals, and keeping the Westerners at bay. And part of this thinking persists even now.

On an early July afternoon recently, during a visit to Okinawa, I wandered around Shuri Castle, the home and headquarters of a

Shuri Castle, Okinawa, built circa 1500

long line of Ryukyu kings. There were glass-encased exhibits and dioramas that established a timeline of the kingdom and attempted to capture some of its colorful past. In the manner of many Japanese museums, the plentiful displays, with their tightly edited texts, elided the nub of bitterness lodged in the heart of this history. When I had finished my tour, I left the castle through the same stone archway gate through which King Shō Tai made his final exit into exile in 1879, bringing to an end five hundred years of unbroken rule in these islands by Ryukyu sovereigns. Shō Tai had spent four years trying to elude Japan's tightening grip on his country, appealing for help repeatedly to China, and even to Western nations. Finally, though, Japan dissolved his kingdom, bundling the king off to Tokyo and seizing his castle. Brought before Japan's Meiji emperor, the deposed Ryukyu sovereign carried out one final and unusual gesture of rhetorical defiance before completing his formal submission. Shō Tai explained that he had sent repeated messages to China to seek its help and guidance in resisting Japan's growing demands, before alleging that "a reply had been received to the effect that China was too busy with internal affairs to act on behalf of Shuri, and that the Ryukyu kingdom henceforth must obey Japan's orders." In this way he was signaling that although Japan's demands would be heeded, it would only be under extreme duress, without admiration or respect.

Aside from its infrequent wars, China paid little attention to Japan throughout most of its history. This was due to Japan's determination to maintain its political and ritual distance from the Central Kingdom. Beginning with the takeover of the Ryukyus, though, Japan became the locus of a fundamental contradiction between *tian xia* and Western-driven modernity, and finally vivid proof of the former's unsustainable nature. Ryukyu was not only the place where Japan commenced its long drive for regional power; in time it would also be the place where Civilization began to crumble.

China's international system and its domestic system, the two integral components of its Civilization, were in fact disintegrating simultaneously. This was no matter of coincidence. As Wang Gungwu and Zheng Yongnian have written, "China's internal order was so closely related to her international order that one could not long survive without the other: when the barbarians were not submissive abroad, rebels might more easily arise within. Most dynasties collapsed under the twin blows of inside disorder and outside calamity, *nei luan wai huan*, that is, domestic rebellion and foreign invasion."

Very soon after Japan's Ryukyu takeover, almost no one, including any well-informed Chinese person, could believe any longer in a China-centered universe. The Sinosphere, in Joshua Fogel's wording, had been something akin to a Bohr atom, in which a thing called China "lay at the center of the sphere but could not conceptually exist without the many orbits around it." The removal from that orbit of Ryukyu, so small and so habitually taken for granted, was like the removal of a linchpin. It destabilized the whole. What collapsed in China was more than simply a dynasty. It was *tian xia* itself, an international system that had proven flexible and dynamic enough to survive in one form or another for two millennia.

Something else had happened too, and it is something that will ensure tremendous resonance for the Ryukyus going forward, helping fuel today's deep Chinese animus toward its neighbor, feeding the need to overcome Japan, the need for revenge. Japan's path to modernity had been opened by snatching something away from China to pave the way for it to become a regional and then a would-be world power, a country that others far and wide would respect.

"Cutting China down to size meant that Japan had joined the great nations," writes Ian Buruma in *Inventing Japan: 1853–1964*. "It also gave the Japanese a new sense of national unity." Buruma quotes a famous Japanese saying: "We are no longer ashamed to stand before the world as Japanese." These words were popularly uttered in response to Japan's victory over China in the Sino-Japanese War of 1895, but it applies just as well to the earlier events in the Ryukyus, where Japan's transformation into a new kind of Asian power had begun.

Today it is China seeking its return to preeminence in Asia and pretending to world power status, and everything suggests that it sees its own path toward modernity retracing this same old fault line, through the tiny islands that dot the intermediate sea separating it from Japan. Like the Japan of the 1870s, China is increasingly determined to brook no rivals in the region, which will first require bringing Japan to heel and then ultimately, mirroring the spirit of *sonnō jōi*—the rallying cry of rebels against the Tokugawa shogunate in the 1850s and 1860s, meaning "revere the emperor and expel the barbarians"—forcing the Americans out of its nearby oceans. Everything now suggests that this old game, so long centered around the Ryukyus, but suspended during the Cold War years of American supremacy, has once again been joined.

CHAPTER TWO

Island Barbarians

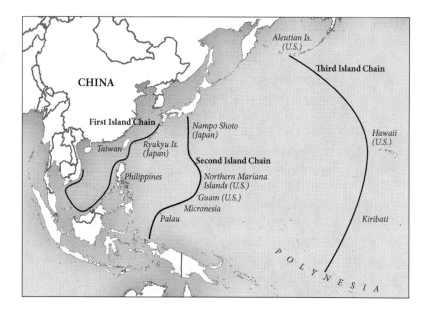

There are many ways to try and grasp the enormity of China's ambitions in the East Asian realm that it once fancied as being entirely its own. They all center on the sea.

Soon after 2010, Beijing began a concerted push toward something that, if it succeeds, will constitute the biggest grab of territory the world has seen since Japan's imperial conquests of the 1930s and 1940s. Territorial expansion by imperialist powers is usually thought of as a land-based matter, involving armies on the march and the large-scale occupations that follow. Japan, for example, invaded China, Vietnam, Burma and the Philippines, among other countries, all constituents at one time or another of China's imagined *tian xia*. But China, which spent much of the 1990s and early 2000s resolving border issues with many of its fourteen terrestrial neighbors, is now seeking to grow dramatically not by making immense claims to land, although that cannot be ruled out in the future, but by stealthily tightening its grip on the surrounding seas to the east and especially to the south.

What most obviously distinguishes China's expansionism from Japan's, slightly less than a century earlier, is that Beijing is hoping to accomplish its grab without the direct resort to force. Military power, though, is an essential tool for China in this effort; indeed, the overwhelming preponderance of strength it is building toward constitutes the very foundation of its strategy. This can be seen in the accelerating rollout of a modern Chinese navy, and especially in the way it has been deployed in the surrounding seas, in classic gunboat diplomacy fashion, as when China's first aircraft carrier, the *Liaoning*, on its maiden cruise in 2013 was sent with a full battle group of accompanying warships straight into many of the most fiercely disputed areas of the South China Sea. Aircraft carriers are new to

Shakedown cruise of China's first aircraft carrier, the Liaoning

China, but in most regards there is great continuity in its approach to the littoral states of Southeast Asia. Today, as in the past, the ideals of the *tian xia* system are being put into effect. This means building up dependency on China among its far smaller neighbors, the better to dominate them peacefully, as much as possible. In the past, China's size, its advanced technology, its brilliant culture, its strong and often patient national will, its long collective memory and its military prowess, whenever they needed to be called upon, together constituted the equivalent of what is known in the jargon of modern Chinese international relations as "comprehensive national strength." Then, like now, attributes like these were not only used to elicit admiration, or even awe from China's neighbors, but also to generate a kind of fatalism or resignation about the futility of trying to defy it.

As heir to an ancient civilization, China has another crucial tool in its long history, which it wields like a bludgeon whenever it wishes to. And in its ongoing attempt to assert itself in this region, the most expressive vehicle, both for recounting that history and for stating expansive claims, has been the map. In order to mobilize a domestic constituency, Chinese mapmakers have busied themselves reconfiguring their country's geographical disposition in the world. The Chinese public and foreigners alike have long been accustomed to seeing China displayed in a way that emphasizes its east-west continental sprawl. But in mounting its push into the South China Sea, Chinese cartographers have adopted a trick from digital photography, where many cameras can change their display ratios, or "aspect," from square to rectangular to panoramic. In China's new cartography, its north-south dimension is emphasized. This has the effect of making the South China Sea appear to hang from the southern coastline like an enormous blue banner. Almost magically, it begins to look more or less like a natural extension of the country and less marginal or incidental as it did on the older, more familiar maps.

To complete the trick, Beijing has mounted an unrelenting campaign of domestic propaganda instructing the Chinese people that the waters the world identifies today as the South China Sea—a name introduced by Europeans in the nineteenth century—indisputably belong to China. In 2015, one of the most striking examples of this was a promotional video for the People's Liberation Army Navy that was reportedly shared online more than one hundred million times in the first week after its release. "China's oceanic and overseas interests are developing rapidly," it said. "Our land is vast. But we will not yield a single inch of our frontiers to foreigners. [At this moment, the video shows a Chinese monument on a coral head protruding from the South China Sea, and then the Senkaku Islands.] China has 3 million square kilometers of ocean under its jurisdiction, including 6,700 islands with a surface area of over 500 square meters. The struggle over sea rights has not ended—we will not give up even the tiniest speck of our resources." [Here it shows pictures of giant oil rigs at sea.]

The domestic campaign focused on this issue follows a time-honored Chinese tactic of whipping up nationalist sentiment to such an extent that the state begins to appear as if it has no room whatsoever to maneuver, which by now may well be the case. China's neighbors are being warned, in effect, that if they do not bend to China's interpretation of its territorial rights, the Communist Party leadership will be forced to take drastic action, to use force. Failure to do so, it is implied, would provoke grave instability in the country, which would be bad for China's neighbors.

The charts that are being drawn up by China's mapmakers are being wielded before international audiences as well. In May 2009, Beijing issued two *notes verbales* to the United Nations stating, "China has indisputable sovereignty over the islands in the South China Sea and the adjacent waters, and enjoys sovereign rights and jurisdiction over the relevant waters, as well as the seabed and subsoil thereof."

This declaration, like the PLA Navy ad, set off alarms throughout the region and drew protests from several other littoral states, each with claims of its own, including most vehemently Vietnam and the Philippines. For documentation of its claim before the United Nations, China attached a map that had been obscure, but that has since become famous, or notorious, depending on one's perspective. It features a drooping, segmented line that encloses about 90 percent of the South China Sea, upon whose history, as two prominent academic experts, Zhiguo Gao and Bing Bing Jia, write in "The Nine-

Dash Line in the South China Sea: History, Status and Implications," "a long shadow has been cast by a heavy Chinese influence."

Since trotting out this claim, via a map that contains what is now popularly known as the "nine-dash line," in 1947, Beijing has ritually repeated that the body of water contained within the dashes has been China's since time immemorial, that China discovered the sea's many islands long before anyone else, and that the waterway and its islands have been traditionally controlled by China, which therefore gives it historic rights over everything there. In defense of these claims, some Chinese research papers harken back to the beginnings of the two-millennia-old tribute system. "The early history of Chinese use of the South China Sea and its islands includes accounts of tributes made to the Imperial Court of various dynasties before the third century AD by 'barbarians' from the southern seas," write Gao and Jia.

These historical claims are not worth exploring because of any legal power they might possess. Almost all non-Chinese experts agree that claiming distant waters as one's own "historic waterway" is not something that international law or conventions governing the sea either contemplate or permit. "China's assertiveness and its reiteration of indeterminate claims do not constitute, from a legal perspective, a position that is even minimally persuasive," write Florian Dupuy and Pierre-Marie Dupuy in an analysis published in the *American Journal of International Law* in 2013.[*]

They merit our attention instead because of how they speak to China's ambivalence about the international system itself, and to the continuing resonance of a certain imperial perspective—*tian xia*. They speak as well of a rising China's desire, like that of any great power, the United States very much included, to selectively exempt itself from widely adopted rules.

A visceral sense of the practical mechanics of China's bid for mastery of the South China Sea came to me on a fifteen-hundred-mile

---

[*] As discussed hereafter, China's claims to rights based on "historical" control of islands in the Spratly chain were vigorously rejected under the United Nations Convention on the Law of the Sea by an international arbital tribunal deliberating in The Hague in July 2016.

flight from Kuala Lumpur to Manila in 2014. The view below, from thirty thousand feet, was all bright turquoise or blue open ocean one moment, followed a few minutes later by the sudden appearance of tiny bits of land, whether outright islands, albeit small ones, in a few cases, or more commonly what geographers often called features or formations. These are wisps of sand that seem to emerge from nowhere, tiny atolls surrounded by light, shallow waters or delicate-looking blooms of coral.

By any conventional legal reckoning, to own the sea, China must own islands, which are the only things under international law that confer ownership of surrounding waters. This fact makes these formations, however insignificant they may appear from above, key. If existing law were to form any part of China's grab, it can be assumed that its strategy until recently was a kind of game of hopscotch that begins at its southernmost province, the island of Hainan, and proceeds formation by formation, feature by feature, through the Paracel Islands, disputed by Vietnam, and down through the Spratlys and their surrounding waters, which are claimed by the Philippines, Vietnam and Taiwan, as well as in part by Malaysia and Brunei. Under this theory, China had reckoned that control of anything deemed to be an island along the way would confer China control of a two-hundred-mile exclusive economic zone (EEZ) of surrounding seas. For the many smaller natural but uninhabitable features it controls, China could claim twelve miles of territorial waters. Beijing's mastery of a combination of islands and features would effectively allow it to dominate the waterway all the way to the doorstep of Indonesia (twelve hundred miles from Hainan). According to the head of the U.S. Pacific Command, Admiral Harry B. Harris Jr., Beijing's creation of three thousand acres of new land in the South China Sea between 2013 and 2015 has placed China on a trajectory to dominate the entire body of water by 2020. "They will control the South China Sea against all the militaries out there with the exception of the U.S. military in all scenarios short of war," he said.[*]

---

[*] In mid-February 2016, just days after Admiral Harris made this remark, Washington announced that China had installed antiaircraft batteries on Woody Island (Yongxing

Here again, China was pushing the envelope in at least two ways. The first was by claiming a range of rights over what goes on within an EEZ that exceeds what most countries recognize. Conventional interpretations of the international law of the sea allow "innocent passage" of vessels from other nations through any state's two-hundred-mile EEZ, including military vessels, which should neither pause or linger nor "launch or recover aircraft, collect military intelligence, distribute propaganda, launch any kind of watercraft, fire weapons, fish or take any action that is not involved in the direct passage of the ship through the territory of the coastal state," according to an article published in September 2015 by the U.S. Naval Institute. China, however, insists that military vessels must receive permission prior to passage through its waters.

In addition to seeking to maximize control over waters surrounding natural features in the sea beginning in 2013, China has also recently built artificial islands on a scale and with a speed that have never been seen before. It is almost universally acknowledged that these afford it no territorial or maritime rights. And yet these outposts, which are often equipped with advanced radar stations, military-grade landing strips and deepwater ports, are designed to allow China to project force to an extent that none of its neighbors can even begin to match. As one recently retired Chinese general said with unusual candor, "If the [People's Liberation Army] wants to achieve its naval supremacy over the South China Sea [in case there is a war], it's a must for the navy to get air control over the Spratly Islands, which is the sole gateway for the Chinese navy to enter the Western Pacific."

If only an airplane ride can provide a sense of the vastness of China's territorial bid, it's necessary to return to earth to fully appreciate its boldness. Toward this end, I traveled to the Filipino island Palawan, 350 miles southwest of Manila. There, 850 miles from

Dao) with a maximum range of about two hundred kilometers, enough to allow China to interdict air traffic from any of its Southeast Asian rivals, such as Vietnam, throughout the Paracel Islands.

Hainan, waters encompassed within China's expansive claims via the nine-dash line come within about twenty-five miles of Philippine shores. This cramped geographic reality is not the only sense in which the Philippines are on the front lines of resisting Chinese expansionism. In March 2013, Manila lodged a case with the Permanent Court of Arbitration in The Hague seeking a ruling by a so-called arbitral tribunal seeking invalidation of China's nine-dash line claims. Manila's argument, in essence, was that the implicit territorial claims under the nine-dash line, as well as its interpretation of exclusive maritime economic zones, violate the United Nations Convention on the Law of the Sea (UNCLOS). Beijing promptly denounced Manila's legal challenge and renounced participation in the case, but this did not prevent a near total rebuke by the court in July 2016, as we shall shortly see.

One brilliant summer morning, I stood at the mouth of a small harbor on Palawan with Edwin Seracarpio, the fifty-two-year-old owner of a modest fleet of wooden *bancas,* simple, low-slung fishing catamarans, as he awaited the return of one of his crews after three days at sea. Seracarpio told me that tuna fishermen who enter waters their forebears have freely used for generations nowadays find themselves at risk in a disputed no-man's-land. "The locals are afraid to

Edwin Seracarpio, owner of a small fishing fleet, greeting his vessels returning to harbor, Palawan, Philippines

go out to the west because there are a lot of Chinese boats—military vessels," he said. "The Chinese say it has always been their property. This is really unfair."

The stories of people like Seracarpio, more than any nautical charts or even legal arguments, best convey the brashness of China's sweeping historical claims, which amount to an argument in favor of a civilizational prerogative grounded in hierarchy. In defending China's nine-dash line, academics working in Chinese state think tanks have routinely argued that it was the Chinese who discovered the rich fishing waters like these that are scattered throughout the South China Sea along with the islands and other formations that dot them. It was the Chinese, they say, who first made traditional use of them, and therefore established a continuous historical claim to them. In effect, according to this view, little does it matter that the waters in question come right up to the very shores of modern-day states, including the Philippines and Malaysia, because such places were once populated by barbarians. It is considered natural that the Chinese, being civilized, would have roamed far and wide in pursuit of economic activity from time immemorial. To follow this argument to its conclusion, the ancestors of the locals who populate places such as these today, unlike the Chinese, never ventured forth in pursuit of their own livelihoods, or if they did, their actions could not be considered consequential, given who they were. The Chinese claim, in this line of thinking, is therefore valid.

For all of China's arguments on behalf of its supposedly ancient claims in the region, the cartography of the nine-dash line is utterly recent. An essentially identical segmented map, albeit with eleven dashes, made its first appearance in 1947, when China was still ruled by the Nationalist government of Chiang Kai-shek. This map was first used officially in 1958 to represent a Chinese view of the country's legitimate territorial claims. (No one knows who first drew it up, and it is crudely imprecise.) The map's real genesis lies in the country's turbulent early-twentieth-century history, when China was struggling to modernize on the fly, under immense pressure from a range of aggressive outsiders, especially Japan.

China's defeat in the Sino-Japanese War was a huge watershed in its modernization process, a moment, as I've said, when the scales seemed to fall from the eyes of the Chinese elite, allowing them finally to see beyond their long-held superiority and aloofness, and abandon, if only temporarily, their traditional hierarchical view of the world, whose default mode called for dealing with foreigners on their terms or not at all. This was clearly no longer possible after Japan had absorbed the Ryukyu kingdom and then colonized both Taiwan and Korea, the most Sinicized state in East Asia. "After the Sino-Japanese War . . . [our former Chinese] arrogance almost completely disappeared," wrote one intellectual, Ou Jujia, in 1899 for the *Qingyi Bao (Journal of Pure Critique)*, an important turn-of-the-century publication for the country's reformers.

The turnabout after China's defeat in East Asia's first modern war took the form of a national *prise de conscience* that was remarkably crisp. In *Staging the World: Chinese Nationalism at the Turn of the Twentieth Century*, Rebecca E. Karl recounts the visit to China in 1881—two years after Japan's summary takeover of Ryukyu—of King Kalakaua of Hawaii, as part of a world tour undertaken by the monarch. Kalakaua's hold on his islands was coming under intensifying threat by American plantation and maritime interests, and Hawaii's population was collapsing due to exposure to unfamiliar diseases borne by the white newcomers. Kalakaua issued an urgent warning to the Chinese about the coming Western-led global transition that he believed threatened to devastate the peoples of Asia, making it imperative that they unite.

The king was received by Li Hongzhang, China's most powerful official outside of the Qing court itself. Li, whom we have already met, was in charge of China's relations with the outside world. Kalakaua had been greeted with pomp and circumstance during a previous stopover in Tokyo, but the Chinese accorded him no such ceremony or importance. "We arrived at Shanghai at noon. . . . No royal salutes were fired as we entered the Woosung river. . . . We dropped suddenly from the pinnacle of royal hospitality to its base, and the royal standard lay dejectedly in its canvas bag," wrote a member of Kalakaua's party.

In a memorandum to the Qing court after meeting with Kalakaua in Tianjin, Li wrote:

> [The king said]: "Since ancient times, the world has been divided into three large continents: Asia, Europe and Africa. . . . We [Hawaiians] are Asians, as are you [Chinese]. . . . [The Europeans] settled Africa, which they have already completely swallowed up in their insatiable greed. Recently they have also been nibbling away at Asia. . . . As of now, white people have settled four and a half continents, and Asians cannot even protect the half-continent that remains. . . .
>
> We cannot be complacent. The past strength of brown peoples [Asians] is gradually declining. The reason we cannot arouse ourselves is because each country relies on its own past strength. We not only have failed to unite together to depend upon one another, but on the contrary, we are cruel to one another. This is a great pity. If we unite, we will be strong; if we persist in division, our energy will be depleted. . . .
>
> We [Asians] should discuss affairs with sympathy for one another and united as one; it is unbearable that China and Japan have lost their good will [toward one another]. [I] have warned the Japanese emperor, and now [I] am cautioning you, Li: if we were able to unite so as not to leave foreigners a single opening, would this not be the best way to arouse our brown Asian peoples? I eagerly await for this to happen."

In Karl's view, it likely came as a shock to Li, easily one of the best informed and most sophisticated people of the day, that Hawaii and China were both "Asian," and that peoples of these two lands could be considered—however loosely—as belonging to the same race. Li, she writes, would have found the king's "claims and pleas not only presumptuous but outlandish. For clearly, Hawaii impinged little on Li Hongzhang's consciousness, and the islands in no way helped structure his thoughts about the world and even less about the Qing empire. Despite the partial loss of territory and sovereignty to foreign powers that had followed the Opium Wars, [the Qing empire] was still relatively secure in its ability to reassert its sociopolitical autonomy and its civilizational universality."

For China, the concept of race, such as it existed, had hitherto been dominated by considerations of culture. Only those who were Sinicized (同文—*tongwen*) could be thought of as being of the same race as Chinese. At a bare minimum, this would have meant that they wrote in Chinese characters and used the Chinese imperial calendar. After their defeat in 1895, the Chinese were able to begin seeing Asians as a category of people whom one could usefully think of as being issued from a common race (同种—*tongzhong*), and therefore people whose destinies were broadly linked in an age of unprecedented global upheaval.

Ironically, just a few years later it would initially be Hawaii, and then shortly afterward the Philippines, that would play a critical role in bringing about this change of consciousness. When the first attempt at reform of the Chinese imperial system in the post–Sino-Japanese War period collapsed in 1898, some of the country's greatest young minds fled overseas to learn whatever they could from other young modern nation-states, to raise money for revolution and to gain new perspective on China. The most important of these figures was Liang Qichao, who fled to Japan in 1898 and traveled from there to Hawaii, where he briefly lived among the Chinese emigrant community on the island and wrote and reflected about nationhood, identity and the urgent necessity that China open itself to change.

Liang's writings cast a sharp eye on two important and intimately related events that were shaping the fortunes of Asia: the emergence of the United States as an ascendant new imperial force, determined to fulfill the nearly fifty-year-old prophecy of Commodore Perry by projecting its power clear across the Pacific, and America's conquest and colonization of the Philippines. The American militarization of Hawaii, beginning with the creation of coaling stations, then of military bases and concluding with the annexation of the islands in July 1898, was closely monitored in the Chinese press of the day. The

American takeover of the Philippines followed almost immediately on the heels of these events, and the combination of the two helped Chinese thinkers anchor a sense of the Pacific as a geopolitical space for the very first time. In one breath, Chinese writers spoke of the dawn of a new imperialist era under the aegis of the United States, which they criticized for betraying its founding ideals by gobbling up territory in Cuba, Hawaii and the Philippines and making common cause with other imperialist nations by intervening in China to help put down the Boxer Rebellion in 1900–1901.[*]

In a 1903 essay in a publication called *Tides of Zhejiang (Zhejiang chao),* a Tokyo-based Chinese author who adopted the pen name Monroe Lover spoke of the growing mutability of the Monroe Doctrine, which had originally been conceived as a mandate to "protect" the Americas from Europeans who might seek to project power there. "Its principles embody the spirit of the physical location of the American continent on which it concentrates. However, its principles also leak into those areas on which the Doctrine has designs but which have not yet experienced it, and are not of the American continent and thus do not pertain to the historicity of Doctrine's era. The Monroe Doctrine is just that sort of subtle thing that cannot be predicted."

The United States had expected its assumption of control of the Philippines to go without a hitch after the defeat of the Spanish fleet there on May 1, 1898, during the Spanish-American War. Prominent American politicians of the day took for granted that its takeover of the islands would be gratefully seen as a civilizing act, a liberation by a just, humane and divinely entitled power. These fin de siècle American expansionists thought it natural that the United States should emulate the imperial mission of Great Britain, and they even were cheered on in this by champions of the British empire, including most notably Rudyard Kipling, whose famous 1899 poem "The White Man's Burden" was published with the far less well-known

---

[*]The name "Boxer Rebellion" lends confusion. These militias mobilized to oppose Western Christian missionaries, but at times supported and were supported by the waning Qing dynasty.

subtitle: "The United States and the Philippine Islands." With that country in mind, the seven-stanza poem urged Americans to "search your manhood" and "send forth the best ye breed," to take colonial charge of a new population of "new-caught, sullen peoples, half-devil and half-child."

"Distance and oceans are no arguments" for reluctance or caution, said a leading American defender of the takeover of the Philippines, Albert Beveridge, a Republican senator from Indiana. Americans were "a people imperial by virtue of their power, by right of their institutions, by authority of their Heaven-directed purposes," he claimed, sounding almost like a pitchman for *tian xia*. Americans, he continued, should "broaden [the] blessed reign" of freedom "until the empire of our principles is established over the hearts of all mankind."

To be clear, the jingoist speech of people like Beveridge was not all about virtue, no more so than was Kipling's poem. It was heavily and unmistakably also laden with racial messaging of a sort that was not lost on Chinese observers. Liang's *Journal of Pure Critique* published one statement by a Filipino that would have had strong and immediate resonance for any Chinese person of the era: "How can this island of ours, insignificant as it might be, be constrained in ways normally reserved for dogs and horses?" Attentive Chinese would also have been aware of the debate that quickly arose in the United States over exclusion of members of the significant Chinese minority in the Philippines from immigration to the United States.

Over a period of a thousand years, God, Beveridge said in 1898, had prepared the "English-speaking and people" to become "the master organizers of the world." The subjects of America's fledgling colonial project, by contrast, were "Malays" debilitated by the "alchemy" of "hundreds of years of savagery, other hundreds of years of Orientalism, and still other hundreds of years of Spanish character and custom."

As it transpired, however, the United States' snap victory over Spain was not taken by Filipinos as their liberation. To the confusion and then consternation of the Americans, the Philippine armed forces mounted a highly spirited and tactically inventive, if ultimately unsuccessful, war of guerrilla-style resistance to rule by their new colonizers. American textbooks often wrongly pass it off as a mere "insurrection," which conforms with the United States' flattering and carefully tended but erroneous self-image of never having been an imperialist power. In fact, the valor and resourcefulness of the Filipino independence fighters caused Theodore Roosevelt in 1902 to describe the prolonged campaign to snuff out resistance in the American colony as "a small but particularly trying and difficult war." The conflict also left telling marks on the American language, with the adoption of such words as "gooks," a slur for Asians that many believe, mistakenly, dates from the Vietnam War, and "boondocks," a Tagalog word for remote rural area that was repurposed to mean at the outer limits of civilization.

To Chinese observers, the conflict had an impact akin to that of the Russo-Japanese War in 1905 much more broadly on many non-white peoples around the world: confirmation that armed, organized resistance to Western conquest and domination was not futile.

"The Philippine sea is close to us," wrote Ou Jujia in Liang's *Journal of Pure Critique* in 1899. "The wind of freedom and independence [emanating from there] will blow over our whole country . . . and then our 400 million compatriots will cultivate patriotism in their hearts and it will have been the Philippines that aided us in overcoming our precarious situation."

Out of the American war in the Philippines grew a very specific Chinese reaction, a consciousness or awareness whose existence the Hawaiian king had found utterly wanting: the notion of being Asian, of belonging, at least loosely, to a race that went beyond old notions of *tongwen,* or shared adoption of Chinese culture. "Not only for Liang, but for many others, in the Philippine insurgency was found the first proximate example of how a 'stateless' people could turn their weakness and 'statelessness' to strength and purposeful activity," writes Karl in *Staging the World.* Ironically, a nation historically seen by China as being populated by uncooked "island barbarians" was now helping the Chinese engineer a transformation of consciousness that would give birth to a modern idea of nationalism of their own for the first time.

As an empire built upon a succession of dynasties, China had never had a fixed name as a country, nor anything like a universally shared national language, nor for that matter anything remotely resembling a national history. Here again, Liang Qichao played a leading role, in essays like his 1901 "Introduction to Chinese History," helping formulate an idea of the nation for the first time. "What I feel most shameful of is that our country does not have a name. The name of the Han or people of Tang are only names of Dynasties, and the name 'China' that foreign countries use is not a name that we call ourselves." From Hawaii two years earlier, Liang had written, "The Chinese people do not even know there is such a thing as a national people [*guomin*]. After several thousand years, there have been the two words *guo jia* [state, family] but I have never heard the two words *guo min* [state, people] ever uttered. *Guojia* is when one family [*jia*] owns the state [*guo*] as private property. . . . *Guomin* connotes when the state [*guo*] belongs to the people [*min*] as public property. . . . This [*guomin*] is then called a national people." He went on to identify the need to mobilize this national people, or nationalism, as one would say in contemporary parlance, as a means of holding China together and allowing it to resist foreign domination and rapidly modernize on its own terms.

A new narrative emerged powerfully from currents of thought like this, one that Karl calls the "frustrated state" narrative. It represented a revolt against two forms of colonization, the one from without that we have already considered, and the one from within. The reaction to supposed internal colonization, however, was based on a surge in Han chauvinism and resentment against what was now being portrayed as usurpation by the Qing (or Manchus) in 1644, by inference an inferior neighboring people who had brought China low. The Qing, according to this narrative, were responsible for China's decadence, its inability to modernize in step with Japan and its inability to fend off aggressive outsiders from tsarist Russia and Europe. The solution called not only for the overthrow of the Qing, but also for the invention of a new nation and indeed a new people to be endowed with a new history.

A major subtheme of this frustrated state narrative was a grievance over the loss of what China saw as its national rights as suzerain over a collection of surrounding "tributaries." The leaders of the late Qing era were derided as bunglers who had frittered away China's rightful patrimony. For example, only belatedly had they mounted efforts to stave off the foreign takeover of China's two most important vassals, Korea and Vietnam, by Japan and France respectively. And in their neglect of their sacred duty to hold close the vassals who constituted the world of *tian xia,* they had failed to realize that both of them had been acting as practically independent states in dealings with foreign powers for several years by the time the Qing aroused itself.

As the Republican era replaced the Qing dynasty in 1912 the emphasis shifted subtly from China's many defeats since the First Opium War to transmitting a message to future generations of their duty to recover China's lost prerogatives. One important work of history from this era, *Diplomatic Documents of Qing,* spoke of the affront of invasions suffered at the hands of peoples who were "inferior to China and used to pay tribute to our nation." The authors wrote that the book had been compiled in order to "alert our descendants." In efforts like these, most Chinese writers devoted special attention to Japan, now China's most threatening nemesis. The 1919 *Textbook of Chinese Language for Elementary School* spoke of China's neighbor this way:

> Japan is an island nation developed after the Meiji Restoration. It placed Okinawa prefecture on our Ryukyu, forced us to cede our Taiwan, leased our Luda [an industrial port in northeastern China], annexed Korea, colonized our Manchuria. It intends to expand its power of transportation and commerce. . . . Japan is a country like a bullet, managed by both domestic and foreign governments. Japan has aimed to target China, and has used any opportunities to invade China as a weak country. Unless we in China come to be a strong country, we cannot remove the shame of our country and enhance our national prestige. Our diplomacy was the most tragic failure

of the Qing Dynasty. . . . Japan . . . has violated our sovereignty continuously.

The insistence here on Ryukyu is due to its being a payer of tribute, and hence a pillar of *tian xia*; Taiwan, inhabited by barbarians, was a mere territorial issue for China. One year earlier, in an exchange on opposition to imperialism and solidarity with other Asian countries published in the *Jiu Kuo Daily,* a Shanghai newspaper, Ceng Qi wrote that "when China was a great power, Korea and Annam [Vietnam] were her tributary states, but China's status was threatened when she lost her national rights during the late Qing. . . . China must struggle and make all efforts to become a great power and become supreme in East Asia, and will not only restore Korea, Annam, Siam [Thailand] and Burma, but make these into Chinese territory. Japan, as well as the countries of the South Seas [,] all received benefits from China. Therefore they are all territories of China."

This seemingly extreme statement was not radically out of line with much of that era's conversation within China about former tributaries and *tian xia*. The challenge of trying to conceptualize a viable country amid the turbulence and depredations of Republican-era China was in part one of reimagining the past through the ready use of selective, idealized memories and outright unsupported notions.

In his March 1924 Principle of Nationalism, for example, Sun Yat-sen, the president of a hoped-for Republican China, stated that "because China had such a peaceful principle toward tributary countries, these countries like Vietnam, Burma and Siam were able to be independent for thousands of years." Later that year, Sun took this thought even further, saying, "These weaker nations surrounding China were influenced by Chinese values and virtue without military menace from China. These nations felt its superiority. . . . Once they were influenced by Chinese values and virtue, they did not send tributary envoys only once or twice, but did so many times from generation to generation." Of the three countries mentioned, Vietnam was the only true vassal of China in any sustained sense, and yet even its relationship with China offered up a record of stark contradiction to Sun Yat-sen's potted history. In *The Birth of Vietnam*, the historian Keith Weller Taylor writes that in dealing with its imposing neighbor, Vietnam "had grown to understand China only as a slave can know its master," and added that "over the past 1,000 years, the Vietnamese have no less than seven times defeated attempts by China to assert its influence by force."

The new China that Republican thinkers were struggling to invent was itself of two minds about China's place in Asia, and these two irreconcilable perspectives live on today in China's self-conception, in the way it engages with the world, and specifically in its territorial disputes with the Philippines and with other littoral states over ownership of the South China Sea. On the one hand, as the 1930s magazine *New East* stated in its first issue, invoking the Pan-Asianism of Sun Yat-sen, "the future of the East is a liberated world where all ethnicities will stand together as equals." On the other hand, there were simultaneous calls for a restoration of China's so-called national rights, which included the recovery and reincorporation of lost tributaries—both real and imagined—under Chinese leadership and control. Indeed, for two decades, Chiang Kai-shek wrote the characters for *Xuechi*, or "avenge humiliation," in the top right corner of each day's diary entry. On March 27, 1934, that entry continued, "Recover Taiwan and Korea. Recover the land that was originally part of the Han and Tang dynasty. Then, as descendants of the Yellow Emperor, we will have no shame."

It is in sentiments like these that we find the real ancestry of the nine-dash line map, and indeed its true significance. It is a lineal descendant of maps from the early decades of the twentieth century, such as the so-called Map of National Shame of 1938, published by the Ministry of Internal Affairs, which indicated a traditional Chinese view of the country's rights under *tian xia* and set forth a cartographic benchmark of territory to be "recovered," by which Chinese governments of the day and governments of the future might be judged.* The territory to be "recovered" traces a broad loop around much of Asia, encompassing all of Korea and Mongolia, parts of

---

*See the "Map of National Shame" on page 13.

Siberia and even chunks of Pakistan and India, before dipping down into Southeast Asia, where it encloses the Nicobar Islands, Burma and the entirety of Indochina and threads its way through the Strait of Malacca, to include the Malay Peninsula and Singapore, before turning northward to take in the South China Sea, Taiwan, all of the Ryukyus and most of the Sea of Japan. It is this map that brings us back to the shores of Palawan.

I met Eduardo Tadem in his office at the Asia Center at the University of the Philippines. He sat at his desk beneath a red-and-black block print poster of Che Guevara as we spoke, Mozart issuing gently from his desktop. From the very outset, Tadem, who is an expert in Southeast Asian studies, made clear his conciliatory views toward China regarding the territorial dispute that pits it against his country over control of the South China Sea. It is people like Tadem, the representative of a distinct but articulate minority throughout Southeast Asia, who incarnate Beijing's best hope of having its interests accommodated, at least peacefully.

"Long before our dispute over Scarborough Shoal, Philippine and Chinese fishermen were taking advantage of the resources of this sea—yes, since time immemorial, even before the rise of states," he said, referring to a chain of reefs and rocks that is the focus of one of several maritime disputes between the Philippines and China. "They got along fine and had their own ways of aiding each other. That is all gone now, with the insistence on sovereignty. Now, no one can fish, because of the presence of naval vessels—Chinese vessels, unfortunately."

Despite this observation, Tadem takes issue with what he calls the realist's view of the region's geopolitics, a confrontational one, which he calls a "recipe for conflict, even all-out war." Countries like the Philippines should meet China halfway, he suggested. Civil societies should bring countries closer together, knowing that China's small and increasingly embattled civil society has almost no voice on international relations. This would mean finding ways to share coveted resources, he said, perhaps even including Reed Bank, an area of the

Spratlys known to be rich in hydrocarbons. (The nearby Malampaya gas field, which is located fifty miles west of northern Palawan, supplies 40 percent of the Philippines' energy needs.) "We have to move away from the world of absolute sovereignty, absolute territorial boundaries," he said.

I asked Tadem why China was pressing its expansive claims almost up to his country's shores, and that brought the conversation to *tian xia*. The good news, he said, is that if China "can be made to hold true to that concept of a tributary system—the giving of gifts to China, the exchange of ambassadors and all that—this did not really affect the sovereignty and independence of the different kingdoms and city-states in the area. Because, you know, if China asserts that historical basis, different states in the region can say, 'Okay, fine, we can go back to what we had before. We'll give you certain presents, recognize whatever you wish us to recognize.' . . . The bad news is that China is probably thinking in a more modern way about the area, thinking about three things: oil, maritime routes and fishing resources. The oil is speculative. The maritime routes are real, and they are already being used. And the fish stocks are also real. So maybe, realistically, it is not so much the oil, the energy reserves in the oil, but the sea routes and the fishing resources that they are after."

Others have placed less stock in scenarios involving a revival of tributary-style relations. The real purpose behind China's recent assertiveness, they believe, is applying pressure on much weaker neighbors until they sue for peace and then in effect divvy up the natural resource spoils in the entire 3.5-million-square-mile nautical region of the South China Sea as China wishes. "It's basically highway robbery, because they have their guns pointed at all of us," said Harry Roque, a Filipino attorney who advised the government on its case under the United Nations Convention on the Law of the Sea. People who have long been involved in the country's foreign policy at a senior level believe that the Philippines was now belatedly doing what most realists would have predicted for it all along: arming itself and upgrading the training of its military so as to raise the price for China of its pushiness, creating a minimally credible military deterrent. It also began to seriously court the United States again. When

President Obama visited the Philippines in November 2015, the two countries announced a ten-year defense pact that reversed Philippine policy on American use of military bases there. Obama's news conference was pointedly staged against the backdrop of the BRP *Gregorio del Pilar,* a former U.S. Coast Guard cutter that is now the flagship of the Philippine navy. "We have a treaty obligation, an ironclad commitment to the defense of our ally the Philippines, who can count on the United States," he said. "My visit here underscores our shared commitment to the security of the waters of this region and to the freedom of navigation."*

So far, China has responded coolly to the stepped-up American support for the Philippines and other South China Sea neighbors with which it has maritime disputes. "It will be up to the United States to decide if it wants to go to war with China for the sake of the Philippines and Vietnam," Yan Xuetong, a prominent Chinese foreign policy hawk told the *New York Times.* "It's not China's call."

Speaking of his country's rush to strengthen its military, a former national security adviser told me, "As to when we need to put everything in place to achieve that minimum posture, we give ourselves until 2020—maybe a little more, to 2025. That's the window when we think China will start making bolder moves, that's the danger period. If a coalition [of regional balancing states] firms up between now and then, and something happens in the South China Sea, we can't be the weak link in that chain. We have to be able to stand our own ground, in our own zone. So the strategy is to beef up our naval and air forces."

On Palawan, Filipino contractors were already building a new naval base that defense officials in the country pretend will be a "new Subic Bay." The phrase jars, because it is so out of proportion with the means that the Philippines can devote to military modernization, but also because it starkly evokes the recent past. There are few countries whose modern fate and fortunes have been more deeply shaped

---

*In March 2016, the Philippines announced that it had agreed to open four air bases and one army camp to American forces, paving the way for prepositioning U.S. troops in that country for the first time in a quarter century.

by the United States than the Philippines. After terminating Spanish colonial rule there a little more than a century ago, the United States embarked on a prolonged colonial project of its own. By defeating Japan in World War II, it liberated the Philippines, only to reassert its influence, which peaked during the Cold War, when being an American ambassador to Manila was akin to being a proconsul. Back then, the naval base at Subic Bay, fifty miles northwest of the capital, was home to the U.S. Seventh Fleet, and it ranked as the second-largest American overseas military installation in the world. Nearby Clark Air Base was number one.

The two bases, which had both played crucial roles in the Vietnam War and in support of American military commitments in Asia more generally, were badly damaged by the eruption of Mount Pinatubo in 1991, which blanketed the immediate area in thick layers of dust. Five years earlier, amid a strong blush of democracy in the Philippines, a movement dubbed People's Power overthrew the dictatorship of Washington's longtime authoritarian client, Ferdinand Marcos. In the wake of the catastrophic eruption, the government decided not to renew the United States' lease on the two bases. The departure of the American sailors and airmen hastened a period of stark disinvestment by the Philippines in its own national defense, ironically just as it was standing on its own for the first time.

Early in the following decade, with Gloria Macapagal Arroyo as president, relations with the United States deteriorated further—mostly as a result of American petulance. In 2003, the Philippines sent a small contingent of humanitarian workers to Iraq to support the Bush administration's invasion of that country. But after a Filipino truck driver was taken hostage, the Arroyo government negotiated his release in exchange for its earlier-than-scheduled withdrawal from the coalition. She was then snubbed by an angry Bush administration. When Arroyo was elected to a second term, she quickly drew closer to China. This reorientation of the country's foreign policy was richly rewarded by Beijing, which was eager to peel away a traditional ally of the United States, all the more because its physical position in the South China Sea forms a major part of the First Island Chain, the long picket-fence-like archipelago we have spoken about that stretches from the Kuril Islands through Japan all the way south to the Philippines and the Malay Peninsula. The chain's geography places it bestride some of the key choke points that govern China's freedom of access to the open ocean.

China generated $8 billion in new lending to back ambitious investment schemes in the Philippines, whose infrastructure was woefully underdeveloped and whose economy lagged badly behind the leading performers of the region. Big Chinese state corporations soon obtained lucrative contracts to build railroads and a national broadband network. Rumors of kickbacks and illicit inducements for both sides began to proliferate. Some of these came back to haunt Arroyo, who became embroiled in corruption scandals and was held in medical custody for nearly five years on charges of electoral sabotage and lottery fraud. She finally won her release in July 2016 on appeal before the country's supreme court.

In 2004, amid the torrent of new Chinese money pouring into the country, Arroyo signed a secretive agreement with Beijing that called for joint exploration for oil in areas of the South China Sea disputed by China and the Philippines. Known as the Joint Maritime Seismic Undertaking, this agreement was joined later by Vietnam, its exact terms to be kept confidential for five years. With allegations of kickbacks swirling around the Arroyo administration's other dealings with China, however, the secrecy did not hold, and before long many in the country's political class were accusing Arroyo of treason and claiming that she had sold out the Philippines' territorial interests in exchange for money from China. Her critics complained that the terms of the agreement were one-sidedly skewed against the Philippines, because the entire 143,000 square kilometers of ocean that it covered all clearly fell within the Philippines' continental shelf according to any conventional definition of its exclusive economic zone under the United Nations Convention on the Law of the Sea, and indeed its control over them had never previously been disputed by either China or Vietnam. By contrast, no waters close to China were to be included in the survey. "China's bottom line on joint exploration," wrote the *Far Eastern Economic Review,* seemed to be "What is mine is mine and what is yours is ours."

The deal for cooperation in oil exploration was allowed to lapse in 2008, two years ahead of time. This angered China, which must have sensed itself in striking distance of a very big coup. If the joint exploration had been pursued to its conclusion, according to its terms China would have won the rights to a big portion of the undersea hydrocarbons in the region. The extent of the reserves is a matter of speculation, but they have been estimated at 35 billion tons of oil in the area of the Spratlys alone, along with as much as 3.4 trillion cubic feet of natural gas in the Reed Bank zone—enough to supply the energy needs of the Philippines for a hundred years. Although the agreement fell apart, Beijing hardly came away empty-handed. China had conducted the seismic surveying using its own technical means, and now it possessed every bit of data. Moreover, invoking its supposed historic claims, it would argue that the zones opened to joint exploration by the Philippines—areas never previously in dispute—were Chinese territory. In seeming payback for Manila's abrupt about-face, China sent ships into the area of Reed Bank to harass and ultimately scare away crews doing exploration under contract with the Philippines. Since then, virtually the entire sea has been officially claimed by China, via the nine-dash line map that it lodged at the United Nations. China was now opting for unilateralism based on disproportionate military and economic power.

In 2013, the Philippines responded to China's moves by filing its case before an arbitral tribunal under UNCLOS to have the nine-dash line discredited. Both countries were members of the convention, which took force in 1994. UNCLOS had been especially popular among developing countries because it seemed to enshrine extended control over the waters off their coasts—from the customary twelve nautical miles of exclusive offshore territorial rights to the two-hundred-mile limit. In the far larger zone (beyond the twelve nautical miles closest to the shore), waters would be open to navigation by all countries, but lucrative activities like fishing and mining would be restricted to the coastal nation. This appealed to weaker countries in part because few of them had the means to prospect for mineral or hydrocarbon deposits in deep seas. This preserved a share for them of the wealth located in or beneath these waters, via deals they could strike with multinational companies, or by gradually developing the relevant mining technologies themselves. China, which itself had a weak maritime presence and poor technology in the 1980s, when the convention was concluded, embraced this vision with particular enthusiasm.

The Philippines' case before an ad hoc tribunal in The Hague, however, put China in an extremely awkward position. Its warnings to Manila against resorting to international law had gone unheeded. Whatever the merits of its historical arguments, Beijing would have surely known from the outset that the vague nine-dash line had no basis in modern international law. Although it was a signatory to UNCLOS, Beijing immediately signaled that it would not present any case before the tribunal and vowed that it would disregard the findings of the tribunal if they were unfavorable to its interests in any way. Moreover, it promptly initiated a campaign to undermine the legitimacy of the process, and hinted darkly that it might even withdraw from UNCLOS altogether. This presented the Hague-based court with a number of serious predicaments, indeed one of them quasi-existential. If it ruled sweepingly against China's maritime claims via the nine-dash line, Beijing might make good on its threat to withdraw from the convention, potentially to be followed by Russia, its frequent tactical ally in strategic matters. At a minimum, that would leave the law unsubscribed to by the world's two most powerful nations—the convention was signed by the United States but never ratified by the Senate—and hence nudging it toward irrelevance.

It seemed theoretically possible, meanwhile, that victory by China in the case, on the other hand, could take one of two forms, and neither of them would bode any better for the convention. The tribunal could employ some dubious logic or fuzzy language to rule in China's favor, even partially, just to keep it in the fold, even though Beijing never put forward its own case or participated in any way in the deliberations. Alternately, the tribunal could simply declare its nonjurisdiction in the matter. Either route would have risked rendering UNCLOS useless for the settlement of major maritime territorial disputes in the future, though, not least because the world's many small countries would conclude that far from being independent, the court defers to great powers in matters where their interests are in play.

Throughout the two-and-a-half-year timespan during which the case was deliberated, this led many to expect that the tribunal would try to somehow split the difference, giving the Philippines satisfaction on some points and China on others, especially perhaps by carefully avoiding making any sweeping statements of judicial principle or strong precedent that could be readily used by other small claimant states in the region, emboldening them to also take legal action against China.

When it was announced on July 12, 2016, though, the decision surprised many for its nearly categorical rejection of China's claims. Although it did not address the nine-dash line frontally, it left it severely discredited nonetheless. Chinese experts had long protested that the case was illegal, because the Philippines had failed to seek a negotiated solution beforehand. The tribunal rejected this argument saying that Manila had indeed sought to negotiate, but in a multilateral framework along with other claimants, which China, in a manner true to its *tian xia* reflexes, rejected. China, being the far larger and more powerful country, had insisted that only bilateral talks would do. Chinese experts then said that the court did not have jurisdiction in the matter, because at bottom this was a territorial dispute, and UNCLOS was not empowered to address questions of disputed territorial sovereignty. Here again, the tribunal rejected Chinese arguments, saying that what was being decided was not ownership of maritime real estate per se, but rather what does and does not constitute an island under UNCLOS, and in function of this determination whether there was any theoretical possibility of an overlap between Chinese claims to rightful ownership of all of the features in the Spratly Islands (plus Scarborough Shoal) and the Philippines' two-hundred-mile Exclusive Economic Zone.

China's final major argument, again, like all of the others made outside of tribunal proceedings, was that the seas contained within the nine-dash line, an area roughly the size of Mexico, was a region over which China had since time immemorial, as the famous phrase holds, demonstrated historical control. This, it dismissed out of hand, saying "although Chinese navigators and fishermen, as well as those of other States, had historically made use of the *islands* in the South China Sea, there was no evidence that China had historically exercised exclusive control over the *waters* or their resources. [italics as per the original document] The Tribunal concluded that there was no legal basis for China to claim historic rights to the resources within the seas falling within the 'nine-dash line'."

The tribunal's five hundred-plus-page unanimous judgment found yet other ways to reject China's history-based arguments. Noting that historical claims such as China's had been the subject of negotiation in the drafting of the UNCLOS laws, and rejected by the signatories, it said that any arguments based upon custom that ran contrary to the law were superceded by the treaty once it took effect.

On the question of what constitutes an island, the tribunal's ruling was just as unfavorable. As promised, it made no determination as to whom belongs which speck of land in the Spratlys, but ruled that none of what China (or other claimants) said were islands met the legal definitions of such. Instead, it said that some of the maritime features controlled by China were mere rocks, meaning modest protrusions of land or coral that can be seen at high tide, and others were mere "low-tide elevations," meaning features that are only visible during ebb tides. This meant that no feature in the Spratlys, Chinese controlled or otherwise, affords any party a two-hundred-mile Exclusive Economic Zone, but at best a twelve-mile zone of territorial control. The low-tide elevations, including several of the features that China had built into impressive artificial islands while the tribunal was deliberating the case, meanwhile, are not entitled to any exclusive maritime zones.

What this meant was that the Philippines' rights within its two-hundred-mile EEZ were restored, at least theoretically. It also meant that the so-called freedom of navigation exercises that the United States Navy has conducted in the Spratlys since China's island-building spree began are on firm legal ground when they enter into the waters that lap the shores of the new Chinese-controlled features there.

China's initial response to all of this was one of both systematic rejection and unrelenting scorn. "The South China Sea arbitration has been a political farce all along, staged under the cover of law and driven by a hidden agenda," said Yang Jiechi, the state councilor for foreign affairs. "Certain countries outside the region have attempted to deny China's sovereign rights and interests in the South China Sea through the arbitration. They have even brought other countries into the scheme to isolate and discredit China in the international community with a view to holding back China's peaceful development. But such attempts are futile, to say the least, and in so doing, they are only lifting a stone to drop it on their own feet." Yang denounced the composition of the tribunal's five-member panel, alleging that it had been assembled by a right-wing Japanese official "intent on ridding Japan of postwar arrangements." Others simply called the judges professionally incompetent, with particular scorn reserved for the presiding judge, an African, Thomas A. Mensah, of Ghana. Still more voices weighed in with the complaint that because the tribunal's other members were all European, the panel was entirely unfamiliar with "Asian culture."

With their strenuous and often strident language, officials like Yang were claiming to be the lone true defenders of international legality. If this was unlikely to impress international opinion, it seemed to pass muster with a domestic audience, partly because due to state censorship of news reports about the tribunal's decision, the Chinese public had been carefully kept in the dark about the legal foundation of the ruling and the arguments deployed to explain it. The Chinese populace was not the only hostage in this propaganda exercise, however. Because the state had gone on for so long, and with such vehemence about China's incontestable and inalienable rights in the South China Sea, Beijing found itself boxed into a corner; rhetorically, there was no plausible way of changing tack, certainly not publicly or quickly. To do so would have brought a denunciation of the Xi Jinping government for selling the country out. This led to chest-beating reaffirmations like this from Yang, in the wake of the unfavorable ruling. "Sovereignty is a bottom line for China. Big as China is, we cannot afford to give away a single inch of territory that our ancestors have left to us. China's sovereignty and maritime rights and interests in the South China Sea have been formed over the course of over two thousand years. They are fully backed by historical and legal evidence. Under no circumstances can they ever be negated by a so-called award that is full of nonsense."

China's response had other important implications beyond immediate tactical questions, though. In fact, Beijing's scornful and paranoia-tinged language had placed it very close to resorting to its familiar old civilizational case: Westerners, not us, created the international system, and despite our fidelity to it, they are now using it as a ruse to deny China of its prerogatives. From here, it is but a small step to more sweeping revisionism as an outlet for Chinese frustration and a cover for its questionable behavior.

The bottom line is that, as an emerging great power, China is determined to have its way in the nearby seas that surround it, and no amount of law or even international public opinion, in the long run, will dissuade it or divert it from that goal.

That view and a kind of imperial perspective—of *tian xia*—could already be discerned in the remarks of the head of China's National Institute for South China Sea Studies, Wu Shicun, when he met with Filipino reporters on Hainan in September 2014, nearly two years before the tribunal ruling. "Suppose the tribunal makes its final judgment, the problem between China and the Philippines will still be there," he said. "Suppose that, as what Philippine scholars have been saying, if everything goes smoothly and successfully, . . . China will not honor that word."

Then, in a clear invocation of the logic of the tribute system, Wu noted that bilateral trade between China and Malaysia had recently surpassed $100 billion annually, while trade with the Philippines was stuck at a mere $20 billion—this despite the fact that Malaysia had twenty-three million people, compared to the Philippines' eighty-plus million. The only way to improve relations and strongly boost trade, he said, was to shelve the arbitration case. This, he said, would allow for the "joint development" of oil and gas deposits in disputed areas. "[This] is a business deal that should be discussed by China National Offshore Oil Company and the Philippine government—

fifty-fifty." Wu added that if then Philippines president, Benigno Aquino, did not wish to deal on this basis, Beijing was prepared to simply wait out his presidency. Perhaps the next national election, in 2016, would deliver someone more pliable (in the vein of Gloria Arroyo).

"The Chinese are saying, 'Let us have joint development, but our fundamental position [within our continental shelf] is that these resources belong to the Philippines—all of the resources,'" Gilbert Asuque, then Philippine assistant secretary for ocean concerns, told me in 2014.

As it happens, a new president took office in the Philippines on June 30, 2016, a mere two weeks before the Permanent Court of Arbitration in The Hague announced the arbitral tribunal's decision. And the country's new leader, Rodrigo R. Duterte, a rough-edged former mayor turned law-and-order candidate who had hitherto placed relatively little emphasis on international relations, seemed from the perspective of China, almost made to order. During his campaign, Duterte strongly criticized the United States for its supposedly neo-colonial attitude toward his country and vowed that he would seek compromise with Beijing. Asked once if he would pursue bilateral talks with Beijing, as China has demanded, he answered: "We have this pact with the West, but I want everybody to know that we will be charting a course of our own. It will not be dependent on America. And it will be a line that is not intended to please anybody but the Filipino interest." At various moments during the campaign and its immediate aftermath it was strongly hinted that where the Philippines' best interest lay was in developing offshore oil reserves and meeting the country's immense needs in the area of infrastructure development, China's specialty, leaving many to wonder whether this would be the basis of a compromise with Beijing by the new president over disputed territory. Not long after taking office, seemingly out of nowhere, Duterte called Barack Obama a "son of a whore," and then shortly afterward said that joint military exercises with the United States would be terminated, although at the time of this writing there had still been no official confirmation of this policy shift.

However the Duterte presidency unfolds, the Philippines will have to live with a steadily more imposing military power right on its doorstep. This, in turn, means potentially accustoming itself to a near-permanent state of uncertainty—and probably to compromise on issues of fundamental interests, as well. After The Hague ruling in his country's favor, the former solicitor general, Florin Hilbay, compared the contest with Beijing to a basketball game. "This game will take time," he said, calling the arbitration proceedings a "game of lawyers," the "second quarter." Now, he added, "we are moving toward the game of diplomats," which he said would be largely played behind closed doors. "The end goal is for the Philippines to be able to effectively assert its maritime entitlements in the South China Sea/West Philippines Sea. That is the ultimate objective."

China has insisted, however, that the arbitral tribunal ruling against it would have no effect on its sovereignty in the South China Sea, and an early test of this is likely to come under Duterte, who faces the risk of a public opinion backlash and potentially legal challenges if he is seen as being too generous in compromising. Perhaps the most obvious potential flashpoint (and promising backdrop for possible goodwill gestures) is a place called Second Thomas Shoal, which is located 105 nautical miles off Palawan, and is hence located

The Philippine navy's BRP Sierra Madre

well within the Philippines' EEZ. Since 1999, the Philippines had managed to sustain what is surely one of the most unusual naval outposts anywhere in the world there: a severely rusted-out World War II vintage tank landing vessel, the BRP *Sierra Madre,* which Manila deliberately grounded, yet kept under commission. The ship houses a small contingent of Filipino soldiers whose job, however symbolic, is to demonstrate physical control of the reef and the surrounding waters, in defiance of Chinese claims.

China maintains a presence of coast guard vessels nearby, and since 2014 it has been given to playing a game of cat-and-mouse with vessels resupplying the Philippine ship, engaging in hot pursuit in hopes of interdicting them. One day, if this keeps up, the Philippine resupply efforts will fail, and the soldiers aboard the *Sierra Madre* will need to be evacuated. If China were to hold the line, preventing their rescue, this might lead to a clash. Beijing could, on the other hand, choose to lower the temperature around the Second Thomas Shoal in the pursuit of later, larger tactical gains. Without renouncing its claims to the shoal, it could quietly allow Manila to resupply its ship, and perhaps even bring in materials for modest repairs to the faltering vessel. Something like this could provide enough maneuvering room for Duterte to deal.

The Second Thomas Shoal is far from the only scenario for trouble, though. As China invests hugely in its navy and coast guard, which is now building ten-thousand-ton vessels with water cannons so powerful they can sink many smaller, ordinarily seaworthy ships, it will gain the ability to sharply raise the pressure on Philippine positions in many other places. As China outfits its coast guard with huge ships built to a standard that would do most large countries' navies proud, the underequipped Philippines is mostly dependent upon hand-me-down coast guard vessels from the United States for its navy. Another small group of islands off of Palawan, Paga Asa, which measures 0.14 square miles and is home to about two hundred Filipino civilians, comes to mind. In 2014, an article in a Chinese publication, *Qianzhan (Prospects),* said that China would soon incorporate Paga Asa by force, helping Beijing assert control over a vast portion of the South China Sea. "The world's largest aircraft carrier, the [USS] Ford, costs $12.8 billion to build but only has a deck area of 0.026 square kilometers," it read. "An airbase established on Zhongye Island (Paga Asa) will be a dozen times larger and cost much less, but it is unsinkable and has a very long service life."

It is far from clear whether or not China would undertake such a frontal challenge to international legality in the wake of the UNCLOS-based ruling against it. Behind the bland surface unanimity of Chinese government statements about the South China Sea a struggle can be assumed to be underway over the best direction for future policy toward the region, with hardliners in the military and in other constituencies with a vested interest in maritime expansion (the state oil sector, the ship building industry, fisheries, coastal provincial governments), all bolstered by fervently nationalist public opinion, unlikely to be chastened by The Hague tribunal ruling.

Instead of deftly seeking compromise, allowing quiet diplomacy to dominate the second half in the basketball game, China could engage in a kind of "lawfare" of its own. One of the most likely scenarios for this would be to declare the Spratly islands an archipelago, as it has done previously with the Paracel Islands, drawing a territorial baseline around the entire group, in explicit if dubious legalistic rejection of The Hague tribunal's ruling that the Spratlys were incapable of generating an EEZ either singly or on a collective basis. Many analysts claimed to see a premonition of this in China's subtle shift to an insistence on its unimpeachable sovereignty over the "islands" in the Spratlys in the wake of the ruling, dropping mention of the sea itself.

This is where the Philippine illusions of a new Subic Bay come into play, as a country with one of Asia's weakest armed forces races to come to terms with the economic and institutional burdens involved in assuring its own defense. No credible deterrent means higher risks of trouble. This is not just a question of huge new outlays for weapons, but the need to create a competent military and defense culture in a society whose modern history as a colony and then semiprotectorate of the United States during the Cold War has saddled it with passive reflexes.

In Manila I was briefed by an admiral who until recently had been the country's national security adviser. As we sat around a conference table together with a dozen or so staff officers, an aide worked his way through a list of the measures the Philippines was taking in order to raise its state of military preparedness. Most of them involved the hasty acquisition of new weapons systems. "We will have two new multipurpose attack craft, perhaps by 2015," he said. "We will have two new frigates, maybe by 2016. We are acquiring eight new amphibious assault vehicles and two antisubmarine helicopters. We are planning the deployment of many more coast guard vessels. And at Oyster Bay [Palawan] we are building a new pier." With that, the admiral interrupted and took control of the meeting. "Judging by the instruments of national power—economic, diplomatic, information, military strength—we are among the weakest countries in Asia. We certainly cannot match Chinese power. But what we can do is try to prevent them from imposing on us. We can try to assure the application of Philippine and international law." The admiral said that his country had placed great store in the idea of developing a common regional position on territorial disputes in the South China Sea, and especially on the idea of strict and binding rules of conduct by neighboring states. "We are having a hard time because some of the countries—Laos, Cambodia, Burma—are under the influence of China."

A well-fed officer in his late thirties with a quick smile who identified himself as Captain Rodriguez then put a question to me. "How long will it be before a war breaks out between us and China?" he asked. He interrupted me as I labored through my response. "I just hope it is after my time."

CHAPTER THREE

The Gullet of the World

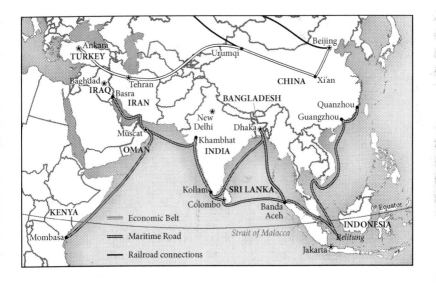

Reaching the top of the steep hill that dominates the mouth of the Malacca River by foot inevitably means sweating copiously in the hot and heavy air of this equatorial region, where the Pacific and Indian oceans converge. At the summit, the hill almost flattens, opening up into a broad plaza where there is a relieving breeze. The view features not just a slowly oozing Malacca River and the narrow streets of the ancient town that clings to it, but the five-hundred-mile-long strait that bears the same name as the river, and beyond it, in the near distance, the Indonesian island of Sumatra.

Statue of Saint Francis Xavier at the hilltop,
sixteenth-century St. Paul's Church in Malacca, Malaysia

Atop this summit, visitors arrive in a place that has served as history's hinge over and over again, a place where globalization began, after a fashion, more than fifteen centuries ago, connecting Persia and the Arab world, Africa and South Asia with China, only to become, much later, an important part of what China fancied as its tributary realm. The plaza on the summit is dominated by the moldering ruins of a nearly five-hundred-year-old church named for Saint Paul. It was built by marauding Portuguese explorers soon after they first came this way, defeating the Malacca sultanate in 1511 and claiming this end of the Malay Peninsula for the crown.

Looking out over this vista is an imposing white statue of Saint Francis Xavier, a Jesuit whose movements in the later stages of his life limned the boundaries of Portugal's new and fast-expanding Asian empire. Five years after Columbus made his first transatlantic voyage, Vasco da Gama set out from Lisbon to discover a route to Asia at the head of an armada that consisted of four square-rigged ships and 170 men. He had received his charge from Manuel I, whose parting words spoke clearly of the audacity of his small, resource-poor kingdom at the southwestern edge of Europe. "The discovery of India and those lands of the Orient" was the "most profitable and honorable enterprise and worthy of most renown," he said. To be sure, there was mention of a desire to spread Christianity, but to judge him from his own words, Manuel's foremost aim was "seizing from the hands of the barbarians' kingdoms . . . those eastern riches so celebrated by ancient writers, part of which, by way of commerce, has made Venice, Genoa, Florence and other Italian cities into great powers."

Da Gama's achievements are far less celebrated, if that is the right word, than those of Columbus, but they belong in the same register of historical importance. Columbus, as every American schoolchild learns, opened up the Western Hemisphere to Europe's budding imperialist project. But with the aid of a Muslim pilot from the East African kingdom of Malindi, da Gama, who died with the title Admiral of the Seas of Arabia, Persia, India and the Orients, furnished proof of concept to the very route that Columbus himself had aimed to establish: a practicable maritime pathway to Asia. "The West had found the East," write Bailey W. Diffie and George D. Winius in an economical description of da Gama's breakthrough in their *Foundations of the Portuguese Empire, 1415–1850.* Through his belligerence along the East African coast, and then in India (Calicut), da Gama also pioneered techniques of force and terror, establishing patterns of behavior that would quickly become fundamental to Western empire in the East. On his second voyage, in 1502, da Gama led to India a fleet of twenty heavily armed vessels designed to awe into submission whichever local leaders it encountered and to exact revenge from the ruler of Calicut for the murder of Portuguese commercial agents there the year before. Despite the Indian ruler's striking a conciliatory stance, the returning da Gama drew his ships close in to the shore and bombarded the city with cannonballs, before senselessly butchering several hundred local fishermen caught at sea.

In the late fifteenth century, the most extroverted European economies were primed by the trade in gold from sub-Saharan Africa, most of which came from the coast of present-day Ghana. According to the historian of Africa Martin Meredith, "by 1487, El Mina, 'the Mine,' as it became known, was sending an estimated 8,000 ounces a year to the royal treasury in Lisbon. By 1500, the annual trade had reached about 25,000 ounces, a significant proportion of the world's supply." This all changed dramatically after the seizure of Malacca in 1511 by the Portuguese conquistador Afonso de Albuquerque, whose signal purpose was to break the stranglehold on Europe's commerce with the Far East created by Venice's trade with Arab merchants. Moving with immense audacity, Albuquerque built upon the foundations laid by da Gama to create a globe-spanning architecture of empire for Portugal in little more than a decade. In its first stage, this involved building fortified stepping-stones along the African coast, constructing a fortress on an island off the west coast of India and creating a base near the mouth of the Red Sea to interdict rival Arab shipping. Just one year after laying out this strategic vision, Manuel I instructed his conquistadors to try to capture and fortify Malacca, a city that no European had ever visited.

For nearly a millennium already a succession of principalities bordering on the Strait of Malacca, places with names like Palembang and Jambi, had grown wealthy and powerful by controlling transit through the waterway, a strategic maritime passage located halfway between the large, agrarian population and cultural centers of East Asia and the Indian subcontinent. By virtue of this position, they were able to provide transshipment facilities connecting not just China and India but the Arab world and even eastern Africa in a gradually thickening web of global commerce. In *Before European Hegemony: The World System A.D. 1250–1350,* Janet L. Abu-Lughod perceptively described these Malayan comprador cities as predecessors of the Hong Kong and (nearby) Singapore of today, writing that they were free ports "in which a wide variety of trading partners exchange externally produced goods free of oppressive restrictions and taxes, store their wealth safely, and switch their capital at will from one trading circuit to another."

In the early sixteenth century, the sultanate of Malacca had held sway in the most famous and lucrative of these entrepôts for just over a hundred years, and Malacca's narrow streets teemed with Gujaratis, for whom it was the terminus of their eastern trade, but also with Javanese, Chinese, Japanese, Arabs, Persians as well, of course, as native Malays. Historians say that Albuquerque arrived here in command of a convoy of perhaps eighteen ships. This fabulously prosperous place, the "gullet of the world," in the phrase of Tomé Pires, the sixteenth-century Portuguese writer and diplomat, was not technically fortified, but it was heavily defended by 20,000 mercenaries and as many as 8,000 artillery pieces. This meant that in a frontal attack, Albuquerque and his 900 or so fellow Portuguese and 200 Indian mercenaries would have had little chance of prevailing. Instead, after an initial assault that produced mixed results, he resorted to ruse, maneuvering a junk supposedly given to him by disgruntled Chinese traders into the mouth of the river at high tide, from which his fighting force burst forth into the heart of the city, making maximum use of surprise. Sixteenth-century Spanish conquistadors, men like Pizarro and Cortés, would become better known for the way they managed to rout vastly larger forces in toppling the Inca and Aztec empires in the New World. But unlike Malacca, those were civilizations lacking guns and other modern weaponry. In total, at the end of Albuquerque's surprise assault, in which he captured Asia's greatest trading city, then systematically looted its warehouses, he had lost only twenty-eight men.

From their experiences in Africa and India, the Portuguese had learned that as long as they could maintain the ability to safely land resupply ships from time to time, a properly built European-style fort was invulnerable to attack using the technologies available to their adversaries far from home, so they scrupulously followed their king's instruction and set about building A Famosa, the fort whose scant ruins one can still see from St. Paul's hilltop. Not long after its capture, Albuquerque wrote of its conquest, "Men cannot estimate the worth of Malacca, on account of its greatness and profit. Malacca is a city that was made for merchandise, fitter than any other in the world." And yet the city did not retain him. Barely three months after his victory, Albuquerque set out to find and capture the Moluccas, a group of small islands in the Malay archipelago that were the source of the spices that Lisbon coveted most.

The trade in cloves, mace and nutmeg, which were found in the Moluccas alone, became an extraordinary new source of wealth for

Lisbon, more valuable even than African gold. Indeed, by the time Ferdinand Magellan, a Portuguese maritime commander who hired his services out to the Spanish, arrived in East Asia in 1521, having circumnavigated South America instead of Africa to establish a new route to the Pacific, the Spanish had reason to consider that they had already definitively lost out to the Portuguese, because Lisbon controlled the Moluccas. Portugal's claims to the Spice Islands were legitimized not only on the basis of their having arrived first, but also by ecclesiastic sanction due to a series of papal bulls dating to 1452 that accorded Lisbon rights to the "Golden East." A beaten Magellan spent much of his time in the region rooting around in the present-day Philippines, where his men discovered that cinnamon grew—a poor consolation compared to the far more prized cloves. He died in battle in Cebu in 1521. In 1529, despairing of ever being able to win an appeal to the Vatican over rights to the Moluccas, and preoccupied by war with France, Charles V, the Spanish king, accepted a payment from Lisbon in order to renounce its rival claims to the Spice Islands.

Following in da Gama's wake, in 1542 Francis Xavier traveled to Goa, building a church there, where he worked to convert Indians. He moved on to Malacca not long after its conquest, founding there the first Western school in eastern Asia. Then, like Albuquerque, he traveled onward to the Moluccas. In the final phase of his missionary life he used Malacca as a base as he tried, with mixed success, to build Christian followings in both Japan and China. Xavier died on a Chinese island not far from Canton and his body was brought back to Malacca, where it was buried for a time at St. Paul's. An empty crypt remains (his resting place was Goa).

Visitors are few at this site nowadays. Such is often the fate of relics of superseded empires. The Portuguese would hold on here for 130 years, and thanks to their fort-building strategy, they would never be defeated by an Asian adversary. One of Europe's smallest countries, they were confronted instead with the difficulty of being woefully overstretched. Although the spices of the Moluccas came from just five closely bunched islands, the far-flung Malay world that Portugal laid claim to was exceedingly vast—comparable in total area, if one includes the seas they span, to all of the United States, including Alaska. The Portuguese inability to hold such extensive territory encouraged probing by the rival Spanish, then takeover by the Dutch, and finally the fall of much of the region to the British. It is hard to imagine either of those northern European powers building the Asian empires they did, however, without the example that Portugal provided of being able to do so with its very limited means.

A short distance from the hill overlooking the Malacca River and the A Famosa ruins below is a historically based tourist attraction that draws big crowds in today's Malacca. There, hordes of people mill around a traffic-choked roundabout to snap photos of a replica of a gigantic ship that visited this strait a century before the arrival of the first Portuguese conquistadors. On most days these crowds are dominated by people of Chinese origin, whether nationals of the People's Republic of China or members of the great Chinese diaspora that suffuses this region, and for anyone who knows the story of the ship in question, there is very little mystery why. The nine-masted vessel looming above the circle is a greatly reduced scale model of a ship commanded by one of the most widely celebrated heroes in all of Chinese culture, Zheng He, a Ming dynasty admiral.

Zheng, a Muslim eunuch who served the Yongle (Eternal Happiness) emperor, arrived in this part of the world in 1405 with an armada that included some of the biggest wooden ships ever built. Under his command were twenty thousand men, most of them professional soldiers, who are described as "crack troops" in the Ming's own accounts. Until a wave of interest from Western historians spurred a revival of Chinese focus on Zheng's exploits early in the twentieth century, he had been largely forgotten to Chinese history. This was due in good part to the sharp reverse course the Ming took after the Yongle emperor's death, when they ended the practice of sending their armadas far and wide and partially restricted travel overseas. The Western scholars wanted to know if ancient archival accounts of ships said to be as large as these could possibly be accurate. And if indeed China had built an armada so formidable, how

Traffic roundabout with large scale model of a
treasure ship from the fleet of Zheng He, Malacca

could it not have been for the purposes of warfare and expansion, whether territorial or mercantile, or perhaps both?

The best modern scholarship confirms both the size of the ships and the fleet's dimensions. The largest of the vessels were 440 by 180 feet, and may even have been as long as 600 feet, the length of two football fields. In *Zheng He: China and the Oceans in the Early Ming Dynasty, 1405–1433,* Edward L. Dreyer writes that Lord Nelson's early-nineteenth-century flagship, *Victory,* was 186 feet by 51 feet, comparable to the smallest class of ships that escorted Zheng. Christopher Columbus's largest ship, the *Santa Maria,* was a mere 125 feet long and could carry only 280 tons, about one-ninth the capacity of Zheng's biggest ships. The Ming fleet that Zheng commanded was a convoy of two hundred or so vessels, which made it seventy ships larger than the famous Spanish Armada of 1588, or roughly equal in size to the combined fleets of Britain, France and Spain that fought the Battle of Trafalgar in 1805.

Chinese interest in Zheng proceeded from an entirely different direction. Many Western historians initially assumed that the behavior of a man so extravagantly armed and equipped would have been similar to that of the European imperialists whose men-of-war seized control of rich trade networks, and ultimately of the entire region, by force, especially given that Zheng had vastly greater means at his disposal than a conquistador like Albuquerque. In the early fifteenth century, a Chinese imperial census registered sixty-five million inhabitants, compared to estimates of one million Portuguese and five million English at the time. "In the language of a later era of navalism," Dreyer writes, "China had the ships, had the men, and had the money" for conquest.

The Chinese looked to the rediscovered Zheng mainly to help build pride in themselves. This urge was fed by China's repeated humiliations at sea in the second half of the nineteenth century, culminating in its 1895 defeat by Japan. In the early twentieth century, this still-fresh legacy of maritime weakness lent a special potency to the Zheng legend. The eunuch admiral and his "treasure ships," as they were called, quickly became an important element in a narrative of Chinese exceptionalism. The country had tremendous strength at its disposal, and yet true to the core of the Confucian ideal behind *tian xia*, it had not beaten up on its neighbors, or even lorded over them in the bullying manner of the West, despite their manifest inferiority. Instead, to believe the narrative created during the early-twentieth-century Zheng He revival, China had lived up to its own hallowed tradition, as reflected in the counsel that the scholar-adviser Wei Cheng gave to the seventh-century Tang ruler Tai Zong: "If the imperial kindness extended throughout the four seas, then there would be no need to seek the pearls; the pearls would come to China of their own accord." For all of his might, following in this tradition, Zheng He had relied on Chinese virtue for winning hearts and minds abroad. Or so it went in the retelling.

A key figure in the Zheng He revival in China, as with so much else in the early-twentieth-century intellectual history of the country, was Liang Qichao. "After Zheng He, no more Zheng He's," Liang lamented in one essay, an epigrammatic summons to the Chinese to recover their historic greatness. For the inventors of modern Chinese nationalism like Liang, who were quickly souring on America's

Pacific imperialism, Zheng was special not just because of his greatness as a figure in naval history, but also due to his supposedly peaceful example, which stood in sharp contradistinction to familiar patterns of Western behavior. Later, Sun Yat-sen too would invoke Zheng's voyages as proof that China was different by nature and, by clear inference, morally superior to the West.

This line of rhetoric continues to the present day, helping explain the popularity of the Zheng He ship replica in Malacca. In this century, the Chinese Communist Party has lavishly celebrated Zheng, highlighting his voyages in school curricula and state propaganda. "These were thus friendly diplomatic activities," said Xu Zuyuan, vice minister of communications, in 2004. "During the overall course of the seven voyages to the Western Ocean, Zheng He did not occupy a single piece of land, establish any fortress or seize any wealth from other countries. In the commercial and trade activities, he adopted the practice of giving more than he received, and thus he was welcomed and lauded by the people of the various countries along his routes." The following year, on the six hundredth anniversary of Zheng's voyages, Chinese state television carried a spate of programs celebrating the admiral. In one of them, part of a popular history series called *Lecture Room,* Mao Peiqi, a professor at Renmin University, in Beijing, hailed Zheng as a "peace ambassador from China, lifting high the flag of friendly communication and collaboration."

As intended, this recent revisionism around Zheng has left its mark on the present generation of Chinese. Attending a conference about China's relations with Africa at Yale University in 2013, I listened as a young Chinese scholar gave her take on Zheng, which was stated as simple fact. "Why are so many people talking about Chinese interests in Africa?" she asked. "China has already proven, since the time of our Zheng He, that we are a friendly country that does not seek hegemony over others. Zheng went all the way to Africa to explore and to make friends, and then he returned home. China did not seek to control anybody."

Recently, Zheng has been pressed into service on behalf of China's claims to sovereignty in its ongoing dispute with neighbors over control of the South China Sea. With a historical record that stretches deeper into antiquity than any of its neighbors, it is able to wield history against them not so much through an abundance of detail, however credible or dubious, but as a kind of trump card over contending arguments. To do this, it simply claims to have controlled the southern seas "since time immemorial," and Zheng He is often enlisted in this cause.

"The term *Nan Hai (Southern Sea)* appeared in the classic poetry book *Shi Jing (The Classic of Poetry)*, a publication of the Spring and Autumn Period (475–221 B.C.), and it has remained the standard appellation in Chinese for the South China Sea ever since," write Zhiguo Gao and Bing Bing Jia in the previously cited *Nine-Dash Line in the South China Sea*:

> In later Chinese dynasties—from the fifth century A.D. forward, as knowledge of the seas was increasingly corroborated by travelers and other seafarers—references to the southern seas and islands became more frequent in geographical and literary works. The clarification of the location and environs of the South China Sea and beyond, together with advances in shipbuilding and the navigational use of compasses, enabled regular journeys to other states in the region and inspired, among others, the famed "Seven Voyages" by the "Three Jewel Eunuch," Zheng He, in the Ming dynasty of the early fifteenth century. The voyages, conducted between 1405 and 1433, were official in nature, as Zheng was appointed fleet admiral by the Ming emperor, Yong Le, with a mandate to spread overseas the knowledge of the emperor's "majesty and virtue."

The problems with enlisting Zheng in modern territorial disputes like this are manifold. The admiral's route, as best as it is understood, would have sought to avoid many of what are today the most hotly disputed areas of the South China Sea, since they are laden with treacherous reefs and shallows that would have threatened ships as large as Zheng's. From southern China, the admiral is known to have sailed to Champa, in present-day Vietnam, hugging the coast, and to have gone from there toward Malacca, and finally into the open Indian Ocean. Moreover, trifling with tiny island groupings would have been contrary to the spirit and purpose of Zheng's missions, and there is no record that he or any Chinese before him laid claim to such territory in the South China Sea, much less administered it.

To decide what meaning to attach to Zheng He's career, it is first necessary to place his life in proper historical context, which is to say, within the frame of early Ming dynasty geopolitics. Zheng's ambitious patron, Zhu Di, who subsequently became known by the reign name Yongle, was a usurper who killed his nephew, the Jian-wen emperor, and seized power in 1402. In need of boosting his legitimacy, he greatly accelerated the Chinese expansionism that had begun in the fourteenth century. In the north, Yongle's armies captured the Mongol capital Dadu, renaming it Beiping (present-day Beijing), and continued to pursue war against the retreating Mongols. In the south, the Ming had recently conquered the present-day Chinese province of Yunnan, which borders on Myanmar, Laos, and Vietnam, and incorporated it into the empire. China had controlled Yunnan at times in the past, but the Chinese migrants there had become "barbarianized" by mixing over time with the local populations. This time, in order to permanently secure its hold on the territory for full incorporation into the empire, China mounted a campaign of settler colonialism, moving eight hundred thousand migrants into Yunnan.

Zheng He was from a Yunnan family often said to have been of Central Asian stock, and he was taken captive during this conflict, eventually becoming a servant of Yongle, who at the time bore the title the Prince of Yan. Under Yongle, China next moved to take over Đại Việt, or present-day northern Vietnam, which was known as Annam, or the Pacified South, to the Chinese, and had been annexed previously under the Tang dynasty. Incorporating it as China's fourteenth province, Yongle renamed Vietnam as Jiao-zhi and imposed a strict and heavily extractive Confucian administration.

While the teaching of Chinese history and the thrust of propaganda across the ages have always spoken in terms of the charms of

Chinese virtue and culture as the irresistible forces that have attracted other countries into China's orbit, the experience of Vietnam, which we will soon explore more deeply, reveals the mailed fist of a classic imperialist power. China's efforts at forced assimilation of the Vietnamese in fact recall in some ways the aggressive behavior of imperial Japan five hundred years later, when it took over Korea, imposed Japanese names on all Koreans and introduced the Japanese language as the official medium of instruction.

Building the largest fleet the world had ever seen was Yongle's final great expansionist initiative, and he did so virtually without regard to cost, a fact that drew mounting expressions of displeasure from the court. Historians of the next dynasty, the Qing, wrote, "The goods and treasures without name that he acquired were too many to be accounted for, yet they did not make up for the wasteful expenditures of the Middle Kingdom." In light of this, the traditional Chinese explanation for Zheng's missions, that they were merely peaceful displays of virtue, is discordant. Imagine the effect upon the leaders of minor coastal states along Zheng's routes at the sight of an arriving fleet of two hundred immense and well-armed ships suddenly filling the horizon. "When thousands of troops marched off the junks and built fortified warehouses (chinakotta), it surely inclined their hosts to consider that a client relationship with the Ming emperor was an offer they could not refuse."

Both archaeological and archival information about Zheng's fleet makes clear that it was designed neither for naval warfare nor even for exploration. The purpose of this foreign expeditionary armada was to transport an army that mostly through sheer intimidation, once landed, could reduce any power it encountered along the way to quick submission, as it was obliged to do in the case of the few potential vassals who failed to immediately grasp that reality.

Zheng's legend as an ambassador of goodwill and friendship simply doesn't hold up. It is Chinese idealization, not history. Zheng's voyages, and those of several other lesser-known commanders of the time, were conceived and funded in order to extend Chinese power throughout the known world, and in doing so to boost the legitimacy and prestige of a ruler who came to power via usurpation.

As China has revived Zheng's memory, among the most persistent claims it has made is that his life and career are proof of its most fundamental distinction from the supposedly inherently aggressive West, that is, that it has never imposed itself on others as a colonial or imperial power. To the contrary, nearly the entire perimeter of present-day China was incorporated via tactics of imperial conquest and subsequent colonialism.

Over a long span of history, Southeast Asia has been a mutable, ever-changing concept when viewed from China's power centers. Ever since the Qin and Han dynasties (221 BCE to 220 CE), Chinese history can be understood as a "march to the tropics," a stop-and-start expansion toward the south that suffered numerous reversals over time, without its fundamental direction ever being called into question. Conceptually, succeeding dynasties have divided the southern periphery into three different realms: a near periphery, like Yunnan, which could be fully assimilated into China itself; an intermediary periphery, consisting of the nearer reaches of mainland Southeast Asia, including parts of Vietnam, Burma and Siam, which could be substantially assimilated, or Sinicized, over time; and the farther reaches of Southeast Asia, including all of the maritime portions of the region, which were too remote and inhabited by people— "southern barbarians"—too unlike the Chinese to make assimilation realistic, but which should nevertheless ideally form part of a consolidated Chinese sphere of influence. The status of many of the lands in the intermediary zone fluctuated according to the empire's power, sometimes being recognized as independent polities, albeit ones that were expected to pay tribute, and at other times being absorbed, or reabsorbed, under direct Chinese control.

Such thinking clearly animated the aggressively expansionist Ming, under whom maritime Southeast Asia "became a sphere of Chinese influence as never before or even after," writes Sun Laichen, and this history still remains useful for understanding current Chinese actions in the region. During Admiral Zheng's time, during the first half of the fifteenth century, in order to pursue newly expansive policies into the Indian Ocean, the Ming needed a way station and stockade for its armies, and toward that end it chose to work with Malacca, which subsequently blossomed on the basis of a sort of premodern favored nation status accorded to it by China. Malacca did not benefit simply via trade, though—its leaders were all but anointed by China, and their very legitimacy (and survival) depended upon recognition by the Ming rulers.

The second pillar of the "voyages of friendship" narrative surrounding Zheng involves the supposed Ming aversion to the use of force. The historical record is quite different. In the Sumatran episode, which occurred during Zheng's very first voyage, in 1407, he attacked a city known to the Chinese as Old Harbor (*Jiu Gang*), which had been the capital of Srivijaya, a Malayan empire that had thrived centuries earlier by cornering the tribute-sanctioned entrepôt trade with China. In the Old Harbor, Zheng's troops captured a Chinese "pirate" named Chen Zu-yi, who was returned to China and beheaded. Chen's real crime was rejecting Ming authority; in capturing him, Ming archives record the killing of 5,000 locals, along with the burning of ten ships. That same year, Zheng violently intervened in nearby Java, killing 170. The toll was not especially large, but the message from the Ming to the king of western Java, in light of the recent subjugation of Vietnam, was particularly chilling. "Immediately pay 60,000 liang of gold in compensation for their lives and to atone for your crime. . . . Fail to comply and there will be no option but to dispatch an army to punish your crime. What happened in Annam can serve as an example." The Ming made similar threats two years later to the ruler of Burma, who was already facing overland pressure from Chinese forces over a contest for influence in Yunnan.

In 1411, on his third voyage, Zheng's forces successfully invaded Sri Lanka (Ceylon). The king of Ceylon was reproached by Zheng for having been "rude" toward his armada on previous passages to India, and to this complaint were added allegations of piracy and of attempting to lure Zheng's armies into an ambush. (The king was replaced by a puppet leader.) Ceylon's true offense was actually failing to bow before China's hegemony in the region. Of a subsequent, similar attack on Sumatra writes the historian Geoff Wade:

Again, we see an instance of the maritime expedition acting mainly as a military force in an attempt to impose a pax Ming on what we now know as Southeast Asia and the Indian Ocean.

... [Zheng's expeditionary armada was] sent abroad in the first third of the 15th century in order to achieve the recognition of Ming preeminence among all the polities of the known maritime world. Those who would not recognize this supremacy of the Ming were subjected to military force. ...

However, the number of Southeast Asian rulers traveling to China with the Zheng He missions suggests that coercion must have been an important element. There are very few other examples of rulers visiting other polities within Southeast Asia in this period, suggesting that some great pressure must have been imposed on them to encourage them to journey to the Ming court, and thereby demonstrate their subordinate status before the Chinese emperor.

Writing in a similar vein, Dreyer says:

The modern idea of Zheng He as an explorer is largely a creation of Western scholarship. Zheng He's fleet was actually an armada, in the sense that it carried a powerful army that could be disembarked, and its purpose was to awe the rulers of Southeast Asia and the Indian Ocean into sending tribute to China. Foreign tributary missions enhanced the legitimacy of the Chinese emperor and received rich gifts in return, yet most of the states visited by Zheng He's fleet sent tribute only under compulsion, and they ceased to do so after the voyages ended.

The fighting of land battles and the capture of recalcitrant local leaders, Dreyer adds later, "was a clear demonstration of the purpose of Zheng He's voyages: to bring the Western Ocean into the Chinese tributary system by overawing, or if need be by overpowering the opposition." Historical records make clear that in just such a manner, the Ming were busily constituting a sphere of influence based on the preponderance of force. It was not like the Portuguese and other empires that would follow in the sense that it does not seem to have regarded commerce for the pure sake of mercantile wealth as its central or primary objective. Nor were the Chinese preoccupied with using naval power to seize control of faraway lands for their own direct administration. Chinese emperors, all of whom embraced *tian xia*, seem to have calculated that holding on to territories separated from them by enormous oceans was too great a task. Holding together China itself, continentally vast and immensely fractious and complex, was already a tall enough order. The missions of Zheng, though, constituted a clear type of imperial behavior that placed politics at the center, following the familiar principle that the strength of an emperor or dynasty in China was measured in good part according to the degree to which it could obtain the deference and submission of nearby peoples. What made this Ming experience so special was its extraordinary range. Before imperial voyages like these were renounced, immediately upon the death of Yongle, Zheng He had pursued his mission into the Arab world and all the way to the eastern coast of Africa, where Chinese diplomacy today enlists his legend to promote the idea of the supposedly peaceful and harmonious behavior of their nation, which they see in clear contradistinction to the West.

As Sun Laichen writes, with echoes of today's Asia, the Ming under Yongle were determined to turn the South China Sea into a "Chinese lake." This was made possible by the leveraging of gigantic technological advances whose foundations had been laid under the Song and were built up further during the Yuan dynasty, placing China well ahead of any potential rivals in terms of both firearms and shipbuilding techniques. As a consequence, during Zheng's time, Sun writes, China became "the first gunpowder empire anywhere on the globe." The Ming, furthermore, left little doubt that they were aware of this fact, as best attested to by the words of Zheng himself:

> The strength of our dynasty has surpassed all previous [dynasties]. It controls the northern and western barbarians, but has

not had to marry princesses to foreigners as the Han did, has not had to make allies [with equal powers] like the Tang, has not had to pay annual tributes like the Song, and has not had to engage in an etiquette of treating enemy states as brothers. They all come to pay tribute and are received with courtesy. . . . How grand is this!

Ever since Chengzu [Yongle] pacified all-under-heaven [*tian xia*] with military power, [he] wanted to control the world [wanfang] with force, [so] he sent envoys to all the directions to solicit [them]. Thus all the large and small countries in the Western region [xiyu] came to kowtow and submit and compete in presenting tribute. [The Ming envoys] reached all the places that could be reached by water and land, as far north as the remotest desert, as far south as the farthermost sea, as far east and west as the sun-rising and sun-setting places.

After Yongle's death, in 1424, his successor, Hongxi, canceled the planned seventh voyage of Zheng He's fleet the very day he assumed the throne. This represented an extraordinary reversal of twenty-two years of Ming policy of southern expansion, but it did not come out of the blue. Not long before his death, Yongle had suspended the voyages in order to focus on challenges to his empire. Vietnamese resistance to Chinese annexation was becoming impossible to suppress, and five campaigns against the Mongols in the north had proven enormously costly in both lives and treasure.

Hongxi died after less than one year in power and was succeeded by Xuande, who dispatched the fleet for a final voyage. Some historians see this move as driven by a concern that the forty-eight states that China claimed as vassals were sending it less and less tribute. Other scholars believe its main purpose was to conclude outstanding business before disbanding the fleet altogether. A generation later, some court officials proposed trying to restore China's maritime preeminence, but this was rejected out of hand by the Confucian court.

Before the end of the fifteenth century, China began dismantling its immense shipyards, which at their height had built as many as six hundred large oceangoing vessels a year in the first half of the fifteenth century. In 1535, an imperial edict ordered the outright destruction of seagoing ships and the arrest of their crews. China began to slacken efforts at technological innovation and investment in weaponry, especially in the use of gunpowder-fired arms, which it had pioneered during the Song dynasty. "The forceful aspect of Yongle's policy—that is his effort to encompass maritime trade within the formal structure of the tribute system—was rejected by his successors, just as his strategy of making forays into the northern steppes was abandoned in place of relying on a Great Wall for defense," writes Robert Finlay in "The Voyages of Zheng He: Ideology, State Power, and Maritime Trade in Ming China." The hyper-activism of Yongle in pursuit of a growing Chinese domination in the region was suddenly replaced by an inward-looking attitude of passivity and fulsomely proclaimed self-satisfaction. Overseas trade was spoken of as something only relished by foreigners, and linked to a deviation from Chinese authenticity that was blamed on Mongol rule during the preceding Yuan dynasty. Overseas commerce was said, moreover, to attract unwanted foreigners to China, like the communities of Arab traders that had established themselves in some southern port cities. In military matters, other rationales were used to justify seclusion, such as this characteristic statement from Yang Shiqi, a court official of the time, explaining the withdrawal from Vietnam. "China should not stoop to fight with wolves and pigs," he said. Others weighed in with the ideological argument that it was enough for Chinese to continue to memorize Confucius; a more perfect embodiment of the sage's notions of virtue would be sufficient to make foreigners fall over themselves in submission.

Why their sudden inward turn, and why the Chinese state's abandonment of the oceans? Some historians, like Bruce Swanson, cite a power struggle within the bureaucracy between eunuchs and conservative neo-Confucians, dubbed "continentalists," with the eunuchs ultimately losing out. Another important factor was probably China's reopening of its enlarged and completely renovated Grand Canal, an extraordinary feat of engineering that connected northern China to the increasingly populous breadbasket of the south. At eleven hundred miles long, the canal was controlled by numerous locks, much like New York's Erie Canal, which measures only one-third its length and was not built until four hundred years later. In 1415 the state banned the shipment of grain to the north by sea to compel use of the canal, for which thousands of barges were built. Such a decision would have dramatically reduced the need for shipping, and hence shipbuilding and the maintenance of fleets, leading to the halting of oceangoing ship construction altogether by Yongle's successor in 1436. If the canal renovation was indeed the principal rationale behind the abandonment of maritime power, it was a decision that would come back to bite China with particularly cruel irony. A monetary crisis brought on by the collapse of China's paper currency was almost certainly another critical factor. This complicated commercial dealings with foreigners, making their goods more costly, strengthening old Confucian arguments about the moral ideal of self-reliance. "A desire for contact with the outside world meant that China itself needed something from abroad and was therefore not strong and self-sufficient," writes Louise Levathes, the author of a book about Zheng He. "The mere expression of need was unworthy of the Dragon Throne."

Whatever the cause for the about-face, however, its consequences were prompt and monumental, one of history's greatest turning points—or as some have characterized it, greatest blunders. Beginning in the thirteenth century, the world had embarked upon the creation of a true global economy. While Europe lagged, the regions we know today as the Middle East and Asia constituted major poles in a circuit of trade and technology exchanges that increasingly connected them. The crucial pivot was the Malay world, or more specifically the Strait of Malacca; it was the universal joint that tied the two axles together. It is impossible to know what shape China's gunboat imperialism would have taken had it not been abandoned. In 1498, however, according to the historian Bailey W. Diffie, when Vasco da Gama first arrived in Calicut, "crew members were told by the natives that about eighty years before some white sailors who resembled the Portuguese had visited their city almost annually for more than a generation. They had worn armor, the Indians said, and came in great vessels with four masts." The surprised Portuguese understood these to be tales of Slavic or German visitors, but of course they were men under Zheng's command. If there had been no prior Chinese withdrawal from the seas, the Portuguese would have heard stories about a powerful Chinese naval presence in the region of South Asia, of a Pax Sinica, in effect, built on the back of regular visits by a two-hundred-ship armada ferrying more than 20,000 crack soldiers. One can only imagine the reaction of an admiral like da Gama who commanded four modest-size ships carrying only 170 men; attempting the use of force would have never occurred to him. The Europeans might even have encountered signs of a Pax Sinica before they arrived in Asia, somewhere along the coast of East Africa, or in Aden, where Zheng had ventured during his latter voyages. Encountering the huge Chinese fleets would have given Westerners pause. Under such a scenario, Albuquerque is unlikely to have made a breakthrough in the Malay world, and the Portuguese would have either understood they were severely overmatched, or they would have paid dearly for their temerity.

Instead, amid the Chinese retreat, many local polities in Asia began to adopt its technological innovations, including more seaworthy ships of their own, and especially gunpowder-fired weapons, narrowing their power disparities with the Central Kingdom.

At the other end of the Eurasian landmass, the mid-fifteenth century marked the start of Europe's early modern era. European naval engineering and weaponry were advancing rapidly and would gradually build insurmountable leads over other regions over the next four centuries. This only happened, of course, because China, so long the premier military power and technological innovator in the world, had essentially dropped out of the race. "The 'Fall of the East' preceded the 'Rise of the West,' and it was this devolution of the preexisting system that facilitated Europe's easy conquest," writes Janet L. Abu-Lughod in *Before European Hegemony*. When Western monarchs and the fortune-hunting explorers and conquistadors they employed completed their longtime quest to reach Asia by sea, they celebrated the interconnection of the world's major oceans, something the Chinese had known about for at least a thousand years.

The impact of the European breakthrough was nonetheless profound, both for China and for global history. The Portuguese enjoyed a brief interlude of near monopoly over the East Asian trade, after which the Pacific Ocean became a "Spanish lake" instead of the Chinese lake it had been on its way to becoming during the time of Zheng He. Once Spain had settled Manila, in 1565, it quickly realized that "its geographical position was the best possible one for drawing together Chinese and Japanese silk from the north, Moluccan spices from the south and Indian cottons and Cambodian ivory from the west, and channeling them toward the seemingly limitless markets of the argentiferous Spanish colonies in the New World."* The project of stitching the world's disparate regions together via long-distance maritime trade had begun in earnest in the thirteenth century, with the efforts of Arabs, Persians and Malays, who were briefly succeeded by the Chinese during the Yuan and early Ming dynasties. But the Middle Kingdom's chance to remake the world on its own terms, to become a global hegemon, in effect, as Europe began to do in the sixteenth century, had been surrendered. Such a chance would not return for another five hundred years.

A prime lesson to be learned from their experience is the importance of sustaining one's strength, of continually developing one's military and technology, and of never letting down one's guard or surrendering a lead once acquired. At least as important is the message of maintaining a hold on one's home region, one's domain. Except for

---

*As the historian Hugh Thomas relates in his 2015 book *World Without End: Spain, Philip II, and the First Global Empire,* Spain briefly entertained the idea of trying to conquer Ming China, which it believed it could accomplish with a small expeditionary force, much as Pizarro is said to have vanquished the Incas. This fantasy was swept away before it could ever be acted upon, however, by the English defeat of the Spanish Armada in 1588, which caused Madrid to refocus its energies in Europe and question, in an almost Chinese way, whether it had lost the mandate of heaven.

Taiwan, whose possession China regards as a top national priority, it is seldom recalled these days that among the first orders of business of Mao Zedong's successful revolution in 1949 was securing the country's continental periphery. "They had watched the great powers (including the United States) colonize some of their neighbors, stake out informal spheres of influence in others, and (most serious of all) steadily extend their control in China itself," write Michael H. Hunt and Steven I. Levine in *Arc of Empire: America's Wars in Asia from the Philippines to Vietnam.* "The prerequisite for overcoming this crisis, Chinese intellectuals and political leaders alike concluded, was the creation of a strong government determined to repossess Taiwan, Manchuria, Mongolia, Xinjiang and Tibet, cut the foreigners down to size, restore Chinese pride and regain China's status as a respected world power."

The term *tian xia* figures nowhere in contemporary Chinese diplomatic discourse, but since 1974, China has seemed determined to gradually assert control over the ocean approaches to the mainland that it had once dominated centuries ago, and above all to keep the barbarians at bay. In abandoning the playing field just before the arrival of the Iberian upstarts, it opened the door for challengers who would follow in their wake—the Dutch, then the British and finally the Americans. These Westerners finally shook the Chinese continentalists out of their complacent and long-held view that the history of the world was the substantial equivalent of the history of China itself.

As late as the Opium Wars, China had no unified fleet, and the junks it sent forth to combat Britain's iron-hulled steamer *Nemesis* brought to the minds of their Western adversaries Roman galleys, "only less efficiently constructed for venturing away from land." As a result, the British were able to bring China quickly to its knees by closing down the Grand Canal, threatening food supplies. In a series of subsequent wars, the French and British took advantage of China's naval defenselessness in order to humiliate the rulers of the Qing dynasty. Toward the end of the nineteenth century the Qing initiated a crash program to obtain a modern fleet, buying vessels from Germany and employing foreign advisers. But it was too little, too late,

as their loss to Japan at sea in 1895 attests. The Treaty of Shimono-
seki, which ended the war, forced China to pay huge indemnities in
silver, as well as to recognize the independence of Korea and cede the
Liaodong Peninsula to Japan, along with Taiwan and the Pescadores
Islands.

China began its career as an energetic oceangoing nation under
the Southern Song dynasty (1127–1279), and in historical terms
that career was very brief, as was its period of serious engagement
with the much-disputed waters of what is known today as the South
China Sea. This history is critical nowadays not just to the Chinese
Communist Party's expansive claims of having controlled the entire
region enclosed by its nine-dash line "since time immemorial"—
which can easily be refuted—as official propaganda holds, but also
in order to comprehend the emergence over time of what would
become a remarkably consistent Chinese worldview, based above all
on notions of centrality and superiority. Under the Ming dynasty,
three centuries later, when the Chinese were confronted for the first
time with a European-drawn map of the world, in 1584, the *mappa
mundi* produced by the Italian Jesuit Matteo Ricci, they were aston-
ished to find their empire positioned at the eastern end of the Eurasian landmass. Out of deference, Ricci drew another map for his
hosts placing China at the center.[*]

Until the second millennium of the Christian era, maritime links
between the Malay-Indonesian world and China for commercial and
diplomatic purposes were assured not by Chinese vessels but by ships
that operated under Malay, South Asian or Arab command. "Information of Chinese participation in maritime shipping to the Malay
region is not forthcoming until the eleventh century, when Chinese

---

[*]Because he had acquired an impressive fluency and literacy in Chinese, the Ming court
recognized Matteo Ricci as a *hua ren* (华人), or civilized man. Ricci graciously accepted
the compliment, but insisted that his civilization derived from his homeland, Italy. This
perplexed his hosts as much as his strange map had, because for the Chinese, *civilized*
simply meant culturally Chinese. There was no other term for *Chinese* at the time, and
in fact *hua ren* is still used, unselfconsciously, by Chinese to refer to themselves. See "The
'Tianxia Trope': Will China change the international system?," by June Teufel Dreyer,
Journal of Contemporary China, Nov. 2, 2015.

provincial accounts, particularly in Fujian and Guangdong, begin to mention the Chinese sailing abroad for the purpose of trade. Archaeologically, no seagoing vessel of Chinese construct, dating to before the thirteenth century, has as yet been discovered in Chinese or Southeast Asian waters," writes Derek Heng in *Sino-Malay Trade and Diplomacy from the Tenth Through the Fourteenth Century.* "The passive stance of the Chinese courts in their diplomatic and economic interaction with maritime Southeast Asia appears to have greatly discouraged active Chinese participation in shipping between the two regions during this period."

The historian Wang Gungwu, in his classic book *The Nanhai Trade: Early Chinese Trade in the South China Sea,* takes a slightly different path to arrive at similar conclusions: "It is not possible to say which ships were most used between the beginning of the fifth and the end of the sixth centuries. The Chinese texts do not mention any Chinese ships carrying the trade."

As mentioned previously, China has had at least a sketchy knowledge of the "great ocean" since the Han dynasty (206 BCE–220 CE), meaning an awareness of western lands that could be reached via the Mediterranean. But ancient accounts from Chinese travelers—mostly from religious pilgrims—are at best fragmentary and sporadic. Most of the slowly accumulating knowledge of maritime geography derived from tribute missions arriving from faraway states, including kingdoms in present-day southern India, Sri Lanka and Indonesia.

It is clear that people venturing forth from China made very little impression on the surrounding maritime region to its south until the second century of the Song dynasty (960–1279) rule. Chinese literature speaks vaguely of inhabited lands in the "southern regions," but emphasizes their remoteness and their near-impossibility of access. "The countries of the barbarians of the southern and eastern oceans . . . are frontier tribes situated at the extreme limits [of the world]," says one official history from the sixth century. "Each tribe has for its borders amazing mountains or extraordinary seas." Taken together, this all seems to convincingly negate today's vague claims about how ancient history legitimizes Chinese control of the South China Sea. More recent history further undermines these claims.

By the end of the fourth century, vessels bearing precious goods from faraway lands were becoming increasingly common in Chinese ports, and people from the Malay world at the southern end of the South China Sea (present-day Indonesia, Malaysia, Brunei and southern Thailand) were emerging as a key interlocutor for the Central Kingdom. Centuries earlier, the Malays had begun to distinguish themselves as highly skilled seafarers, starting with a thriving trade with the Indian subcontinent, which became the source of their early Hindu- and Buddhist-influenced culture. Their superb navigational skills, combined with a strong martial culture, allowed the Malays to control passage through the Strait of Malacca, taxing ships for their cargo or charging port fees before permitting them to proceed, and attacking anyone who dared to balk. Given the rudimentary nature of maritime transportation, few of what might be considered emerging world cities at the time were directly connected with one another. This created lucrative opportunities for ports that could serve as intermediate transit centers, enabling the Malays, who sat astride one of the world's great crossroads, to position themselves as masters of the emporium and to emerge more or less as China's main provisioners.

The Malays' opportunities were enhanced by China's own peculiar politics, which throughout history have repeatedly imposed seclusion that has variously meant denying foreigners access to China, denying exit from the country to Chinese, or both. This traditional desire on the part of the Chinese state to tightly control or carefully mediate all relations between Chinese people and foreigners helps explain the conservative impulses that underpinned tributary relations. It also helps explain the appeal that China first saw under the Tang of establishing a privileged relationship with a single barbarian race to the maritime south, the Malays, who were allowed to approach China with goods for trade, as opposed to keeping its ports open, which had led to unrest with Arab trading communities that set themselves up in the country's south. The Tang reverted to a posture that has been common to a number of dynasties and has been something of a bedrock of the tribute system: rejecting trade with nonsubservient parties. The Malays quickly got the drift, however, and honored China's Confucian values, including the protocols of tribute, securing a commercial role by conducting themselves in suitably civilized—meaning docile and submissive—ways.

By the latter half of the Tang period, from the late eighth to the early tenth centuries, the Chinese economy had embarked upon what would become known as a golden age of technological innovation. The list of advancements was breathtaking. It includes the discovery of gunpowder; the development of firearms; a revolution in agriculture based on the mastery of hydraulics; the invention—centuries before the Europeans—of early forms of paper money, first in the form of promissory notes used by long-distance traders; and the invention of the compass, which was quickly put to use on Chinese ships.

The explosion of wealth that followed on the heels of these advances powerfully boosted the status of merchants in China and fed a booming new demand for foreign goods, for which Srivijaya, an important south Sumatran Buddhist entrepôt city-state that controlled the Strait of Malacca, was only too happy to become the purveyor. With the fall of the Tang dynasty, there was no economic letup under the Song (960–1279) and the Yuan (1271–1368). Under the militarily weak Song, however, a decisive shift occurred in China's continental power, with a succession of northern peoples mounting increasingly bold attacks against them. These had the effect of cutting the empire off from its important traditional trade links with peoples to the west, the long-established overland routes known collectively—if misleadingly, because of the singular form of the title—as the Silk Road. Conflict in the north of China and the severing of Central Asian trade drove a huge internal migration from northern to southern China. In the space of four centuries, from 800 to 1200, the population of the coastal provinces of the south, Zhejiang, Fujian and Guangdong, soared by 700 percent. These developments hugely boosted Chinese interest in the fast-emerging maritime alternative to the Silk Road—overseas trade via the Strait of Malacca. As Wang Gungwu wrote lyrically in *The Nanhai Trade,* "The South China Sea [became] the main route of what may be called the Asian east-west trade in commodities and ideas. It was the second Silk Route. Its waters and its island straits were as the sands and mountain passes of Central Asia; its ports were like the caravanserais."

In 960, the very year that the Northern Song took power, Srivijaya sent a mission to signal its fealty. The tribute on offer included some of the most coveted luxury items in China, including ivory, rhinoceros horn, rosewater and frankincense. The timing of the mission, which arrived in the ninth month of the year, signaled the urgency the Srivijayans attached to getting into the good graces of the Song. Ships traveling from the far south ordinarily sailed in May or June to take advantage of favorable monsoon winds during that season, but the Srivijayans apparently felt they could not wait.

In 987, having fully consolidated power, the Song sent emissaries out into the region bearing the message that now that it was firmly in charge of China, the Song court was ready to begin receiving tribute missions. The Song were of course simply doing what other new Chinese dynasties had done in the past, attempting to bolster the emperor's claim to possessing the mandate of heaven by having foreign leaders come and bow to its authority. Srivijaya was the first to arrive.

By 1017, the maharajas who ruled the Srivijaya thalassocracy had grown so flush and confident that one of them described himself grandly in correspondence with China as "the king of the ocean lands." This they could get away with, in part, because although China had already begun assembling a powerful navy by the time of the Tang dynasty, it had not so far sought a direct role for itself in the booming trade of the strait, and neither had it projected force anywhere near the southern reaches of the South China Sea. We know this partly because Chinese archives, which richly document all manner of state affairs, make no claims on either of these topics. The previously mentioned total absence of Chinese shipwrecks or other archaeological evidence of a Chinese maritime presence, furthermore, supports this view. Finally, there is a surviving description of Palembang from the tenth century by an Arab trader who colorfully depicts it as a secure merchant community so cosmopolitan that the parrots commonly found there spoke a wide variety of languages. Among those that he enumerates, though, Chinese is conspicuously absent. The Arabs called Palembang "the port that looks upon China," but even into the eleventh century surviving inscriptions from the harbor omit mention of Chinese among the varied nationalities of foreign visitors.

The tributary relationship that bridged the South China Sea signified the Central Kingdom's manner of understanding the world—the graceful ratification by a lesser people of the natural order of things. In substance and in ceremony, this of course meant recognition that China was "the source of all political virtue and the ultimate protector of mankind." A view less clouded by chauvinism would have revealed a somewhat different reality. The Malays had in fact been the ones, starting in the fifth century, who established a successful trading relationship sanctioned through the elaborate and sometimes costly theater of tribute, and they had done so by developing their own shipping industry and by policing the strait. In his influential book *The Fall of Srivijaya in Malay History,* O. W. Wolters wrote:

> The Malays did so not because they wanted to be loyal vassals, though they were, of course, familiar with the institution of vassaldom, practiced everywhere in "Indianized" Southeast Asia. They were prepared to allow the Chinese to regard them as vassals for a very practical reason. The China trade was the source of their power. The emperors thought that they were manipulating their vassals by techniques of indirect control; the vassals were manipulating the China trade, the reality behind the tributary trade, to amass wealth as a means of asserting their authority in the fragmented and restless Malay society. . . . Their quest for power therefore required the cooperation of the emperors, and formal submission by overseas rulers was the sole condition for cooperation demanded and understood by the Chinese. Thus the Maharajas were prepared to receive marks of imperial favor, which were no doubt

sometimes flaunted to enhance their prestige in Asian commercial circles.

What looked like the basis for a stable and mutually profitable equilibrium—a win-win, in the common parlance of contemporary Chinese diplomacy—unraveled with startling speed beginning late in the eleventh century. This was the consequence of rapid political and economic changes in China under the Song, linked to the insecurity in the north and the previously mentioned population movements, which rendered the imperial patron and peripheral client relationships obsolete.

The Southern Song badly needed new sources of revenue, and after overcoming long-standing cultural biases in favor of state control and against private commerce, they rapidly developed the means to carry out a booming, globally oriented maritime commerce on their own. In doing so, the Central Kingdom jettisoned its privileged intermediary, Srivijaya, without the least sentimentality or fanfare. It did this by liberalizing foreign trade, first by allowing Arab ships into Chinese ports again, and then by encouraging Chinese merchants to venture out in search of profitable markets. Chinese traders wasted little time setting off for the South China Sea, and for Sumatra and Java in particular, where they quickly established small merchant communities and began buying goods from India and the Middle East, as well as local luxury items like spices and aromatics for sale in China.

By the thirteenth century, Chinese merchants dominated the maritime trade in the region of modern-day Indonesia, obtaining everything China desired by way of imports in local ports, rather than in the form of consignments carried from afar by others to southern Chinese ports, like Guangzhou, as had long been the tradition. The shipbuilding industry of the Mongol Yuan dynasty was in full expansion, enabling it to build large ships faster than anyone else. Developments like this prefigure recent changes in the global economy during the present era, when the size of China's manufacturing sector and its labor pool make it all but impossible for its Southeast Asian neighbors and many others to compete with it over industrial economies of scale. By 1330, Chinese merchant shipping was conducting a thriving business even farther afield, throughout much of the Indian Ocean. Places like Palembang and Jambi, once the rich trading capitals of Srivijaya, were reduced to run-of-the-mill ports of call.

Although it had once distinguished itself as an ultraloyal vassal, the "empire" of the strait was no longer of any use to its patron, China, providing a premodern example of the dictum attributed to nineteenth-century British statesman Lord Palmerston: "Nations have no permanent friends or allies, they only have interests." By the time Zheng He's armada showed up in the Malay-Indonesian world in the early fifteenth century, all that remained of the once fabulously wealthy Palembang was a pirates' lair. A little more than a century later, after the Portuguese had taken over, Tomé Pires, the most alert and perceptive chronicler of the early European imperial experience in East Asia, visited Palembang without ever suspecting that it had been a great city, about which an Arab visitor early in the tenth century would write that "one would not hear of a king who was richer, stronger, and with more revenue."

The power of this story lies in the example it provides about the transitory nature of the imperial networks that from era to era have served to stitch the world together, and especially about what is perhaps their most ephemeral component, the world city. Malacca, the successor city to Palembang and Jambi, rose as a kind of Chinese proto-colony, and it too burned brightly, albeit briefly. But whether viewed from the hilltop church of St. Paul, or from the narrow streets that were stormed by Albuquerque and are now overrun with tourists loading up on knickknacks who are almost as oblivious to the rich history here as Pires was, little hint remains of Malaccan agency, its vitality or its connectedness to things. This place represented the last gasp of the Malay world's claim to global relevance, and time, in its own brutal way, passed it by.

The aforementioned networks of trade and finance built by Europeans in Asia could create their own global centers in Manila, Jakarta and Macau, among other places, and later in Hong Kong and, nearby to Malacca, in Singapore. Now, after a five-hundred-year run, though, the tide of history seems again to be turning. With each passing year, the Western Pacific looks less and less like a place configured for the needs and ends of the West and ever more like the world briefly dominated by China from the late twelfth century until the early sixteenth. China is already the biggest trading partner of almost every state in the region, and as will be explored in detail later, its military, despite still being far weaker overall than that of the United States, is steadily putting itself in a position to make forward American deployment in a time of conflict a thing of extreme risk.

Today, in ways that are increasingly unmistakable, China's geopolitical play draws on Chinese conceptions of the world and of the country's own past traditions of power. Everything about its diplomatic language says that it views the Western Pacific as it once did its ancient known world, its *tian xia*, and that it intends for this region to return to its status as a place where China's paramount standing goes unchallenged. Such things are still not stated altogether directly, but it takes little imagination to fill in the blanks given the sorts of things that are already being said. Speaking at a conference in Shanghai in May 2014, President Xi Jinping, for example, all but called for the United States to give way to China in Asia when he said, "It's time for the people of Asia to run the affairs of Asia."

As under *tian xia*, China's new and unfolding power comes in two varieties, soft and hard, and just as in the past, there is little doubt which one China would prefer to employ, following the ancient precepts of Sun Tzu, which hold that "the supreme excellence consists in breaking the enemy's resistance without fighting." Toward this end, as with the old maritime tribute system, China's aim is to maximally leverage access to its immense market. In doing so, the none too subtle message it radiates to its neighbors is a familiar one that can be summed up in the following way: *In order to ensure your prosperity, hitch your wagons to us. Yes, we expect deference, but isn't that a small price to pay for stability and co-prosperity?* It is a message that in substance could have been penned by an emperor of old.

To modern China's neighbors the story of Srivijaya should probably be read as a tale of caution, of the hazards of overdependence and of being drawn too closely into the apron folds of the Central

Kingdom. The attraction of a fast-growing market as large as China's and of a new Pax Sinica, especially one led by a country that professes to benignly abstain from involvement in the internal affairs of others, is obvious. Over time, though, the price to pay could prove higher, indeed much higher than what's suggested in the soft pitch, and if the example of Srivijaya is indeed relevant, the price is the loss of control over one's destiny.

In this light, the entrepôts of today, Hong Kong and Singapore (along with the autonomous democratic statelet, Taiwan), warrant especially careful watching, for where China's emerging power is concerned, they are not unlike proverbial coal mine canaries. Like the South China Sea states that preceded them hundreds of years ago, both have thrived by arbitraging their geographic positions and cultural connections to China, and yet their insecurity is as manifest today as is their wealth. In Hong Kong's case, the signs are already abundant of a growing struggle to remain economically viable and politically at least semi-autonomous from China. British colonial rule and the relatively liberal cosmopolitanism that has deepened there—to the surprise of many—since the reversion of the territory to China in 1997 have fortified a local sense of identity in Hong Kong that already strongly differentiates it from the rest of China. Paradoxically, at the same time, Hong Kong's fate and fortunes are hitched more tightly now to the mother country than they have ever been in modern times.

Whether gamely or foolishly putting out of mind that they probably have no choice in the matter, Hong Kong's younger generations are pushing to have it both ways. Given their druthers, Hong Kong would continue to enjoy the role of the privileged intermediary for China—not the riverside warehouse sort of intermediary familiar from the history of the Malacca Strait, but a financial, jurispruden-tial, design and service halfway house between China and the rest of the world—while evolving toward a steadily more Western-style political dispensation for itself, meaning free and direct elections, unrestrained speech and independent courts. Alas, this is not the kind of bargain the Central Kingdom has in mind when it uses the iconic phrase "One Country, Two Systems" as political shorthand for the kind of limited autonomy it is willing to allow. China's response to this challenge has been pure *tian xia*, warning ominously about the threat that instability and disorder in Hong Kong pose to prosperity there, all the while trying to sweeten the pie economically for Hong Kong's people, hoping that their pocketbook sense of things will prove decisive in shaping their political attitudes.

In response to a wave of enormous protests in 2014 in favor of electoral reforms, China linked the Hong Kong stock market to mainland markets, and it has also signaled that it will push ahead with another favorite from its co-prosperity playbook: massive infrastructure development. In substance, this means creating a high-speed rail connection linking Hong Kong to Shanghai, and moving toward the creation of a new megacity in the Pearl River Delta that would fuse Hong Kong with a collection of nearby large young cities that includes Shenzhen, Dongguan, Zhuhai and Foshan along with Guangzhou. The fifty million people this megacity would comprise would account for fully a tenth of the Chinese economy and cover an area twenty-six times as large as Greater London.

From the perspective of Beijing, an approach like this has the merit not only of buying off Hong Kong via regional integration and the shared sense of prosperity that presumably comes along with it, but also of strongly eroding its individuality via immersion in a far greater, interdependent whole. The use of human inundation via state-organized migration and the deliberate concentration of people, the better to control them, in newly resettled areas are time-honored strategies of China, both dynastic and contemporary. Usually it has been used to bring about assimilation, first of China's southern provinces early in the country's history, then of its west-central regions, and now of peripheral areas like Tibet and Xinjiang, which are populated by restive ethnically and religiously distinct minorities.

If this hearts, minds and pocketbooks approach does not work, though, Beijing also retains a number of sticks to supplement its ample supply of carrots. As if by way of preemptive warning, in recent years China has been publicly airing the idea of transforming Shanghai, or alternately Tianjin, or perhaps both, into global financial centers, which would strip Hong Kong of one of its most important and lucrative vocations. Such plans would require challenging reforms in China. Many of these, however, such as the floating of the currency, the lifting of other capital controls and the introduction of more stringent regulations governing financial reporting, are seen as inevitable in the long run, and they could surely be accelerated to increase pressure on Hong Kong. In a similar vein, albeit somewhat harder to pull off, without challenging the power of the Communist Party, China could always strengthen its own rule of law in financial matters. This could be tried out initially on a limited and experimental basis via enclaves, much like the special economic zones used in the early 1980s to accept overseas private investment and experiment with capitalist-style industrial production without the risk of subverting the Leninist system that prevailed in the rest of the country.

It is not hard to imagine Beijing allowing foreign companies to register their businesses in China in special economic zones that would guarantee them something like a global standard for financial due process. Even moderate progress in an endeavor like this would threaten Hong Kong's other main pillar: its unique status within China as a relative haven of judicial independence and transparency. To forestall changes like this, the Hong Kong elite will go to great lengths to appease Beijing, including playing the heavy in turning back popular demands for democratic reforms, as it has already begun to do. In embracing this role, it would spare the Chinese Communist Party some of the cost and direct blame for the repression. In the meantime, however, no one should suffer the illusion that Beijing will be unwilling to play the heavy itself if ever the need arises. This could be seen in 2015 and 2016, with the disappearance of five Hong Kong booksellers whose stores carried works critical of China's rulers. One of them, Gui Minhai, a Swedish citizen of Chinese origin, whose publishing company was preparing to issue a book about Xi Jinping, turned up mysteriously in China, where he "confessed" on television to turning himself in over a twelve-year-old traffic case. In January 2016, a website of the Chinese Public Security Ministry announced that it had established a special bureau for tracking down "suspects" who had fled across mainland China's borders.

China's stepped-up pressure on freedom of expression in Hong Kong, as seen in efforts like these to rein in publishers, as well as in parallel efforts to take over the city's universities, has heightened a mood of pessimism among Hong Kong residents about their future. This was reflected in the surprise huge success of a movie released in late 2015 called *Ten Years,* which was built around five dystopian scenarios imagining life in Hong Kong in 2025, each filmed by a different director. In one of them, Mandarin has replaced Cantonese as the city's official language, and anyone not speaking it is marginalized. In another, Beijing interferes heavily in local government, working through obsequious Hong Kong officials and employing thugs to intimidate dissenters. "The movie is a reminder that if we do nothing, Hong Kong will become another Shenzhen," a viewer of the film told the *New York Times.*

Assessing Hong Kong toward the end of the 1980s in *Before European Hegemony*, Janet L. Abu-Lughod had already seen the writing on the wall. The city's role, she wrote, "is similar to a 'free trade' zone whose chief function is to serve as a 'gateway' to China, which, until recently, restricted the access of foreign traders and, even today, channels it through international ports such as Shanghai and [Guangzhou]. Hong Kong's prosperity is thus completely tied to her privileged access to an otherwise restricted market. In this, it bears considerable resemblance to Palembang or Jambi, whose importance derived from their special relationship to the tribute trade preferred by pre-Song dynasties. It is easy to understand why such positions are politically fragile."

One key to survival, and it is something that eluded all of the old comprador states of the strait, is what Abu-Lughod called "envaluation," or what is more commonly known as value added. This has been a key element in Singapore's strategy, which has been far more entrepreneurial than Hong Kong's, probably as a result of what might be called its advantage of distance. For a long time, Hong Kong seemed to thrive, collecting rents based almost purely on its geographic position as a portal into China. Over time, however, experiencing no urgent pressure to evolve or to innovate has exacted its own steep cost: Hong Kong became, like Palembang or Jambi, a place with no hinterland of its own, which traded plenty but could produce relatively little once China's own reforms priced it out of most industrial pursuits. Singapore, by contrast, constantly labored to develop new industries, placing a special focus on high-value-added fields that drew upon sophisticated research and development, innovative design, and advanced technology. The distinctive brand of soft authoritarianism that has emerged under the Lee family's leadership of the country has so far succeeded brilliantly in outrunning the curse of complacency. Of course its success in the longer term is anything but assured.

Unlike Hong Kong, not being part of China has allowed Singapore to apply another lesson derived from the rise and fall of comprador states in the region, and that is to avoid being subsumed into any gradual resurrection of the tribute system. In the language of modern international relations, Singapore has hedged its bets, or balanced. It is one of the region's most ardent cheerleaders of a continued strong U.S. posture in the Western Pacific, managing it so far without alienating China. It has also maintained its own strong and independent defenses, built upon a foundation of compulsory national military service and steady technological renewal.

It is hard to say what would happen, though, if anything remotely like recent global trends were to continue for another couple of decades (China's economy has quintupled in size since 1990, ballooning from one smaller than Italy's to one larger than the United States', by one common if not universally accepted measure), and the Chinese economy were to clearly surpass America's, and Washington could no longer sustain the kind of military expenditure required to remain competitive, or perhaps even relevant, in the Western Pacific. The history of the region offers us no good precedents or parallels for a Singapore under such a scenario. The question that would then loom is whether a *tian xia*–like situation would be any more escapable for Singapore than it is for a Hong Kong that today is not even remotely in charge of its own destiny.

A possible glimpse of this future came in an exchange at a security forum of the Association of Southeast Asian Nations in Hanoi in 2010 that some treated as a mere lapse in diplomatic message discipline. When the Singapore delegate made a statement supporting a maritime code of conduct in the region, something that Beijing had already signaled it was unenthusiastic about, the Chinese foreign minister, Yang Jiechi, fixed his gaze on his Singaporean counterpart, George Yeo, and let slip his country's view of the rules of the game: "China is a big country and other countries are small countries," he said. "And that's just a fact."

CHAPTER FOUR

A Pacified South

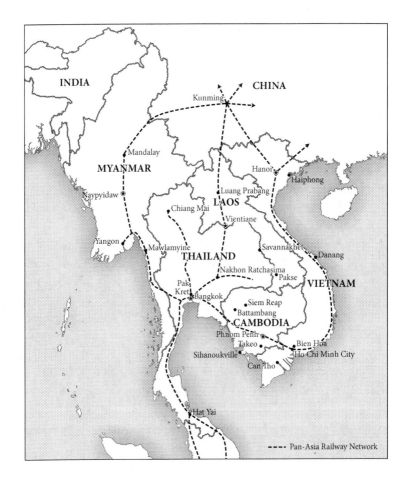

INDIA

CHINA

Kunming

MYANMAR

Mandalay

Hanoi

Haiphong

Naypyidaw

Luang Prabang

LAOS

Chiang Mai

Vientiane

Yangon

Mawlamyine

Savannakhet

Danang

THAILAND

Nakhon Ratchasima

Pakse

VIETNAM

Pak Kret

Bangkok

Siem Reap

Battambang

CAMBODIA

Phnom Penh

Takeo

Bien Hoa

Sihanoukville

Ho Chi Minh City

Can Tho

Hat Yai

---- Pan-Asia Railway Network

The cemetery popped into view on a late winter afternoon in 2005 as we rounded a country bend. There, in the sunshine, stretching as far as the eye could see, loomed serried hills decked in graves, concrete crypts. Two Chinese men in their early forties met us at the bottom of a slope. They were veterans of the People's Liberation Army and they had come, as they said they did every few years, to hike the hills together and look for the graves of comrades along whose sides they had fought in the war their country waged against Vietnam in 1979. China's neighbor was just a few miles away to the south, and the concentration of Chinese burial grounds in this border region was designed to keep this unpleasant history out of sight and out of mind.

This was a war for which the authorities in Beijing wanted no monuments or heroes. They had done a good job of burying it in the folds of time. This I knew, in part, because I was visiting the area with Liu Hui, a well-educated Chinese friend, and she had little sense of what had happened between her country and Vietnam a generation earlier. When I invoked the official name, "the Self-Defense and Counterattack Against Vietnam War," as it is called whenever referring to it cannot be avoided, it produced a nod of recognition from her, but, like almost any Chinese person of her generation, she could tell me little more about it.

We spent a couple of hours quietly climbing the hills with the veterans that day, a gentle breeze rustling through the bamboo groves all around. There were 957 graves on our chosen hillside alone, and whenever the two men found the tomb of someone they knew, they would stop to reminisce, before lighting a cigarette, which they placed upright as an offering at the base of the concrete headstones, each of which was emblazoned with a large red star.

During one pause I asked one of the veterans, Long Chaogang, who had seen heavy combat, what the war against Vietnam had been about. "I don't know," he said. How had he explained it to his family, to his twelve-year-old daughter? I asked. "It's none of her business," he said bluntly, followed by silence.

———

Without China there is no way of defining Vietnam. And without longtime tributaries like Vietnam, we would see China in a very different light. Where one of these countries begins and the other ends has been an almost irresolvable question, and this puzzle remains with us today in the disputed waters of a sea whose name they cannot even agree upon: the South Sea for China, and the East Sea for the Vietnamese.

The earliest recorded events in what we now know as Vietnam came under the rule of a Chinese king late in the seventh century BCE, which was more than four hundred years before the place we now know as China was itself first unified. The traditional legends that the Vietnamese sustain about the founding of their nation possess a Joseph Campbell–like resonance. Like most legends, they are unreliable in their finer details, but as people like Campbell have tried to demonstrate via the exegesis of myths, that does nothing to detract from their power or even higher truth. The first lineage of rulers was said to have been founded by Lac Long Quan (Lac Dragon Lord), a hero who resided in the seas off of what is now northern Vietnam. When he visited the Hong River plain, he brought with him the gift of culture and civilized the local people there, instructing them in the intricacies of tidal paddy rice cultivation and in many other matters. Before returning to his mythical abode in the sea, he delivered a pledge to his new wards that he would return to help them whenever they faced a crisis, and before long he was called upon to make good on his vow.

The occasion was a bid to take over the land by a king arriving from the north, meaning from the land we now call China. According to the legend, Lac Long Quan lived up to his promise, returning from the sea to kidnap the wife of the "Chinese" sovereign, Au Co, whom he sequestered atop a sacred mountain. Unable to find his wife, the Chinese king retreated to the north, after which Au Co gave birth to the child of Lac Dragon Lord. This child later became the first of the Hung kings, a bronze age dynasty said to have been founded around 2879 BCE. "This theme of a local culture hero neutralizing a northern threat by appropriating its source of legitimacy foreshadowed the historical relationship between the Vietnamese and the Chinese," writes Keith Weller Taylor in his book *The Birth of Vietnam*. "The mythical origins of the Hung kings reflects a maritime cultural base with political accretions from continental influences."

The rule of the Hung kings would end in 257 BCE, when they were replaced by a short-lived dynasty founded by a prince from what is today China's Sichuan Province. But as much as the legend can suggest successful resistance to takeover by northerner usurpers, it also reflects another contradictory, long-term historical process of major significance.

Beginning with a series of wars in China in the third century BCE, the northern part of today's Vietnam gradually became the scene of successive waves of settlement by new elites arriving from farther north. These Sinicized peoples were in effect the losers in a series of battles for control of southern China. "China" had been locked in the throes of a struggle for consolidation, in which peoples of the north began forcibly extending their control over the peoples of the south. This process was greatly accelerated after China was unified for the first time by emperor Qin Shihuang, in 221 BCE. Following his victory over a collection of rival states in central China, Qin, from whose name the word "China" is itself perhaps derived, dispatched an army numbering a half million soldiers in pursuit of conquest farther to the south.

The kingdoms of the southeast and their inhabitants, residents of present-day China's Fujian and Guangdong provinces and extending southward all the way into the northern reaches of present-day Vietnam, were the main target of this conquest, and these diverse and loosely related peoples were referred to by the conquerors not by their own names but by a portmanteau description, the *Yue*. The term survives as an etymologically obscure label for the south still in popular usage in modern China (as an abbreviation for Guangdong Province, for example, used there on vehicle license plates), and in the name of Vietnam itself. The word *nam* contained in the country's name simply means "south." The word "Viet," meanwhile, is in effect the Vietnamese version or analog of the same word, *yue,* and its literal meaning, "barbarian," makes clear Chinese attitudes toward the region. In the early nineteenth century, when Vietnam first began to adopt these two words to form its modern name, even this became a subject of contention with China. As the historian and political scientist Benedict Anderson wrote in his book *Imagined Communities,* "On his coronation in 1802, Gia-long [the Vietnamese king] wished to call his realm 'Nam Viet' and sent envoys to gain Peking's assent. The Manchu Son of Heaven, however, insisted that it be 'Viet Nam.' The reason for this inversion is as follows: 'Viet Nam (or in Chinese Yue Nan) means, roughly 'to the south of Viet (Yue),' a realm conquered by the Han seventeen centuries earlier and reputed to cover today's Chinese provinces of Guangdong and Guangxi, as well as the Red River Valley. Gia-long's 'Nam Viet,' however, meant 'Southern Viet/Yue,' in effect a claim to the old realm."

The brief-lived Qin and subsequent dynasties characteristically regarded the Yue denizens to the south of the Yangtze as incipient subjects who were merely awaiting the gift of civilization from the descendants of the mythical Yellow Emperor. But to the conquerors and settlers from the north, civilization did not only mean the adoption of certain basic cultural traits that we think of as essentially Chinese. Rather, it meant outright assimilation, which to a large extent implied forgetting whoever you once thought you were and "becoming" thoroughly Chinese in thought and self-image.

Although it took centuries to play out, in most places this project worked so well that the prevalent identity that people of China's southeast hold of themselves today is that they are simply Han, or "descendants of the dragon," as over 90 percent of the rest of "Chinese" would say. This is true despite their speaking a distinctive patchwork of languages, most famously Cantonese, along with a myriad of other tongues in Fujian Province, all of which are mutually incomprehensible with Mandarin (a northern dialect that was made the national language after the Republican revolution).

The process of incorporation of southern China into a larger whole was accomplished only by the continuous and at times large-scale movement of peoples from northern and central China southward. It wasn't until the Tang dynasty that the great south began to feel more or less reliably "Chinese," meaning culturally and politically assimilated beyond the city centers and into the hills and valleys, by the peasants who resided there.

Many of the half million troops sent by the Qin emperor settled in northern Vietnam, manning garrisons in towns there. But instead of becoming the vanguards for a process of deep Sinicization, after the Qin emperor died, the freshly unified China fragmented, leaving the former Qin armies that had been deployed in the far south stranded. Those who were left behind, along with their descendants, gradually became acculturated by the locals instead. This is where one can think of Vietnam beginning.

Similarly, by force of demographics, and also as a matter of securing their own legitimacy, the displaced elites who had arrived from China found themselves intermarrying with the local people and assimilating into the emerging local culture, rather than spreading a uniquely Chinese identity. Possession of the keys of Chinese civilization, including reading and writing and mastery of the classics and of ritual, were essential gauges of elite cultivation and prestige, but elites who were too thoroughly acculturated as Chinese and who moreover were too directly perceived as surrogates for northern power rendered themselves vulnerable to revolt. This all favored the steady emergence of a distinctive and, from the perspective of China, refractory culture, one that would never truly accept foreign control.

Ruling Vietnam then, and many would say now, required a careful balancing act between independence and deference, between local authenticity and the embrace of northern ways. This was the lesson applied early on by Chao To, the flinty and resourceful leader of the southern Yue at the end of the Qin dynasty. His "success rested not only on his ability to rally the Chinese immigrants in the south, but also on his popularity among the non-Chinese population," wrote Taylor in *The Birth of Vietnam.* In 196 BCE, when Chao To received an envoy of the Han dynasty, the successor to the Qin, he wore his hair in a bun and squatted, in the manner of the Yue people. To the accusation that he had forgotten his "true ancestry," he replied that "after so many years of living in the south he no longer remembered the proper usages of the north."

The Han eventually put an end to Yue self-rule, an event that is usually dated to 111 BCE, when northern Vietnam was proclaimed an administrative district of China. Formal direct control began in 42 CE, and would continue for the next nine centuries, a period during which China exhibited extraordinary patience and determination in a nonetheless doomed effort to achieve what it had managed to do with so many other vanquished subjects: annex their territory and culturally absorb the population into the Sinic world. Across the centuries, China applied almost every imaginable tactic in order to overcome persistent local resistance to its project, and none of them enjoyed lasting success. These included scorched-earth military campaigns, cultural indoctrination and stern, top-down administration, as well as softer approaches to win the hearts and minds of the locals by, among other things, applying light taxation.

Even early on, astute local Chinese administrators were already taking a skeptical view of the project's long-term prospects. In *The Birth of Vietnam,* Taylor quotes at length from a memorial to the Chinese emperor written to this effect in 231 CE by a recently retired administrator, Que Song. China had labored hard to convert the southern Yue peoples to their supposedly superior ways but faced resistance in even the most basic of things. For men, this meant wearing their hair long; for women, it meant wearing trousers instead of skirts. It also meant imposing the strict patrimonial patterns that prevailed in China in place of the more egalitarian practices of the Vietnamese.

"The people are like birds and beasts; they wear their hair tied up and go barefoot, while for clothing they simply cut a hole in a piece of cloth for their head or they fasten their garments on the left side [in barbarian style]," reads one characteristically frustrated passage. In another, he bemoans that "according to the records, civilizing activities have been going on for over four hundred years, but, according to what I myself have seen during many years of travel since my arrival here, the actual situation is something else."

Que's pessimistic memorial raises the question of why China had even bothered with such a daunting challenge in a place that was, from the perspective of its own culture, "beyond the realm of normal government," according to Taylor. The spread of Chinese political and cultural hegemony faced limits in the steppes of Central Asia, a topography that favored modestly populated settlements and nomadic lifestyles, and not the zones of readily taxable, intensive, fixed cultivation anchored by densely settled urban areas that were characteristic of Central Kingdom culture. To the southwest, Chinese expansion was contained by an even more imposing geographic reality—forbidding mountainous terrain that culminated in the high Tibetan Plateau. To the south, though, there were no fixed obstacles. To the contrary, Vietnam was extraordinarily well suited to wet rice cultivation—a mainstay of Chinese civilization. Moreover, it was peopled by inhabitants who, superficially at least, appeared to be *mi mi,* in the words of a Chinese emperor, meaning closely related to the Chinese themselves. Such inviting conditions redoubled China's determination to impose itself, seemingly at whatever cost.

A sense of manifest Chinese entitlement, of course, is implicit in the very phrase *tian xia.* But beyond this lay yet more practical incentives. Annam, as Vietnam was known to the Chinese, possessed natural resources of sufficient abundance and variety that it could support an economy heavily based on lucrative extraction, as even Que, in his otherwise skeptical memorial, recognized. "This place is famous," he wrote, "for precious rarities from afar: pearls, incense, drugs, elephant tusks, rhinoceros horn, tortoise shell, coral, lapis lazuli, parrots, kingfishers, peacocks, rare and abundant treasures enough to satisfy all desires. So it is not necessary to depend on what is received from taxes in order to profit the Central Kingdom." Additionally, by virtue of both its geography and its maritime culture, it seemed to offer China a vital corridor onto the South China Sea and the rich new trade possibilities that existed there and beyond.

China's hold on Vietnam unraveled during the Tang dynasty, a millennium after it had begun. This was the result of a confluence of factors. The Tang had been both distracted and weakened by the An Lushan Rebellion, a costly and hugely disruptive domestic revolt. A trend toward more and more naked extraction, and other forms of misrule of the Vietnamese, including the use of forced labor in mining and the sudden doubling of taxation, also helped drive an alliance between Sinicized local elites and the rest of the population. Hitherto aloof Vietnamese mandarins began to adopt the language of the common people, and stressed their shared interest in casting off foreign domination. Ironically, the Annamese were freed to direct all of their energies into revolt against the Chinese by the Tang's defeat of their longtime rival to the immediate south, the strongly Hindu-influenced society known as Champa. Once independent, Vietnam would remain so—albeit still as an uneasy tributary of China—with only brief interruption for another thousand years, until the nineteenth-century takeover of Indochina by the French.

The details of how Vietnam, or Đại Việt, as it called itself, managed independence during this era are essential for understanding China's conception of power and the workings of geopolitics in the region down to the present day. The price of peace with China was adherence to the rules of *tian xia*. This meant acceptance by Vietnam of its inferior and subsidiary status, which included ritual submission and flattery of Chinese prestige and power. In fact, the Vietnamese were playing an elaborate double game. Despite the skepticism of Chinese administrators like Que Song that the Vietnamese could ever master the Yellow Emperor's culture, the Vietnamese had consistently proven themselves tremendously applied learners. The elite's conceptions of power and statecraft were richly informed by China's Confucian model. That, coupled with Vietnam's deeply rooted sense of its own uniqueness and its own stubborn right to autonomy, led to a kind of mini *tian xia* of its own.

Vietnam set out on a southward march. Through a process of ruthless conquest and assimilation, Đại Việt campaigned to establish the hegemony of its northern culture over the rest of the elongated territory that we now recognize as modern Vietnam. Like imperial China, its directional thrust was heavily dictated by geography. To the north, of course, lay China, with its vast expanse and immense population; conquest there was impossible (although in several wars, Vietnam conducted offensives into Chinese territory). To the west of the Đại Việt homeland around the Hong River sat the formidable Annamite mountain range, precluding easy expansion in that direction, and to the east lay the sea. This left a concerted push to the south as the only possibility for increasing the country's wealth and power. The Vietnamese readily perceived a compelling geopolitical imperative for southward expansion as well. Long-term survival in the face of the ever-present threat of an overbearing neighbor to the north required achieving a kind of strategic physical depth for the country. China might (and did) invade during the centuries of independence, but possessing a hinterland could enable the Vietnamese to retrench and regroup, hence survive.

The Song first sought to recover Vietnam in 981, just forty years after the Tang had lost it. Shortly before launching an invasion, the Song emperor, Taizong, sent a letter to the Vietnamese king in which he likened China's southern tributaries to limbs attached to a Chinese body. "Does a sage ignore one sore toe?" the letter read. Next came a request that Vietnam submit to China so as to preserve China's health, followed by a litany of threats describing what would happen if Vietnam did not comply:

> Our command must be to cut up your corpses, chop up your bones, and return your land to the grasses. . . . Although your seas have pearls, we will throw them into the rivers, and though your mountains produce gold, we will throw it into the dust; we do not covet your valuables. You fly and leap like savages, we have horse-drawn carriages; you drink through your noses, we have rice and wine; let us change your customs. You cut your hair, we wear hats; when you talk you sound like birds, we have examinations and books; let us teach you knowledge of the proper laws. . . . Do you want to escape from the savagery of the outer islands and gaze upon the house of civilization? Do you want to discard your garments of leaves and grass and wear flowered robes embroidered with mountains and dragons? Have you understood? Do not march out and make a mortal mistake. We are preparing chariots, horses, and soldiers.

When the threatened invasion came, for all of that bravado, it was defeated by the forces of the Vietnamese king, Le Hoan. This was only the first of a score of invasions from the north during the ensuing millennium of Vietnamese independence. The next major wave came during the rule of Kublai Khan (Yuan dynasty), when Mongol-led armies numbering from three hundred thousand to half a million men repeatedly invaded Đại Việt during the second half of the thirteenth century. The Vietnamese survived in part by abandoning major cities and towns during each Mongol offensive and falling back, typically southward, into the countryside, where they harried and ambushed the invaders and took advantage of China's overstretched supply lines.

As we have already seen, in 1406 under the Ming, China mounted yet another major invasion and occupation, sending two armies totaling as many as a million soldiers, many of them equipped with firearms for the first time, to occupy the country and imposing what Vietnamese popularly regard today as the harshest regime of foreign rule their nation has ever experienced. Efforts by the Ming to restore Chinese dominance to Annam were prompted in part by unrest in the region to its south. In 1400, Hanoi had fallen to Annam's longtime rival, Champa, giving the Cham control of the South China Sea and disrupting lucrative Chinese maritime trade there.

As many as seven million Vietnamese may have died during this invasion and in resisting the subsequent twenty-one-year-long annexation. As colonial master, China instituted a strict registration system and compulsory carrying of identification papers, allowing it to monitor every household. Able-bodied young men were forcibly conscripted into the imperial army, and artisans and others with special talents were deported to China. The chewing of betel nut and the blackening of teeth, both deeply entrenched local traditions, were banned. In addition, the Vietnamese were forced to begin sacrificing to Chinese deities. "Schools were permitted to teach only in Chinese. All local cults were suppressed. What national literature Vietnam had produced was confiscated and shipped to China. The women were forced to wear Chinese dress, the men to wear long hair," writes Joseph Buttinger in *A Dragon Defiant: A Short History of Vietnam.*

Despite its investment of immense military and administrative means, China's attempt to bring about assimilation was finally defeated by a resistance movement launched in 1418 by a man named Lê Lợi, a wealthy farmer. His rebel forces laid siege to the Chinese colonial capital, Dong Quan, present-day Hanoi. The Chinese emperor sent a large army of reinforcements, but in one of the most celebrated feats of Vietnamese history, its commander was captured in an ambush and the Ming army was defeated. In 1428, a triumphant Lê Lợi established a new dynasty that both restored Vietnamese sovereignty to the land and established a definitive separateness from China for the first time.

The new Lê dynasty quickly redirected its energies southward. Under a variety of guises, Vietnam had been nibbling away at Cham territory since the seventh century, but now sensing an opportunity for much more substantial expansion, it launched a great migratory drive known as Nam Tien (the southward movement), which eventually resulted in a full-blown war with its Hinduized (and later Islamicized) neighbor to the south. Champa, which had itself only recently been at war with China, appealed for Ming intervention against the Vietnamese, which was granted, but only in the form of naval support, which proved unable to tip the balance in the Cham's favor. This episode, and its aftermath, reveals a number of enduring themes about the ways of power in this region. Although Champa was defeated by the Lê dynasty and annexed in 1471, along the way it became the first Southeast Asian state to grasp and try to take advantage of what would become long-term Chinese policy toward the region: siding with smaller neighboring states in order to constrain Vietnam's growing geopolitical ambitions.

Đại Việt had begun the fifteenth century as one of a number of roughly comparable Southeast Asian principalities. By the end of the century it would stand out as the subregion's preeminent power. The takeover of Champa proved to be the first step in a lengthy reordering of its own neighborhood, mimicking the ways, albeit on a far smaller scale, of its former master, the Central Kingdom. Successfully carrying out its aspiration to dominate Southeast Asia demanded of the Vietnamese not only all of the necessary military and economic means that one might imagine, but also great deftness in managing relations with China, which would win them a 360-year period of freedom from war with their neighbor.

Bitter history dating to the 1406–07 takeover of Vietnam by the Ming furnished a powerful cautionary tale of the possible consequences of insufficient deference or attention to decorum toward their imperial neighbor. The short-lived Ming takeover of Đại Việt had powerful ideological roots that related to the conceptual integrity of *tian xia* itself. Yongle, the emperor who would soon launch Zheng He on his series of sea voyages, took strong offense at what he regarded as the Vietnamese claims of political equality with China. This feeling was based on the public reinterpretation of the Confucian classics by the Vietnamese dynast Hồ Quý Ly, an act that the Chinese felt deviated from the proper universal order of things. "Yongle regarded Ly's ideology as an open challenge to his own legitimate right to assert moral control over the entire world," wrote Alexander Eng Ann Ong in *Southeast Asia in the Fifteenth Century: The China Factor*. The severity of the Ming colonial conduct in Đại Việt following its takeover had a clearly punitive aspect. One of the most infamous episodes, the systematic destruction of Vietnamese literature, was a form of payback meted out for this apostasy. Yongle's commander in Đại Việt, Zheng Fu, gathered "every single written work and stele he and his armies could find. He then had personnel inspect each item before deciding whether to burn or destroy it."

From the earliest times, in the interest of conflict avoidance and indeed of survival, as we have previously seen, Vietnamese dynasts did not often represent themselves to the Chinese as being their imperial equals, or even as their very remote counterparts. After the threatening rebuke over the impossibility of "two emperors appearing simultaneously" that was delivered by a Han dynasty emperor in 179 BCE, for example, the Vietnamese king issued this groveling acceptance of his demotion: "I called myself emperor for the purpose of giving myself pleasure," he wrote in apology. "I have lived in Viet for forty-nine years. Now I carry in my arms my grandchildren. Still, I rise early and bed late. I lie down and find no peace on my mat. I eat and find no flavor. My eyes do not perceive the brilliant colors. My ears do not hear the sounds of bell and drum, all because I could not serve the Han. Now Your Majesty graciously restores my old title and communicates through an ambassador as of old. Therefore, when I die my bones will not rot. I change my title and dare not call myself emperor [follows a list of tributary items sent to the emperor]. . . . With a temerity worthy of death I twice worshipfully inform Your Imperial Majesty of all of this."

Moments like these, though, have alternated with far greater self-assertion by the Vietnamese, and sometimes outright aggressiveness, such as a preemptive invasion of southern China by Vietnam during the Song dynasty, lending a cyclical dynamic to the relationship. There are extraordinary stories from early in the millennium of Vietnamese independence, which commenced in the tenth century, when the country's rulers would not completely abase themselves in dealings with their Chinese counterparts, as China expected under its conception of *tian xia*. Throughout the ages, many Vietnamese rulers have declined to perform the ritual kowtow, infuriating the Chinese. Proper protocol theoretically called for Vietnamese kings who had opposed China to make a journey to the imperial capital and beg for pardon, but there is only one example known to history of compliance, during the Qing dynasty, in 1790, and even in this case the Vietnamese later insisted that they had sent a body double or impersonator in place of the king.

A challenge for the Lê dynasty was finding the right vocabulary in its dealings with China now that Vietnam was morphing into a regional hegemon, with an increasingly imperial manner of its own toward its neighbors. One traditional approach to this problem is summed up in a phrase that long enjoyed currency: *"truong de ngoai vuong,"* meaning "inside as emperor, outside as king." "This postulate is illustrated by the fact that the first act of a Vietnamese ruler was to proclaim himself 'emperor,' while his second act was to seek investiture as 'king' from the Chinese ruler," according to Alexander Vuving, a political scientist who specializes in Vietnamese affairs. Viet leaders would strive for an acceptably submissive pose in their dealings with China while maintaining their imperial pretensions at home. Under the Lê, this included going about the rough business of intermittently rolling up their weaker neighbors and forcing them to assimilate or submit. Vuving writes:

> What developed from this was a kind of play-acting on both sides.
>
> The Vietnamese world vision contradicted the Chinese world view at a crucial point. In the Chinese view, the Chinese emperor was the universal ruler. He alone ruled the entire world in heaven's name, and "nobody else could claim the title of emperor." The Vietnamese, however, asserted that the world was naturally divided into north and south and each domain was ruled by its own emperor. According to the Vietnamese view, the Vietnamese emperor was the legitimate ruler of the south, while the Chinese emperor the legitimate ruler of the north.

To the extent that Vietnam *asserted* such things, though, it avoided doing so in ways that would prevent it from keeping up appearances with China. Following victory over the Ming, for example, the Lê dynasty went to great lengths to avoid humiliating China. Many in Vietnam were calling for revenge on the Chinese, including the execution of Chinese war prisoners. But a close associate of the Vietnamese leader (Lê Lợi), the poet Nguyen Trai, won the day by counseling a conciliatory approach instead. Describing this episode, Nayan Chanda wrote in his 1986 book *Brother Enemy: A History of Indochina Since the Fall of Saigon*:

> "In the present circumstances it is not difficult to attack the enemy and to quench our thirst with his blood. But I am afraid that that way we will incur the profound hatred of the Ming. To take their revenge, to save the prestige of a great empire, they will send a new army. For how long will the evil of war last? For the good of our two nations it is better to take advantage of this situation when the enemy is at the end of its tether to make peace with him." Lê Lợi accepted this counsel and

gave the Chinese army five hundred boats, several thousand horses, and some food for their return.

Not long afterward, as he prepared to push southward late in the fifteenth century, the Vietnamese "emperor" took the precaution of sending an envoy to the Ming court to explain his plans for what amounted to a full-scale invasion of Champa and thereby preemptively gain China's acquiescence.

In the way it went about constructing a worldview of its own, one that placed it at the center of its own realm, Vietnam was behaving in the manner of a devoted student that had internalized the values of its master. As we have seen, it had been a successful apprenticeship. This learning process was dramatically accelerated during the harsh colonial occupation that followed Đại Việt's annexation by China in 1407. While China failed in its ultimate task of once and for all wiping out Vietnamese culture and along with it any notions of separateness, during this twenty-year occupation it succeeded to a degree that any of the world's present-day nation builders could only envy in grafting onto Vietnam a new ruling culture based on neo-Confucianism, intensive agriculture and rigorous and energetic bureaucracy. It was this culture of governance that ironically allowed the Vietnamese state to render its own society much more "legible," to borrow the language of the Yale political scientist James C. Scott, meaning enabling it to administer, police and especially tax its population more thoroughly. And it was these capabilities, along with the rapid adoption and mastery of guns and other gunpowder-based weaponry borrowed from the Ming, that quickly elevated Vietnam vis-à-vis some of its more traditionally ruled regional neighbors. This meant that as Vietnam grew in power and amplitude, it too came to see itself as naturally sitting at the center atop a hierarchical system of international relations within its neighborhood. Like the Middle Kingdom itself, it began to regard its culture as the reference and its power as the last word.

From the Chinese perspective, Vietnam, being non-Chinese, was barbarian and belonged to the world's peripheries. From the Vietnamese perspective, however, Vietnam also belonged to the world's center. The Vietnamese called themselves the "metropolitan" (*kinh*) people and regarded their country as a "domain of manifest civility" (*van hien chi bang*). "The Vietnamese court employed the hallowed term *trung quoc* (central state), which was identical with the Chinese term *zhongguo,* to refer to Vietnam," according to Vuving.

After the conquest of the Cham, who were massacred and dispersed, the Đại Việt expansion proceeded apace. "Vietnamese history has flowed across Indochina like a flood carrying off other people wherever they occupied a lowland rice field or where it could be put under rice," wrote the French historian Paul Mus. The next to fall victim were the Lao people, whose lands lay to the west and southwest. By the end of the sixteenth century, the territories of the Cham had been fully integrated, lending Vietnam its peculiarly elongated, dragon's neck form. Vietnamese settlers had begun moving into Cambodian lands in the heavily forested far south even before this had been fully accomplished, though. Then, from 1650 to 1750, Vietnam took over the Mekong River valley, including the Cambodian fishing village of Prey Nokor, which would later become known as Saigon.

A long seesaw contest between Vietnam and the region's other aspiring power, Siam (Thailand), ensued over Cambodia. In an earlier era, the Khmer empire had been Southeast Asia's most powerful and ambitious state, controlling territory that stretched from the Malay Peninsula to the Kingdom of Laos. By the early nineteenth century, when Thailand and Vietnam were gearing up for their competition, the Khmer polity had already entered into an advanced state of decay. The Cambodian king turned to Vietnam to protect his country from the encroachments of Siam, and in 1813 the Vietnamese drove the Siamese army out of Cambodia. A Vietnamese historian of the time wrote, "Our troops built two walls and constructed a Pavilion of the Pacified Frontier [at Phnom Penh], and on this pavilion they built a structure called the Yu-yuan-t'ang, to be a place where the barbarian king [the Cambodian king] will look toward Hué [the Vietnamese capital], worshipping." The historian Mark Mancall points out in "The Ch'ing Tribute System: An Interpretive Essay," in John King

Fairbank's book *The Chinese World Order,* how thoroughly Vietnamese behavior by this time had come to mimic that of imperial China, relegating neighbors to the status of *fan,* or barbarians, and the price Cambodia paid:

> Following an unsuccessful Thai attempt to bring Cambodia under their control in 1833–34, the Vietnamese embarked on a process that, unchecked, might well have led to the disappearance of Cambodia altogether. Fortresses were built throughout the country, and a garrison was installed in Phnom Penh. Independent Cambodia was turned into Vietnam's "overlordship of the pacified west." [The Vietnamese king] Minh Mang launched a vigorous campaign to bring the "barbaric" Khmers into the civilized world. Vietnamese teachers were sent in to teach "the [Confucian] way" to Cambodian officials. The Vietnamese emperor tried to impose the Vietnamese style of dressing the hair and Vietnamese attire on the Khmers, to introduce a system of taxation modeled on Vietnam's, and even to force peasants to grow the same crops as were grown in Vietnam. Severe punishments were meted out to those who refused to accept the new order.

By now, Vietnam's sense of hierarchy within its own neighborhood had begun to reflect a strikingly thorough internalization of the *tian xia* mind-set, down to the creation of that demeaning appellation for Cambodia, "the pacified west," a name that ironically mirrored China's own longtime patronizing use of the name for Vietnam, Annam, which meant "the pacified south." At its worst, the high-handed condescension and severity of the Vietnamese strongly echoed the haughtiest excesses of the Tang and Ming who had worked so hard to forcibly "civilize" Vietnam. Vietnamese actions produced in the Cambodians much the same result—a deep and lasting enmity toward their neighbor that down to this day, as we will see shortly, conditions the geopolitics of the region every bit as much as does Vietnam's defiant, perpetual underdog attitude toward China.

These trends were compounded after the end of Vietnam's millennium of nominal independence by the colonial policies of France, which became the country's new master in the late nineteenth century. In 1871, France administratively reorganized the subregion (Vietnam's three main constituencies, Tonkin, Annam and Cochin China, plus Cambodia and Laos) into a federation, which it named Indochina. Within Indochina, Vietnam not only received a disproportionate share of French investment, but Paris also allocated land that had historically been part of the Khmer empire to Cochin China and employed Vietnamese heavily in the colonial administration to help it run its two smaller neighbors more cheaply, contributing to their long-standing fears of being swallowed by the country they regarded as the region's aspiring hegemon. As Benedict Anderson wrote in *Imagined Communities,* "The French made no bones about expressing the view that if the Vietnamese were untrustworthy and grasping, they were nevertheless decisively more energetic and intelligent than the 'child-like' Khmer and Lao."

France had staked its claim to Indochina in the midst of a generalized European scramble for colonies around the world, one in which China had always been considered the biggest prize of all. Britain and France were the most ambitious of Western imperialists, and they competed ferociously throughout the nineteenth century. But in 1860, during the Second Opium War, the two European powers made rare common cause in launching an assault on Beijing. It was the French and their artillery that overwhelmed the courageous last stand of the Qing empire's Mongol cavalry, setting the stage for the sack of the Chinese capital and the pillage and destruction of the imperial Old Summer Palace on the outskirts of the city. This large complex of temples, palaces and pagodas, known in Chinese as the Garden of Eternal Brightness, or *Yuanmingyuan,* was one of the greatest symbols of Qing achievement and splendor. A French soldier who was witness to its destruction wrote at the time, "I was dumbfounded, stunned, bewildered by what I had seen, and suddenly Thousand and One Nights seem perfectly believable to me. I have walked for more than two days over more than 30 million worth of silks, jewels, porcelain, bronzes, sculptures, [and] treasures! I do not think we have seen anything like it since the sack of Rome by the barbarians."

Like other European powers of the day, France used military might and blackmail to obtain special "rights" within China, via the series of unequal treaties that the Qing were forced into signing, but its concessions did not compare with those of its perennial rival the British, whose interests stood preeminent in the country. Against that backdrop, Indochina, from China's perspective a core component of its tributary world, suddenly loomed attractively for Paris as a somewhat neglected and potentially lucrative concession prize, and one that might even offer, via Vietnam, a backdoor route for France into China itself.

All around China's perimeter, the tributary ties that formed the very foundation of *tian xia* were dissolving. As Liang Qichao said of his country and its disintegrating realm, "Here is a big mansion which has lasted a thousand years. . . . It is still a magnificently big thing, but when wind and rain suddenly come up, its fall is foredoomed. Yet people are happily playing or soundly sleeping . . . quite indifferent." This statement came just before century's end, suggesting that even premier Chinese intellectuals such as Liang had failed to fully measure the tremendous size and power of the storm, or indeed to recognize how long ago its arrival had begun.

Decades earlier, Burma, which was never a fully fledged vassal, and Siam (Thailand) had already grasped that the Qing empire was a declining force in Asia and consequently abandoned the pretense of ceremonial deference in their ties with the Central Kingdom. The Burmese had defeated the Qing in a major border war late in the late eighteenth century, after which the Qing, even in humiliation, somehow convinced themselves that Burma had agreed to conduct itself as a vassal. In fact, it had only agreed to exchange goodwill missions every decade, and not to the formal payment of tribute. Moreover, there was certainly plenty of historical precedent for its diffidence. During the Ming dynasty, a Chinese envoy named Yang Xuan traveled to the Burmese capital, Pegu, to demand submission, stating, "The son of heaven of the great Ming is sending envoys to notify all the barbarians, why do not you kowtow to the edict bearer?" To this, the Burmese king, Rayadazit, replied, "Ruling this country, I only understand that others kowtow to me, how do I kowtow to others?"

Siam sent the last of its tribute missions to China in 1851, on the accession of King Mongkut to the throne, under the ceremonial name Rama IV. In one of the last decrees before his death, however, Mongkut denounced tribute as a "shameful" practice, and said the Chinese had distorted the meaning of Siam's courteousness to preserve the illusion that a tributary relationship was still in force. The turnabout on the Siamese side could be partly explained by the experience of members of that ultimate mission to Beijing, where the Siamese felt slighted at every turn as its envoys were humiliatingly forced to wait for an audience while a French delegation was being received instead. On the return voyage home, the Siamese stopped in Hong Kong, where they received a briefing on Westphalian diplomacy and legal principles from the British governor, John Bowring, who emphasized above all the equality of states, urging that "you should not go to pay tribute to China any more."

The two most notable holdouts under *tian xia* were the two countries that had been closest to China and had been most profoundly influenced by it all along, Korea and Vietnam. But even for them, with the Qing position so weak, a relationship based upon ritual fealty could not hold. By the early 1870s, prominent figures in Meiji Japan had begun urging that their rapidly ascendant country should invade and occupy Korea. In 1875, after Koreans had shelled a Japanese warship that had sailed to the mouth of the Han River, which leads straight to Seoul, the Japanese avenged themselves with a show of force by their new imperial navy that obliged Korea to sign an unequal treaty with Japan much like those previously forced upon Japan and China by the Western powers. Under the 1876 Treaty of Ganghwa, Japan thrust Korea into the world of Westphalia, in which it was treated by outside powers as an independent state and not as a tributary of China, as it traditionally had regarded itself. Five years later, with their country under ever-growing pressure from Japan, Korean Confucianists petitioned the government to ignore demands that it deal with China and Japan on an equal basis. "We are a tributary state in our relations with China. For two hundred years we have sent tributes . . . and maintained our faith as a dependent state," one petition read. "If we are to accept official communications from Japan in which such honorifics as 'the emperor' or 'imperial' are used, suppose China questions our acquiescence. How are we to explain?" As Japan modernized and strengthened, its interests in Korea continued to expand rapidly, but it would take Tokyo another fifteen years to sever the traditional bonds between Korea and China, and only then by way of a major conflict, the Sino-Japanese War.

In 1862, the Vietnamese emperor, Tu Duc, was forced to cede three southern provinces of his country, subsequently known as Cochin China, to Paris. Twelve years later, in 1874, France proclaimed the opening of all of Vietnam to its trade, causing Vietnam to appeal to the Qing for help. At a time when reformist voices were already beginning to demand an end to the official use of Chinese writing and urging modernizations of all kinds, Tu Duc, known for his extremely conservative Confucian worldview, sought to draw even closer to China. This stands in stark contrast, of course, to the country's most recent defiance of the Qing a century earlier, when Vietnamese resistance leaders launched a surprise attack on Chinese invaders during the Tet New Year celebration, foreshadowing one of the most important events of their war with the United States in 1968, nearly two centuries later. Rising up against the Qing then, Vietnamese troops marched to a tune whose defiant, proto-nationalist lyrics proclaimed:

> FIGHT TO KEEP OUR HAIR LONG,
> FIGHT TO KEEP OUR TEETH BLACK,
> FIGHT TO DESTROY EVERY ENEMY VEHICLE,
> FIGHT TO LEAVE NO ENEMY ARMOR INTACT,
> FIGHT TO LET THEM KNOW THE HEROIC SOUTHERN
>   COUNTRY IS ITS OWN MASTER.

Now, though, rather than mobilizing the populace to resist the French, or moving the capital from seaside Hué to a more defensible location, the king, as described by one historian, was "tarry[ing] over all the geomantic problems and disruptions of ancestral ceremony" that any such efforts would require.

At first blush, Vietnam's pendulum swing toward China, including its pleas for intervention and hewing even more tightly to its culture, seems oddly out of phase with the age, and especially with events in the surrounding region, as others floated out of China's orbit. But the story of Tu Duc serves as a potent reminder of the fundamentally conflicted character of Vietnam's attitudes toward its patron and neighbor, which continue even today: ever balancing between resistance and dependence, subservience and noncompliance, almost irrespective of whatever might divide the two countries at any given moment. Striving to stay in tune with China is as deeply consonant with the country's culture as is its customary defiance, and historically Vietnam's leaders have paid a high price for leaning too far in either of these directions.

The Qing answered Tu Duc's request for assistance by putting the French on notice that he was their loyal and duly invested vassal—and then by sending in troops. After an initial victory in battle against the Chinese, setbacks to the French army caused consternation in Paris and brought down the government of Prime Minister Jules Ferry. This was followed by a series of clashes between China and France on land and at sea, including fighting in Taiwan and in China's southeastern coastal region, where French naval operations blockaded rice shipments from southern China, threatening famine and unrest in the north. This French tactic, which had already been employed by the British, ultimately brought the contest between the two countries to a conclusion, and Beijing was forced to concede Vietnam (Annam and Tonkin) to Paris as French protectorates, respecting the Tientsin Accord, which had been signed a year before, in May 1884. In another treaty that year, one less often noted by historians, the defeated Vietnamese, in the Treaty of Hué, had conceded the right of the French to station troops in their country. During the ceremony following the signing, the Vietnamese were obliged to publicly melt the seal provided to their king decades earlier as a patent of his authority, thus symbolically ending the country's tributary relationship with China.

For Paris the value of Indochina went beyond the question of territory or of the region's direct economic potential whether as a market for French goods or as a source of raw materials. All along, it saw this now conquered territory, centered around Vietnam, as a valuable gateway into China and its vast, from the perspective of the French, underexploited markets. Paris's designs on China were never fully realized, but France was able to consolidate its hold on Indochina without major difficulty until the 1930s, by which time the colony had become far more integrated into the global economy due to soaring demand for rubber, coal and other commodities than the region had been at any previous time in its history. In the meantime, Vietnam was buffeted by a number of international currents that steadily nudged it onto a path that would lead to war with France and ultimately to independence. First came the final demise of imperial rule in China in 1911–12 and the formation, however unsteady, of Republican government there. With that development, powerful waves of Chinese nationalism began flowing into Vietnam, especially from the adjacent provinces of that country's south. The rise of Japan was also influential, providing the unique and powerful example of an Asian culture that was able to modernize while retaining its sovereignty, a country able to defeat Western power, as it did Russia in 1905. Japan had thereby provided rare proof that Western colonization was by no means a prerequisite to development or modernization. Even here, China played its quasi-perpetual big brother role, with important Chinese reformers like Liang Qichao urging the Vietnamese to send students to Japan and learn from its example.

Eventually the most important influence on the direction of events in Vietnam by far was the Chinese Communist Party, from its foundation in Shanghai in 1921 to the Red Army's victory in civil war nearly three decades later under the leadership of Mao Zedong. North Vietnam's eventual liberator, Ho Chi Minh, met Mao's closest revolutionary comrade, Zhou Enlai, in Communist circles in France in the early 1920s, and although it is not widely known, Vietnamese fought in China in Mao's armies in the 1930s and 1940s, with one officer, Nguyen Son, participating in the 1934 Long March and rising to the rank of general. In fact, the Chinese Communists had been seriously influencing their revolutionary brethren in Vietnam well before. The Vietnamese Communist Party was itself established in Hong Kong in 1930. Even before then, from the mid-1920s onward, Ho had recruited Vietnamese nationalists who, like him, bridled at French repression and placed them in training at the Whampoa Politico-Military Academy in Canton, where Zhou Enlai was the director of the political department.

Mao's victory in 1949 spelled a clear death knell for French colonialism in the region and, seen in the light of broader currents of history, seemed to temporarily restore Vietnam, or at least North Vietnam, for the time being, under its Communist leader, Ho Chi Minh, to a kind of near-tributary relationship with its traditional patron to the north.*

In the face of strong initial Soviet skepticism about what was suspected to be his essentially nationalist character, Mao won Stalin's endorsement for Ho in 1950, a year after Stalin had deemed Vietnam to be within China's sphere of influence and anointed his Chinese counterpart as leader of Communist revolution in Asia. In order to conserve his newly won welcome into the Communist internationalist fold, Ho was obliged in exchange to demonstrate a strong degree of ideological conformity. This meant that both in party organization and in rhetoric, the Vietnamese Communists were called upon to toe an orthodox line.

Mao's first ambassador to Hanoi, Luo Guibo, not only closely oversaw the provision of military assistance and technical expertise desperately needed by the North Vietnamese in order to defeat the French, but also substantially drafted an ambitious land reform program in 1952 that was patterned closely on China's own recent, violent experience of land reform. It might be going too far to call Luo a proconsul, but Vietnam once again found itself in a historically familiar position: under China's unmistakable imprint. French rule came to an end in Indochina in 1954 following France's defeat

---

*In the 1960s, in a distinct echo of a venerable tribute system practice, Mao Zedong is said to have had the Chinese Communist Party offer a wife to Ho as a way of strengthening the patron/client relationship between Beijing and Hanoi. Vietnam declined the offer.

at Dien Bien Phu earlier that year. This then led before the end of the decade to an intensifying insurgency aimed at overthrowing the American-supported government of South Vietnam.

Widespread skepticism among American policymakers about the prospects of preventing the unification of Vietnam on the North's terms dated as far back as the early 1950s. "Indochina is devoid of decisive military objectives and the allocation of more than token U.S. armed forces in Indochina would be a serious diversion of limited U.S. capabilities," read a Joint Chiefs of Staff memorandum for the secretary of defense in May 1954. Despite such precautionary sentiments, of course, in the 1960s the United States became steadily more involved in the pursuit of that very cause. By the decade's end, support among Americans for the war had dramatically eroded and the position of the southern government in Saigon became increasingly imperiled. From a perspective that takes in the sweep of centuries, the decades of French colonialism, followed by the briefer Japanese and American periods in Vietnam, can be seen as imposing a mere pause in the longer-term currents of this region's history, brought about by varying degrees of Chinese incapacitation lasting from the Opium Wars until the end of the Cultural Revolution in 1976. The first inklings of the resumption of this history appeared just as American ardor for the war faded.

In the late 1950s and early 1960s, North Vietnam faced little pressure to choose between its two big Communist patrons, the People's Republic of China and the Soviet Union, leaning very strongly in the direction of Beijing, the familiar big brother next door. China continued to be the main supplier of both war materiel and economic assistance. Chinese engineering crews consisting of tens of thousands of men built and maintained highways, airfields and other defense installations, and in 1967, 170,000 Chinese troops were deployed in North Vietnam, more than at any other time, freeing up that country's own armed forces to press the war against the United States and its client government in Saigon. Hanoi ultimately made most of its own decisions on the battlefield as well as in policy matters, but such massive assistance, when considered along with the long and intimate ties with the Chinese Communist Party, strongly inclined the Vietnamese to draw lessons from China on everything from the Maoist strategy of "people's war" to matters of party organization and political line. During a banquet in Beijing in 1968, Mao went so far as to tell the Vietnamese ambassador, "Your struggle is our struggle. The Vietnamese people have the powerful backing of seven hundred thousand Chinese; the vast Chinese territory is Vietnam's dependable rear-area." Vietnam had begun to lean so much in China's favor, in fact, that it briefly adopted its neighbor's acrimonious language toward the Soviet Union under Khrushchev, labeling Moscow as "revisionist."

Despite appearances, though, by the time Mao Zedong had boasted at the Beijing banquet of his support for Vietnam, ties between the two countries were already under increasing strain. In 1966, Mao launched China's decade-long Cultural Revolution in a radical attempt to defeat perceived revisionist enemies within his party's leadership and in the bureaucracy and restore his personal authority, which had suffered badly following the debacle of the Great Leap Forward in the late 1950s. That effort had sought to drastically boost agricultural and industrial output, but led to a famine that killed at least thirty-four million people instead. Amid the suffocating cult of personality that was erected around him in the Cultural Revolution, Mao's zealous followers treated their leader as virtually infallible and insisted on absolute compliance with his wishes and policy pronouncements. The strident radicalism of this period began to close China off from much of the world, eventually leaving Egypt as the only country where it kept an ambassador. In early 1969, Mao himself grumbled that "now we are isolated and no one shows an interest in us." China's problems with North Vietnam, supposedly as close to it as lips are to teeth, as an expression of the era would have it, were unique. Toward this hitherto dutiful understudy, which had depended upon it for war support, Beijing adopted a hectoring tone that demanded servile fidelity to the patron's guidance. For North Vietnamese leaders, China's overbearing behavior dredged up memories of the two countries' unpleasant past. As the historian Odd Arne Westad wrote in his book *The Third Indochina War: Conflict Between China, Vietnam and Cambodia, 1972–79*:

The Chinese Maoist leadership began insisting on the universal applicability of their new model for transforming state and society. Mao Zedong and the Cultural Revolution Small Leading Group in Beijing, which in reality served as China's government during these turbulent years, saw the lesson of their new "revolution" as particularly relevant for Vietnam, because it was a neighboring state and because it shared many cultural traits with China. The Chinese leaders allowed their soldiers and aid workers who were stationed in Vietnam to propagate the Chinese road to Communism as an example to the Vietnamese. In other words, only through a complete acceptance of Mao's new revolution in their own work could the Vietnamese Workers Party become a truly revolutionary organization.

China's relations with the Soviet Union had become deeply acrimonious by this point over what Beijing denounced as the USSR's aforementioned "revisionism." This bill of accusation included Khrushchev's renunciation of the crimes of Stalinism in February 1956, Moscow's policy of seeking "peaceful coexistence" with the United States instead of risking nuclear war, and its corresponding refusal to support protracted warfare in pursuit of global revolution to China's satisfaction. The falling-out between the two countries would lead to a series of violent border clashes in 1969, in which Beijing ordered a general mobilization of its armed forces in provinces bordering the Soviet Union, and Moscow subsequently let it be known that it was contemplating a nuclear strike against China, most likely as a tactic to force the bellicose Chinese leadership to the negotiating table.

The spiking tensions heightened Chinese paranoia about Soviet influence over North Vietnam, which had been growing steadily for at least three years. In 1966, in one of a series of degrading conversations between senior officials in Beijing and Hanoi, Mao's lieutenant, Deng Xiaoping, berated the general secretary of the North Vietnamese Communist Party, Le Duan, ordering him to make a choice for "true" socialism by siding with China. "Why are you afraid of

Chinese cemetery from its war with Vietnam

displeasing the Soviets, and what about China? I want to tell you frankly what I now feel: Vietnamese comrades have some other thoughts about our methods of assistance, but you have not told us." But China's strident new tone produced the opposite effect than intended, pushing the North Vietnamese in the direction of Moscow in order to avoid complete dependence on a Chinese patron that had grown both increasingly imperious and erratic.

The ensuing China-Vietnam divorce resulted from a complex mix of factors. In addition to China's deepening rivalry with the Soviet Union, and often self-defeating chest thumping by Beijing, there was the direct entry of the United States into the Vietnam War in 1965 and the war's subsequent escalation, which scrambled everyone's prior calculations. Under heavy American pressure, North Vietnam now needed more military and economic assistance than China alone could provide. China, accustomed to the role of patron and sponsor of Asian revolution, became obsessed with the idea of losing its regional franchise to the Soviet Union, and went so far as to impede the supply of arms to Hanoi from Moscow. Amid their escalating tensions with Beijing, the Soviets, by contrast, deftly played their hand; instead of obliging North Vietnam to choose sides, as the

Chinese persistently tried to do, they sharply increased their assistance to Hanoi between 1965 and 1968, which further infuriated the Chinese, producing more rash behavior at each turn. This fed Chinese concerns about being encircled by Soviet allies, from Mongolia and North Korea to India, but its very behavior was pushing Vietnam in the direction it wished for it to avoid.

China's displeasure with Hanoi worsened rapidly in 1968, a year of major events both in the Vietnam War and in the broader Communist world that wrenched the two countries further apart. First came Tết, North Vietnam's surprise simultaneous offensive against sixty-four of the largest population centers in South Vietnam, which was launched on January 30, the start of the traditional Lunar New Year holidays. China had strongly counseled against an all-out attack like this and in private continued its sharp criticism after its launch. It opposed the actions ostensibly because they did not follow the Chinese example of "people's war," given the reliance on large-scale mobilization, intensive logistics and conventional battle tactics. The more genuine source of its reservations, however, was that Hanoi was relying ever more on Moscow's assistance and embracing its counsel. For Beijing, Tết stood out as a shift in the war that would ineluctably lead to far greater North Vietnamese dependence on advanced Soviet armaments and other forms of support. In the logic of *tian xia*, China feared that Vietnam was rapidly becoming a Soviet vassal.

The Chinese once again hectored their Vietnamese allies, with Zhou Enlai this time telling the Vietcong commissar, Pham Hung, that Hanoi should have stuck with Maoist doctrine, and calling the offensive a gigantic blunder. "The Soviet revisionists are claiming that attacks on Saigon are genuine offensives, that the tactics of using the countryside to encircle the urban areas [classic people's war strategy] are wrong and that to conduct a protracted struggle is a mistake. In their opinion, only lightning attacks on big cities are decisive. But if you do [that], the US will be happy as they can concentrate their forces for counter-attack thus causing greater destruction for you. The losses that you would suffer will lead to defeatism on your side."

This Chinese criticism had some merit. The tactical mobility of the Americans and other allied forces allowed them to quickly fall

back from areas under assault and regroup for counterattack. Vietcong and North Vietnamese regular army losses mounted quickly and
disastrously for Hanoi, eventually rising to nearly two hundred thousand troops. But Tết had another kind of impact, a political shock of
largely unforeseen depth that would shift the terms of the war dramatically yet again, leaving China feeling one step behind events and
ever more at odds with Hanoi. Although by most conventional military reckoning the Americans prevailed on the battlefield in 1968,
the scale and intensity of the northern offensive, including Saigon,
stunned political elites and public opinion in the United States. This
drove a series of deeply impactful subsequent events, beginning on
March 31, when in a speech outlining steps to "limit" the Vietnam
War, Lyndon B. Johnson declared that he would not seek reelection
as president. In both North Vietnam and the United States, Tết had
created a new momentum for diplomacy, and this led to the Paris
talks between Hanoi and Washington that opened on May 13, and
an accord between the two sides that eventually resulted in an end to
direct U.S. military involvement in the war.

When the North Vietnamese revealed to the Chinese the existence
of exploratory discussions with the United States aimed at bringing
the war to a negotiated end, Beijing once again forcefully expressed
its displeasure. The diplomacy was a ruse, the Chinese warned. The
Americans could only be defeated on the battlefield through continued application of Maoist doctrine, which meant protracted war.
Once again, Zhou Enlai leaned on a senior North Vietnamese official, this time Pham Van Dong, the prime minister, his threats barely
veiled as he told him that Hanoi must wait until it has fought its way
into a stronger position. "It is for the sake of our two parties' relations that we take every opportunity to remind you of this matter.
And when we tell you this, we tell you all what we think."

In a subsequent conversation, the Chinese foreign minister, Chen
Yi, spoke in even stronger terms to Le Duc Tho, the North Vietnamese
general and diplomat who would be awarded the Nobel Peace Prize
in 1973, together with Henry Kissinger, only to decline it. "In our
opinion, in a very short time, you have accepted the compromising
and capitulationist proposals put forward by the Soviet revisionists.

So between our two parties and the two governments of Vietnam and China, there is nothing more to talk about." Le counseled patience, telling his Chinese counterpart, "On this matter, we will wait and see. And the reality will give us the answer." By this point the level of suspicion was such between the two allies that Hanoi only gave Beijing one week's lead time in revealing plans for its coming peace talks with the Americans.

Afterward, China quickly made good on its threats, drawing down the number of engineering and antiaircraft units it maintained in North Vietnam later that year, and reducing its supply of guns, artillery and ammunition. Because China cherished its image as the leading patron of revolution worldwide, it struggled to impart a positive spin to these moves, explaining them as a bid to strengthen Vietnamese self-reliance, but the element of punishment for disregarding guidance proffered by the Central Kingdom was unmistakable.

In August 1968, when the USSR invaded Czechoslovakia, Vietnam applauded the action despite Beijing's claim that this proved Moscow's "hegemonic" intentions. Moscow justified the Czech invasion with what came to be known as the Brezhnev Doctrine, according to which the Soviets claimed the right to intervene in Communist states that deviated from Marxism-Leninism. Mao took this as an implicit threat to China, which had worked hard at establishing itself as a rival pole in the Communist movement. From this moment on, North Vietnam appeared in Chinese eyes to have irrevocably chosen sides. Scarcely a decade after Moscow had put forward the idea of a special sphere of influence in Southeast Asia for China, something that flattered China's own traditional sense of its place in the world, Beijing saw in these events the beginnings of a hostile revocation.

The next major crossroads in the Sino-Vietnam relationship came with word that China was conducting serious diplomacy of its own with the United States, a process that had begun with an exploratory message sent by the State Department to the Chinese embassy in Warsaw in September 1968, a month after the Soviet Union's takeover of Prague.

Following the outbreak of tense border clashes between their two countries in March 1969, Moscow and Beijing each began an ardent search for ways to make common cause with the United States in what was increasingly becoming a triangular global power contest. This lent strong impetus to the discreet and limited Chinese political contacts already under way with Washington, leading to a recommendation by four Chinese marshals that China must attempt to "play the card of the United States." After a second series of clashes with the Soviets that August, Chen Yi pressed the seniormost leadership to strive for a quick resolution of tensions with Washington, lest the United States be left "sitting on top of the mountain to watch a fight between two tigers," as Michael Pillsbury, a former Pentagon official, wrote. Amid the shifting complexities of this geopolitical situation, China had rapidly recalculated its own interests. This was the spark on the Chinese side that helped produce Henry Kissinger's famous secret diplomacy with China, and not long afterward, of course, Richard Nixon's historic visit to the country.

Hitherto, Beijing had been focused on draining the United States by keeping it bogged down in Southeast Asia. Now its priority switched to helping husband American strength as a counterweight to the Soviets. Where Vietnam was concerned, this meant trying to tamp down the conflict with the United States and help bring about a successful conclusion to the Paris peace talks that Beijing had only recently fiercely opposed. The North Vietnamese complained bitterly and persistently about being sold out, creating a complicated diplomatic challenge for the Chinese, who by no means desired to see an outright public rupture in relations between the two countries. This comes across powerfully in the emotional and defensive case that Zhou Enlai made to Vietnamese leaders in explaining China's search for common ground with the Americans:

> Recently Kissinger visited China and it was he who took the initiative, and why can't we have some discussion with him? [Nikita] Khrushchev traveled to Camp David in the United States to have talks, [Alexis] Kosygin went to Glassboro to hold negotiations, and you go to Paris to negotiate with the Americans. I, Zhou Enlai, did not travel to Washington. It is they [the Americans] who came to China. Why can't we have

talks with the Americans in Beijing? We will not make deals by trading our principles, and we will never sell out our friends.

If only to maintain its own prestige in the mounting competition for global and regional influence with the Soviets, China could not afford to simply drop its ally, nor did it want it to prevail outright. The ideal interim situation in Vietnam for Chinese strategists was a stalemate, in which South Vietnam continued to exist and the Americans exited the country with all deliberate speed. In February 1973, Australia's prime minister, Gough Whitlam, said that Zhou Enlai told him that a withdrawal of American forces from the region would create local instability that would benefit the Soviets. Remarkably, China had already discreetly given vent to such views as far back as the Geneva talks that ended the First Indochina War, and French colonialism there, in 1954. During that diplomacy, Zhou Enlai told French prime minister Pierre Mendès-France:

> Ho is getting too big for his britches. He does not listen to us ... even after all that we have done for him. He listens too much, we think, to the Russians. So this is what we propose. Indochina should be cut into four zones. Ho will be allowed to keep North Vietnam, of course. But Laos and Cambodia should stay independent ... and continue as members of your French Overseas Union. The South of Vietnam should be partitioned off. A separate government could be formed there. We could talk of eventual unification by elections ... but China would not mind if this unification did not actually occur.

China managed to preserve appearances with North Vietnam from late 1971 through early 1973, while both Beijing and Hanoi pursued their separate diplomacy with the United States. Once the Paris Peace Accords were concluded in January 1973, though, relations promptly entered into a sharp downward spiral. By the end of 1973, or early 1974 at the latest, China initiated low-level clashes along their border, prefiguring the brief but intense war they would fight in 1979. By early 1975, Hanoi had become eager to take advantage of the American withdrawal from Vietnam and bring the division of the country to an end, but once again Beijing proffered strongly contrary advice, and was urging it not to launch an offensive as late as early April, just three weeks before Hanoi's final victory and the capture of Saigon.

From that point on, there was no concealing the sharp divide that separated North Vietnam—and eventually the reunited Vietnam—from its big northern neighbor. Indeed, some of these differences even shone through in Beijing's congratulatory telegram upon Hanoi's final triumph in the war. "We sincerely wish that the South Vietnamese people will ceaselessly win new and greater victories in their continued struggle to carry through their national and democratic revolution," it read, addressing the transitional authorities in Saigon more than North Vietnam and saying nothing about quick reunification, which of course had been Hanoi's firm objective from the outset. Here were ominous echoes of China's support for Champa as a counterweight to Đại Việt centuries earlier.

"One of the great ironies of history was that more than the United States it was China who lost the Vietnam War," wrote Nayan Chanda. "The American pullout in 1975 seemed to bring about all the Chinese policymakers' nightmares about Vietnam—a strong, reunified Vietnam challenging China from the south in cahoots with China's bitter enemy in the north [the Soviet Union]." Beijing stressed and fretted over Southeast Asia throughout the 1970s, revealing its insecurities about maintaining its habitual, one might say civilizational, sway over the region, and laying the foundation for future conflict with Vietnam, much of which was arguably unnecessary.

China began moving to preempt Vietnam even while it was still formally North Vietnam's cosponsor in the late stages of the war against the United States. When Cambodia's government fell to the Khmer Rouge, also in April 1975, Beijing hustled to draw the radical Khmer leadership under Pol Pot into its embrace as a counter to Vietnam and as a platform for sustained Chinese influence in the region. In August of that year, even as it pleaded austerity in explaining to Vietnam's new leaders why its postwar aid had to be so modest, China pledged $1 billion to assist the new Khmer Rouge government, including a number of generous outright grants—the largest foreign aid commitment in the history of the People's Republic up until that point. When Mao received a visit from Pol Pot, the praise he lavished on his murderous guest for his "communist" policies contrasted sharply with the tightlipped congratulations offered to Vietnam upon its winning its war. "You have achieved with one stroke what we failed with all our masses," Mao told the man who would become known as Cambodia's butcher. Then, insultingly, given the sense of hierarchy that pervaded relationships in the region, Mao even urged Vietnam's leaders to "learn from the Khmer Rouge how to carry out a revolution."

North Vietnam's defeat of South Vietnam came nearly three weeks after the Khmer Rouge's seizure of power in Cambodia, and that only exacerbated the mounting tensions between the two countries. Hanoi had sought to achieve its triumph first, urging the Maoist revolutionaries who would become known as the Khmer Rouge to defer to their big brothers and patrons next door. But with Beijing's encouragement, Pol Pot's fighters deliberately raced ahead as fast as they could so as to consolidate control of the country while upstaging their larger neighbor.

North Vietnam had long played patron to Cambodia's revolutionaries, often under difficult circumstances. In the early 1950s, in conformity with the strong spirit of the Marxist internationalism that still existed then, Mao encouraged Ho Chi Minh and his cohorts to oversee the creation of Communist parties in Southeast Asia, a task that the North Vietnamese undertook with enthusiasm. The North Vietnamese cadres sent to Cambodia in the 1950s were virtually obliged to start from scratch. As late as 1944, only five hundred Khmer students completed primary school each year, and nationwide there were not more than a thousand secondary school students. Marxism had few roots in the country, and for the Vietnamese, Cambodia's strong overlay of Indian-derived culture was alien and, from the chauvinist perspective of heavily Sinicized Vietnam, implicitly inferior.

Already, during French rule over the region in the 1930s, Vietnam had created the Indochina Communist Party, which incorporated

Cambodia and Laos (much like France's colonial Indochina Federation), but it consisted almost entirely of Vietnamese leaders and members of the Chinese diaspora. In 1951, the Vietnamese founded the Khmer People's Revolutionary Party. By being patron and sponsor, Vietnam stood a good chance of protecting its own interests, and not just narrow, immediate ones. Just as China had come to see the situation of being surrounded by smaller, deeply deferential states as ideal, Vietnam too had acquired its own *tian xia*–style vision for relations with its western neighbors in Indochina. These attitudes evolved over the course of centuries, and were robust enough to coexist alongside Vietnam's traditional acceptance of one degree or another of Chinese suzerainty. "The rulers would call themselves *vuong* (king) when communicating with the Chinese but *hoang de* (emperor) when addressing their own subjects or other rulers in Southeast Asia," wrote Nayan Chanda. "The Vietnamese court's cultural pretensions were as great as China's."

In the Vietnamese Workers' Party, though, there appeared from the start to be a clear element of internationalist true belief; one did one's duty to support world revolution, and that began, naturally enough, next door.

By the time its efforts to sponsor Communist movements among its smaller neighbors resumed in the early 1950s, however, North Vietnam had come to understand that its formal tutelage in Indochina would be unacceptable to its Southeast Asian neighbors, and it began recruiting and training numerous Cambodian cadres both locally and in Vietnam, where they were brought for ideological indoctrination and schooling in military and technical matters. Many of these cadres stayed on in Hanoi, serving theoretically as the core of a regime-in-waiting, ostensibly to be delivered into power at the right moment by a unified Vietnam. The politics of revolutionary internationalism would grow extraordinarily complicated, though, as time went by and as Cambodia was sucked into the vortex of the Vietnam War. Cambodia steered an increasingly precarious course of neutrality under Prince Norodom Sihanouk into the late 1960s under an arrangement that allowed North Vietnam to use his country as the route for funneling weapons into South Vietnam via

Laos, along what became known as the Ho Chi Minh Trail. The price Sihanouk exacted from Hanoi for having him turn a blind eye to this activity was putting its support for armed insurgency in Cambodia in abeyance. This eventually created an opening for Saloth Sar, the man who would later become known as Pol Pot, to promote a hitherto nearly marginal organization that was still secretly known as the Workers Party of Kampuchea (later renamed the Communist Party of Kampuchea) on the basis of fierce independence from Vietnam and an uncompromising will to power.

Pol Pot, who had been schooled and worked in France for a stint beginning in 1949, returned to his country in the mid-1950s, where he engaged in Phnom Penh's volatile leftist politics until heading underground in 1963 following a government crackdown. Operating from a "liberated" area across the border in South Vietnam that was under the protection of Vietnamese Communists, which his partisans called "Office 900," he began to plot his conquest of power. The following year, Pol Pot began a long pilgrimage through Communist East Asia, spending months in Hanoi before traveling to China, where he appears to have been personally handled by the president, Liu Shaoqi, and his close deputy, Deng Xiaoping. Pol Pot remained in China for much of 1965, before secretly visiting North Korea. During a stop in Beijing before returning home, Pol Pot was the featured guest at a banquet to which Vietnamese delegates were also invited. "On this occasion . . . Mao was particularly effusive about the merits of the Kampuchean Party, causing the Vietnamese guests to believe that he had held important discussions with Pol Pot and had for some reason been rather impressed. The Chinese message was clear: the new leadership of the Kampuchean Party enjoyed their protection." Later, speaking to a member of the Communist Party of Thailand, Pol Pot said of his first Beijing sojourn that "we were reassured to have made friends in the world and on the inside we were reassured to have Chinese friends who would bring us strategic, political and spiritual aid."

Clearly, as far back as 1965 there was a lively, if still mostly sub rosa, rivalry playing out between China and North Vietnam involving control over the destiny of the former French Indochina. Pol Pot returned to China the following year, just as the Cultural Revolution was getting under way, and the violent vigilantism in the name of radical egalitarianism that had gripped China had a strong effect on his still-evolving ideology. From this point onward, he cast his lot with China, whose politics he called "authentic Marxist-Leninism," by way of bluntly differentiating China from the Soviet Union. Just as Prince Sihanouk, the man he hoped to eventually unseat, had understood before him, Pol Pot had become convinced that only by bandwagoning with China could Cambodia preserve itself from the kind of domination by Vietnam for which Laos already served as a strongly cautionary example. China, with its centuries of experience in balancing against Vietnam in the region whenever Vietnam became uppity or recalcitrant, was eagerly obliging.

In March 1970, Prince Sihanouk was overthrown while on a visit to Moscow, and this thrust his country into play, with the Americans and South Vietnamese invading Cambodia the following month to try to eliminate North Vietnamese sanctuaries there and destroy the Ho Chi Minh Trail. Hanoi and Beijing both threw their weight behind insurgents in Cambodia, but, caught off guard and with few other options on the ground, for North Vietnam this meant backing Pol Pot's still small and fragmented Communist Party of Kampuchea, and not the Marxist cadres that Hanoi had been patiently training for so long in exile. Around the time of the anti-Sihanouk coup, which placed the general Lon Nol in power, the opposing Khmer Rouge had only between 2,500 and 4,000 troops, and they were dispersed in various parts of the country.

The North Vietnamese, who were desperate not to lose their sanctuaries in the country, intervened in Cambodia with an intensity to match that of the Americans and their South Vietnamese allies. One of the first signs of contretemps with the Khmer Rouge came when Hanoi offered to occupy the northeast to create a liberated zone there on behalf of the Cambodian Communists. The Khmer Rouge may have possessed feeble means, but they insisted nonetheless that they would only accept weapons. The Vietnamese took no heed of this, though, and sent thousands of soldiers to seize control of Cambodian borderland territory.

Despite their fierce opposition to it, the Khmer Rouge benefited greatly from the North Vietnamese intervention, and with China's support they quickly won standing for themselves as members of a coalition government in exile under Sihanouk's leadership, the Front Uni National de Kampuchea (FUNK), which he mostly led from the comfort of exile in Beijing. What the Khmer Rouge now feared most was that Hanoi flood the country with people it had trained in exile, resulting in a co-optation.

Pol Pot had deliberately remained in the shadows and was still largely unknown to the outside world. Still, the intensely secretive group centered around him in the Khmer Rouge began to signal its determination to remain free of Vietnamese influence. The first of what would become scores of clashes between the two parties broke out in September 1970, with Khmer Rouge units attacking North Vietnamese patrols from the rear. Around the same time, the Khmer Rouge had begun developing what would become its murderously xenophobic political line. Much of its venom stemmed from a well-spring of historical romanticism about the great Khmer empire, which had once controlled much of Laos, bits of Thailand and a large chunk of South Vietnam encompassing the agriculturally rich Mekong Delta and even Saigon itself. Other elements, though, were founded on a uniquely Cambodian realpolitik that was the product of being stuck between two powerful and jealous neighbors, Vietnam and China, each with its own Middle Kingdom complex. In addition, there was no small amount of simple opportunism on the part of Pol Pot himself. The Khmer Rouge would gradually refine and amplify its xenophobia, and soon raise it to a fever pitch. At first, though, it served the party's purposes better to mute its anti-Vietnamese rhetoric in meetings with its neighbor in order to continue profiting from having Hanoi shoulder the brunt of the war against America's "strongman" ally in Cambodia, Lon Nol.

By the late 1950s, Beijing was already alive to Cambodia's potential as a future counterweight to Vietnam and occasionally worked at sowing rivalry and distrust between the two countries, encouraging Prince Sihanouk, for example, to make irredentist claims on what had hitherto been undisputed Vietnamese territory, and duplicitously engineering misunderstandings between communist parties in Vietnam and Cambodia. But as the Cambodia–North Vietnamese clashes began, China was not yet giving explicit encouragement to Pol Pot for aggressive anti-Vietnamese behavior; indeed, the opposite may have been true.

By the early 1970s, duplicity had become the name of the game in the region, and Pol Pot had become its keenest practitioner. He managed to maintain a façade of loyalty within the coalition led by Sihanouk, display fealty to Beijing in both ideological and geopolitical matters and do just enough to assuage the North Vietnamese, even as his fighters harassed their troops, liquidated the cadres who returned from exile there and generally laid the groundwork for a style of rule based more than anything else on blood enmity toward his eastern neighbor. Against all evidence, Hanoi persuaded itself that things would work out with time.

In 1973, during the height of the devastating American aerial bombing campaign of Cambodia, Pol Pot would change his strategy. North Vietnam's fight against the increasingly besieged Lon Nol government had opened up space for the Khmer Rouge to recruit members and build up its army. From its tiny and relatively recent beginnings, it had already managed to amass a force of more than 200,000 regular troops and guerrilla fighters, and it was still growing. After Hanoi's conclusion of a peace agreement with the United States in January 1973, Pol Pot set out on an explicitly independent course and urged the North Vietnamese to leave his country immediately, while turning on his nominal coalition ally, Prince Sihanouk, whom he now labeled an enemy of the people. By the middle of the year, Hanoi, although still maintaining its policy of placating the Cambodian rebels, had drawn down its troops in the country to 3,000 or so, from a high of about 150,000.

According to the terms of the Paris Peace Accords, North Vietnam was charged with obtaining the signatures on it of its Communist allies in Laos and Cambodia, but the Khmer Rouge made plain that they had no intention of supporting a negotiated peace. Pol Pot's goal all along had been to seize power by force, and having hollowed out the coalition with Sihanouk from the inside and made maximal—if utterly cynical—use of Hanoi's determined war effort in his country, he was now in an almost undreamed-of position to do so. The United States had dropped 257,500 tons of bombs on Cambodia in 1973, but having just withdrawn from Vietnam amid deep national opposition to the American war, it was in no position to fight against communism in another Southeast Asian nation. North Vietnam itself was focused on bringing about the demise of the Thieu government in Saigon. And China up until this point was not too particular about who would rule Cambodia. In the words of the historian Ben Kiernan, it merely wanted to make sure that its influence in Indochina was intact.

Five days after the United States closed its embassy in Phnom Penh, on April 12, 1975, Cambodia fell to the Khmer Rouge, which announced itself to the world by evacuating the capital of all of its inhabitants. The country's new leadership still clung to the shadowy name Angkar, meaning simply "the Organization," and its head and founder, Pol Pot, had as yet still not gone public or proclaimed his central role in any way. The outside world interpreted many of Angkar's early moves—such as the abolition of money and the violent purge of educated people—as expressions of an ultraradical variant of Maoism, which they were, in part. But there were more directly pertinent factors for the emptying of Phnom Penh than the Khmer Rouge's Maoist ideology, most notably the fact that the evacuation had coincided with a series of Cambodian attacks against Vietnam, whose final victory in its war still lay several days ahead.

Khmer Rouge records show that the party had long hoped to win its civil war before Hanoi could conclude its own war. Khmer Rouge radio justified the hostility toward its neighbor, saying that North Vietnam planned to capture Saigon and then sweep into Cambodia, grabbing control of more of the rich Mekong Delta and even seizing Phnom Penh. In fact, it had been Pol Pot's aim to seize power in Cambodia and then quickly sweep into adjacent areas of South Vietnam, lands known to irredentist Cambodians as Kampuchea Krom, and reclaim them for the motherland well before the North Vietnamese could seize Saigon. Evacuating Phnom Penh of its two million residents can perhaps be best understood as a ploy to deprive

Vietnam of a huge and vulnerable strategic target in the inevitable counterattack on Cambodia foreseen by Pol Pot in what he imagined would become a protracted struggle between the two Southeast Asian neighbors.

The opportunism evident in China's quick pivot from being a major backer of Vietnam to being, in rapid succession, a source of encouragement for the Khmer Rouge, then its leading supporter in its struggle against Hanoi, and finally, as we will see shortly, guarantor of the Khmer Rouge's survival, laid bare a truth that remains with us today: Ideology explains little about Beijing's strategic choices in the region. China's real motives stemmed from a calculus that was far older and ran much deeper. Its basic instinct, which is still operative today, was to cling to and shelter states that behaved like tributaries and to oppose, cajole, subvert or subdue those that stood in the way of its project to hold on to an old-fashioned realm.* By invading Cambodia, Vietnam's "crime" in China's eyes was effrontery; usurping China's self-appointed role as leader of Vietnam's own subregion; pretending there could be two emperors simultaneously.

The Khmer Rouge's first outright military assault against Vietnam took place on April 19, just two days after the surrender of the last remnants of the former Khmer Republic to Pol Pot's forces. The first of these took the form of an artillery attack on Phu Quoc, a large, previously undisputed island near the mouth of the Mekong Delta. Other attacks took place widely across the land border divid-

---

*This pattern is as evident on the Korean Peninsula as it is in Southeast Asia. China would prefer even an extremely nettlesome client in North Korea to any plausible alternative, and hence goes to great lengths to shield it from international pressure over its nuclear weapons program. A testy Pyongyang not heeding advice is better, in China's eyes, than a united Korea linked with the United States. Beijing simultaneously pressures South Korea, whose economy has become increasingly dependent on trade with China, against reinforcing its alliance with the United States, warning in 2016, for example, that if Seoul accepts the installation of sophisticated anti–ballistic missile systems to protect itself from North Korean attack, this could "destroy bilateral relations" with China. In July 2016, the United States and South Korea announced their decision to deploy the missile defense system over China's strong objections, saying it was meant to "protect alliance military forces from North Korea's weapons of mass destruction," and was not "directed toward any third party nations."

ing the two countries, but Pol Pot's bigger ambitions were thwarted by Hanoi's rush southward into the vacuum created by the rapid crumbling of South Vietnamese defenses, resulting in the capture of Saigon on April 30. North Vietnam's final victory over the South made large-scale revanchism by the Cambodians impractical, but the Khmer Rouge continued to mount a string of provocations, mostly offshore, involving other islands in the mouth of the delta.

Meeting with Vietnamese officials shortly after Hanoi's victory, Khmer Rouge leaders blamed these incidents on local commanders and their faulty knowledge of geography. Meanwhile, Vietnamese were being expelled from Cambodia, as rhetoric against the ancient enemy was ratcheted up to a fever pitch.

Cambodia's attack on Vietnamese islands signaled a seaward shift in the competition between states of the region, several of which, nominally at least, had formerly been close allies, and surely few at the time could have fully anticipated the importance of this for the future. While Beijing lent crucial backing to the new Cambodian regime, helping embolden it in taking a fiercely hostile stance toward Vietnam, China was making its own critical moves against Vietnamese-controlled territory.

In January 1974, two weeks after Hanoi notified Beijing that it had entered into discussions with an Italian oil company over exploration possibilities in the Gulf of Tonkin, Beijing issued a statement claiming all of the islands of the South China Sea as its own, and dispatched troops to seize control of positions in the tiny Crescent Group of features, which are part of the Paracel Islands. This immediately drew a bid by the navy of South Vietnam, which also claimed the islands in this area, to expel the Chinese. As Bill Hayton wrote in his book *The South China Sea: The Struggle for Power in Asia,* a richly detailed account of the ongoing contest between China and several of its neighbors over this body of water, "Beijing's relations with North Vietnam were deteriorating fast and South Vietnam had lost American military support. January 1974 was a moment when the Beijing leadership could act without fearing the consequences."

South Vietnam officially requested the assistance of the U.S. Seventh Fleet, pleading for Washington to use it to form a picket line to prevent the Chinese from reaching the disputed islands, but this came late in what the United States had already long recognized was a losing war, and no aid was forthcoming. Hayton's story continues with the showdown at sea that ensued between China and South Vietnam, with Chinese ships interdicting Vietnamese vessels that were attempting to land members of that country's SEALs unit on one of the islands: "Using signal lamps, they started a historical argument in English. 'These islands have belonged to China since the Ming Dynasty. Nobody can deny' they flashed. The Vietnamese replied with the blunt and decidedly less erudite 'please leave our territorial waters immediately.'" The South Vietnamese were forced to back down. This conflict turned violent as it played out over the next several days, and concluded in China's favor.

Beijing's victory over Saigon produced a highly awkward moment for Hanoi, which had no choice but to remain mute for the time being in the matter. The government in Saigon was its sworn enemy, and Beijing had long been Hanoi's overbearing but generous longtime ally. Still, Beijing's move was seen in Hanoi as an unmistakably hostile act. An expansionist China was now showing its true face, moving opportunistically to take over Vietnamese territory at a moment of acute national vulnerability. At a military gathering that July, the North Vietnamese leader, Le Duan, spoke of "other countries which are trying to gain influence in this area," and said that "even though they did not speak about their strategy, [they] all have secret strategies regarding the Southeast Asian region." After this unmistakable reference to China, he urged the quick defeat of Saigon, and then invoked an ancient Vietnamese argument for southward consolidation. A unified Vietnam with a population of fifty million, Le Duan said, "would not be an easy target for any prospective invader." Here was an echo of the original rationale behind Vietnam's southward expansion, or *nam tien,* under the Lê dynasty.

In June 1974, leaving little room for ambiguity, a North Vietnamese official declared, "Southeast Asia belongs to the Southeast Asian people. . . . China is not a Southeast Asian country, so China should not have such big territorial waters as it claims." This was a self-serving statement, to be sure, but as such it eerily reverse-mirrors traditional Chinese rhetoric, rhetoric that has recently been updated for this very same dispute by the current Chinese leader, Xi Jinping, who declared in 2014 that "it is for the people of Asia to run the affairs of Asia, solve the problems of Asia, and uphold the security of Asia."

Each of these two old rivals was positioning itself to push for historical geostrategic priorities, securing preeminence in their home regions. The trouble was that they had conflicting definitions of home. For Vietnam, notions of home are bound up with the idea of holding sway in Southeast Asia. This only begins with the promise of rich deposits of oil and gas presumed to lie beneath the disputed seabed off its coast. Vietnam's extensive ocean frontier serves, more fundamentally, as the basis for the country's deep-seated identity as a seafaring nation. Most important, from the Vietnamese perspective, Southeast Asia, with Vietnam at its helm, offered it the strategic depth it had always sought to hold its own against China.

For China, the language used by President Xi also fit within a long tradition. "Everything under the heavens" meant first and foremost sitting atop an East Asian hierarchy, and having others, including Vietnam and the rest of Southeast Asia, defer to it. Xi's statement equally embodied a thoroughly modern Chinese priority, though, and that is keeping the United States—the overwhelmingly dominant power in the region—at a figurative arm's length. In fact, the one idea nowadays utterly depends on the other. There are technical and strategic reasons why China feels it necessary to achieve a mastery of the maritime approaches to the Asian mainland that involve guaranteeing the security of Chinese trade as well as the sanctity of its homeland. And then there is that far older notion, expressed in a lecture by a Chinese sovereign to a peripheral southern upstart more than two thousand years ago: There can only be one emperor at any given time. In East Asia, if not quite yet in the broader world, China is bent on playing the role of the emperor, and Vietnam, the United States or anyone else who would stand in its way would do well to be forewarned that the Central Kingdom cannot accept this.

The end of the Vietnam War, it seems clear, marked the revenge of this history in the region, and by the end of the 1970s the slide toward yet another Indochina war was consummated. In this conflict, unlike in previous modern wars in Southeast Asia, all of the frontline players were local. Vietnam, driven to exasperation by uninterrupted Khmer Rouge provocations, mounted a full-blown invasion of its neighbor, sending a 150,000-man army into the country on Christmas Day 1978. This action was taken despite a blunt warning from China two weeks earlier against behaving in an "unbridled" fashion.

The Vietnamese, who had prepared their action well in advance, though, would not be deterred. Among other measures, they had assembled a Cambodian government in exile ready to be installed in power the moment victory came, and benefited from stepped-up aid from the Soviet Union, with which Hanoi had just signed a comprehensive mutual defense pact. This explicit challenge to China's hegemony in the region predictably enraged Beijing, but despite a huge infusion of Chinese materiel and advisers in support of the Cambodians, that country's capital, Phnom Penh, fell swiftly. What followed was a virtual reenactment of the region's nineteenth-century history. The Khmer Rouge leadership fled to Thailand, where it was instantly embraced, and for the next ten years Cambodia was run for all intents and purposes as a protectorate of Vietnam, much as it once had been. Both China and Thailand, which were lined up on opposing sides during America's Vietnam War, quickly put that history behind them in the interest of a higher priority: blunting Vietnamese influence in Southeast Asia. This was because Thailand was Vietnam's nearest peer rival in the region, and because China wanted hegemony for itself, of the old tribute era kind. Beijing quickly found ways to funnel arms and money to the Khmer Rouge via underworld elements in the Chinese diaspora in Thailand.

After three million casualties in two long wars against major Western powers, Vietnam felt that it had earned its independence the hard way, and this included the right to carve out its own distinct sphere of influence. Independence, to the Vietnamese leadership of the late 1970s, meant a measure of equality with the Central Kingdom, just as it had during previous periods of self-confidence and assertiveness in the country's long history.

What China desired at the end of the Vietnam War, by contrast, was a return of the region to what it imagined as its own natural realm, and from the perspective of Beijing, the generous benefactor, Vietnam had shown no deference or even enough ordinary gratitude for its assistance. China had long bristled at Vietnam's closeness with the Soviets, and took Hanoi's defense pact as the final straw. For Beijing, this was the place to draw the line, and it began doing so with more open and robust encouragement to the Khmer Rouge, a useful thorn in the side of an impudent, upstart Vietnam. For the leaders of Vietnam, with Ho Chi Minh, the Communist founder who had always maintained serviceable ties to Mao, now dead, this was enough to bring out strong latent feelings of hostility toward what it now called "the Great Han expansionists." In its propaganda, Hanoi began to speak of China as a "chauvinist and hegemonistic" power, and explained its own role in Cambodia strictly in terms of socialist international solidarity, eschewing any mention of spheres of interest or legitimate historical rights.

In February 1979, less than two months after Vietnam's invasion of Cambodia, Beijing tried to make good on its threat to punish its southern neighbor for not recognizing its subordinate place. Militarily, China's punitive invasion of northern Vietnam quickly turned disastrous, but such was Beijing's determination to restore its hierarchical vision of proper order in the region that it took little heed of what might be considered conventional cost calculations. Chinese troops advanced rapidly in the initial phases of their operation, appearing as if they might even reach Hanoi, but they did so with insufficient mechanized support and little backup from the air. As a result, they soon found themselves at the end of overextended supply lines, harried from every direction by an adversary that had been hardened by long years of war against France, the United States, the South Vietnamese and the Khmer Rouge. The Vietnamese army was steeled even further by its own civilizational story, an existential narrative as old as Vietnam itself that centered on standing up to the eternal, overbearing empire next door.

The main thrust of the Chinese campaign concluded in a mere three weeks, and as Beijing withdrew its forces from Vietnam they did so licking their wounds, just as they had so many times during the previous shared history between the two countries. In the brief but intense fighting, approximately seventy-five thousand Chinese were wounded or killed, the bodies of the deceased buried in terraced hillside graves in the immediate border region rather than transported to their home provinces, where the full dimension of the losses might have risked generating a backlash. During the fighting itself, China's propaganda machine put the best possible face on the offensive, declaring victory, in effect, even amid the considerable losses, and proclaiming that Hanoi had been taught its much-needed lesson. This was a war that many a rational calculus might have suggested China could ill afford to fight at the time. The country was just emerging from the chaos of the Cultural Revolution. Its economy was so weak that in 1975 Mao had told the Vietnamese Communist Party chief, Le Duan, that "the poorest nation in the world is not you, but us." And its military was ill-equipped and seriously dispirited. But struggling to maintain China's position at the top of the pile in its old realm was an impulse that could simply not (and still cannot) be resisted.

Although the intense phase of direct, armed confrontation was brief, the struggle between the two countries had scarcely commenced. Once the guns fell silent, China, making common cause with the United States, set about punishing Vietnam in every way it could. As these two big powers pursued rapprochement, in the interest of weakening the other major global power, the Soviet Union, they each provided strong political backing to the Khmer Rouge (and to Thailand, which hosted its leadership and served as a vital conduit for weaponry), in spite of what was already by then irrefutable knowledge of the scope of the genocide perpetrated by the Khmer Rouge. Vietnam made entreaties to the World Bank for loans in order to jump-start its national reconstruction, but financial help was denied at Washington's quiet insistence. For the better part of a decade, meanwhile, with China's backing, Pol Pot's fighters harassed Hanoi's occupation army in Cambodia, even though everyone involved knew that it had no prospect of victory. This was how China realized its punishment aims: a long and devastating campaign of bleeding—physically, in the form of fallen soldiers—as well as economic loss and destruction. Beijing exulted that Moscow supplied arms to Vietnam, but Beijing knew that this exacerbated the Soviet Union's overextended imperial missions in Afghanistan, Cuba, Ethiopia and elsewhere; it simply did not possess the sufficient wherewithal to rebuild its Southeast Asian client. So while much of the rest of the region was creating wealth, and China's own openings to the world market were gathering pace, Vietnam, isolated and forced to carry Cambodia on its back, remained stuck in the mud. In time, it became clear to Hanoi that the price for pursuing its interests in defiance of China's position in Asia was not worth the trouble.

For Hanoi, the next big blow was the withdrawal of the Soviet Union from Southeast Asia. With its economy sputtering, Moscow was desperate to reconcile with China and begin to do profitable business with it. In the interval between these sharp swings in their relationship, China had gone from being the far poorer and weaker junior partner in an alliance of Communist powers, a supplicant almost, during the 1950s, to becoming an increasingly rich East Asian-style developmental state run by a Leninist party in the freewheeling late 1980s. Now it was impecunious Moscow's turn as the hobbled party. At its peak, the Soviet Union had supplied as much as one-quarter of Vietnam's gross domestic product in the form of aid. But as early as 1985, Moscow informed Hanoi that it would have to begin fending for itself. Initially this message was understood to refer only to the country's economy, but in 1988, when China sank two Vietnamese vessels in an armed takeover of Vietnamese-controlled features in the Spratlys, the Soviet Union made no moves to fulfill its mutual defense obligations and counseled moderation to Hanoi. The next year, Moscow gave up its longtime dream of having a warmwater fleet in the Pacific, surrendering basing rights in Cam Ranh Bay as a major concession aimed at finally getting into Beijing's good graces. The Soviet Union imploded two years later.

That event, simply unimaginable during the long years of turbulent rivalry between Beijing and Moscow, meant that within little more than a decade, China had successfully dealt with the threat to its southern flanks from its two imperial rivals. A chastened United States had withdrawn from Indochina, and done so on surprisingly friendly terms with China. Under Presidents Richard Nixon, Jimmy Carter and Ronald Reagan, and even part of the presidency of George H. W. Bush, the prevailing sentiment in American foreign policy was in support of ways to help strengthen China. Meanwhile, the Soviet Union, China's most immediate and dangerous threat in the 1960s and 1970s, disappeared. In the 1960s, the United States had fought in Vietnam in order to prevent China from dominating Southeast Asia. In the 1980s, spurred by its competition with Moscow, Washington made common cause with China. For Beijing, this all amounted to a geopolitical boon that brought China to the threshold of realizing its century-old dream of cobbling back together its old tributary realm and restoring its rights of paramountcy in East Asia. With the Soviet Union now absent, Vietnam was brought to heel with relative ease. Secretly and tentatively at first, Beijing and Hanoi began to explore normalization of their relations in 1988, and in 1991, largely on China's terms, they finally reestablished diplomatic ties.

By 1986, Vietnam had begun to emulate certain aspects of Chinese political and economic reforms, adopting a policy called *doi moi*, or renovation. By the middle of the 1990s, Vietnam's Communist Party–led government had adopted an approach toward China that was beginning to edge back toward old-fashioned fealty. A Vietnamese diplomat even used historical analogy as a rationale, saying, "Remember after defeating the Chinese we always sent tribute." This was a reference to the care Vietnam always took in victory over China to give face to the Central Kingdom, so as to forestall future reprisals. But given the degree of obsequiousness involved, with Communist Party and government officials making huge numbers of pilgrimages north to study and praise China's example, even this was putting too kind a face on things. Delegation after delegation had begun making its way north to Beijing to kowtow and pay homage, toasting their Chinese Communist Party hosts with remarks like this one from Le Kha Phieu, the Vietnamese party secretary: "If China succeeds in its reform, we succeed," he told a member of the Chinese Politburo. "If China fails, we fail."

In the end, both Cambodia and Laos were pried from Hanoi's

orbit, not by force of arms, whose limitations had been demonstrated against Vietnam, but rather through the irresistible power of China's growing economic strength, enhanced by both diplomatic persistence and occasional finesse. This was classic bandwagoning, in international relations terms, and a foundation of the tribute relations of old. Forget the Chinese tales of the attractive power of their country's virtue, as well as the interpretations of Western historians, in the mold of Fairbank, who for so long accepted that "Chinese empire grew by the acculturation of its borders. Its expansion was an expansion of a way of life," which meant that neighbors willingly, even eagerly, submitted to China because they wanted to emulate it. In fact, wrote historian Yuan-kang Wang, "Tributary states lived next to the strongest power in East Asia and there were no other allies of significance that could be counted upon to balance Chinese power. Lesser states submitted to Chinese authority and accepted hierarchy because they did not have better alternatives. Relative weakness, geographic proximity and lack of a counterbalancing ally forced them to accept Chinese dominance."

The strategic realignment of the region that had begun with the American defeat in Vietnam and was followed by the Soviet pullout at the end of the 1980s deepened with the 1994 American withdrawal from its oldest overseas naval base, at Subic Bay. This came after a referendum showed a strong Filipino desire to recover national sovereignty. The Americans carried out the closure of Subic Bay, and that of the neighboring Clark Air Force Base—two of its most important forward positions in Asia—without any great show of angst. The creation of Subic was in line with a long succession of similar Western imperial projects in Asia, an aspect of naval strategy. These began with the Portuguese and Spanish, and the conquistadors like Albuquerque and Magellan. They were followed by the Dutch, British and Japanese, each leaving a bigger mark than the last. All of these powers had sought to establish dominant positions in the region through maritime supremacy. The final attempt by a Western power to do so was launched by Washington in the nineteenth century, when the United States embarked on a long process of building or acquiring bases stretching from the Aleutian Islands to Hawaii and Guam and onward into the Indian Ocean. From the start, Subic Bay had a very specific vocation within this project, one of "securing privileged access to the China market," a policy that annoyed Britain and helped lead to war with Japan.

The base was a key forward staging and resupply point for the United States during the Vietnam War, throughout which it received intensive use, in part to check Chinese power. Late in the Cold War, as we have seen, Moscow acquired naval basing rights in Vietnam, at Cam Ranh Bay. In addition to fulfilling the age-old Russian dream of possessing warm-water ports, it provided a way for the Soviet navy to "overcome the choke points of the Soya, Tsugaru and Tsushima Straits," which impeded free access for its warships to the Pacific. The arrival of the Soviets in Southeast Asia, with a deployment of twenty-five hundred permanent personnel at Cam Ranh Bay, was a major spur to the rapprochement between the United States and China, and of course an even greater factor in the breakdown of relations between Hanoi and Beijing. After a period of gentle downsizing, Washington beefed up its presence anew in the Philippines and focused on a strategy of containing the Soviets, which still has relevance for China's security thinking today. For this purpose, the United States guarded three checkpoints in waters around Indonesia, at the Malacca, Sunda and Lombok straits, and relied on its forward base presence at Subic for additional potential force projection. Once the Soviet Union disappeared, however, the value of maintaining bases in the Philippines seemed to fade and Washington acquiesced to the demands to withdraw from the country. During those years of modest retrenchment, few in the United States imagined China becoming a full-fledged economic competitor in the foreseeable future, and for the time being, even in security matters, it regarded China in mostly nonthreatening terms.

Although they were little heeded at the time, there were in fact already important changes under way in China that bespoke both of the country's ambitions and of its evolving geopolitical strategy. Deng Xiaoping, leading the country at this point, had already shared his view with colleagues in the senior Chinese leadership that the United States was fated to gradually decline, a prediction that required some boldness at the time, coming as it did just as Washington was about to embark on a period of global unipolarity. Deng's vision, like Mao's before him, called for a fundamental redistribution of power in the world in China's favor. For the time being, however, he urged that China should be prepared to advance opportunistically, to fill any voids that presented themselves without setting off anyone's alarms and without overreaching. The spirit of his strategic thinking was captured in a famous twenty-four-character instruction from the early 1990s. "Hide our capacities and bide our time. Be good at maintaining a low profile. Never claim leadership." This was the statement not of a man who was content to make peace with an American-led international order, as it came to be widely read, but rather that of someone who saw conflict between major powers involving China, possibly as soon as two decades hence, as essentially unavoidable. The essence of Deng's thought was that China should avoid any confrontation until it was in a position to prevail.

After the Tiananmen Square incident in 1989, Beijing took fresh stock of its relations throughout its immediate neighborhood and began to piece together a new strategy. Hitherto, China had behaved warily toward the Association of Southeast Asian Nations (ASEAN), regarding it as just one among many pieces of the multilateral economic and security architecture that Washington supported in the region for the purpose of containment. The fallout from the massacre of the student demonstrators, however, sharpened distinctions in China between friend and foe. Japan was the only neighboring country to condemn the violent suppression of the student movement outright. South Korea merely "regretted" it. Other Asian countries were largely silent in their response, with Malaysia calling it an "internal affair." Amid heavy public outcry, even the Americans took a relatively accommodating view in the wake of the crackdown. "Our foreign policy must really keep open the possibility and indeed encourage China's full return to the international community," said Bush administration secretary of state James A. Baker. Taken together, these reactions created a new sense in Beijing that the region was not arrayed against it, and might soon even be susceptible to Chinese powers of attraction. China's foreign policy toward its Asian neighbors had evolved very slowly since the 1960s, but now it began to move with alacrity.

The next important watershed came with the Asian financial crisis of 1997–1998. Following the counsel of what might be called an emerging "Asia-first" lobby within China's foreign policy and national security establishment, Beijing played a proactive role in stabilizing the region's economy, and through its adroit crisis response began to fashion a new image for itself as a generous and reasonable power, easing the image of go-it-alone revanchism that had clung to it for decades. China "acted responsibly and in a stabilizing way by not devaluing its currency and by offering aid packages and low-interest loans to several Southeast Asian states," writes David Shambaugh in his book *China Goes Global: The Partial Power.* "These actions not only were appreciated in the region but also stood in stark contrast to the dictatorial posture taken by the International Monetary Fund and international creditors in response to the crisis. This assistance punctured the prevailing image of China in the region as either aloof or hegemonic."

Economic largesse like this was backed by a number of important political gestures. Perhaps most important, Beijing resolved long-standing border disputes with a number of neighboring states, including Laos, Tajikistan, Kyrgyzstan, Kazakhstan and Russia. In almost every case, the concessions it made were in fact small, but this did nothing to detract from the spreading notion that China's rise might be accomplished without inflicting undue trauma on its neighborhood. Indeed, from 1997 to 2008, in fulfillment of Deng's wishes, there was widespread and growing acceptance of the view that China was becoming a new kind of power, almost benevolent, and certainly not aimed at harshly imposing itself on others, as most of the imperialists of the past had been.

The most obvious tool in this image remake was trade. China had become a fast-rising manufacturing powerhouse, and almost every observer of the region in this period has remarked that the country's trade with its neighbors exploded in parallel with its goodwill diplomacy. In this regard, for the purpose of influence, imports are more important than exports. In 1990, China purchased a mere 5 percent of the exports of its neighboring countries. By 2013, that figure had mushroomed to 22 percent and was rising. Less widely remarked, at least early in the post–Asian financial crisis decade, and yet even more important than trade, was Chinese lending to its neighbors. Beijing does not report its lending totals for individual countries, but after starting from a very modest base, by 2008 it was widely regarded as the most important source of lending in the region.

In remarkably little time, the Asia-first strategy, or Good Neighbor Policy, as it was sometimes called, had begun paying huge dividends. China was on its way to becoming the true center of gravity in its region to a degree that had not been seen for a century and a half. The country had come in from the cold in Asia first by attracting investment from Japan to produce raw materials for its neighbors' advanced industries. Its next step was to lure manufacturers from throughout the region to take advantage of China's well-trained and inexpensive labor. Along the way, it was able to absorb lots of technology and know-how, through means both legitimate and illicit, meaning intellectual property theft and piracy. As Chinese industry began to take off and the income levels of its people rose, Beijing started playing on an idea as old as the Opium Wars—the dream foreigners have had of selling an untold amount of goods to tens of millions of Chinese people. Even as China began to draw investment away from nearby countries and produce goods at such low cost that those countries' industries struggled to compete, China's neighbors continued to buy into the idea that demand from a rising class of consumers on the mainland would fuel prosperity for all in the region steadily into the future. Under the circumstances, few were in the mood to ask hard questions of China on geopolitical grounds or indeed to rock the boat in any other manner. China was well on its way to reestablishing an ancient game played by the Central Kingdom, one that leveraged access to the world's biggest market in exchange for the deference of its neighbors and acceptance of its primacy. By the end of the 1990s, the tables had been largely turned, and the member countries of ASEAN were being converted into commodity suppliers for China instead of the other way around, as had been the case early in its takeoff. This was the first big step in much larger plans for an ambitious economic integration of the entire region, with China at its center. In his 2015 book *China's Coming War with Asia,* the prominent European analyst Jonathan Holslag laid out a remarkable vision of what China's ambitions might mean, should they succeed, in a not so distant future.

The area from Shanghai to Chengdu and from Shenyang to Kunming, he imagined, would be turned into a high-income zone, saturated with middle classes and boasting advanced industries, internationally renowned brands, and quality services:

> Its main cities would specialize in different lucrative economies: Shanghai, for instance in financial services, Chongqing in clean cars, Kunming in advanced machinery, Chengdu in software, and so forth. Between them, the towns and villages would offer comfortable and healthy living conditions in green garden estates. Meanwhile, fast trains and airlines would channel millions of tourists and billions of spending to quiet places, to Tibet, emerging as the Chinese Pyrenees, to the Northeast, the future Chinese Alps, to Xinjiang, the new Andalusia, and to the southern beaches, China's Club Med. The China seas would be patrolled by a powerful navy, cheap workers from Vietnam would operate Chinese oil platforms, and Filipino waitresses serve Shandong Mary's or Beijing Bellini cocktails on new tropical resorts on the Spratly Islands. Taiwan would be a contented autonomous region of the People's Republic— oyster pancakes and bubble tea still being generously served.

> The economy would be more efficient and thrive largely on domestic demand. That demand would gradually raise up the development of neighboring countries. China's new international champions would have tied them to the motherland by means of roads, railways, pipelines, and endless flows of visitors. They would control most of the production chain, from the mines to the retail chains, and trade mostly in Chinese currency. Russia's fate is obvious; Japan's would be compara-

ble to a depopulating version of the United Kingdom, quietly musing on its great imperial past. Southeast Asia, China's Italy, would be vibrant and enthralling, yet heavily penetrated by Chinese companies, banks, and high-livers.* The stretch from Bangladesh to Kazakhstan could well be China's Northern Africa and Middle East. . . . At the same time, a modus vivendi will have been developed with the United States, which allows China to establish de facto control over the disputed parts of its maritime margins and to turn Taiwan into another autonomous region, like Tibet and Xinjiang. In other words, the most effective form of revisionism would thrive on economic power politics, keeping military force as the feared tool of last resort.

When Holslag's book came out, the easiest response to a passage like this might have been something to the effect of, "Hey, not so fast," or "Isn't this a tad ambitious?" But in the months that followed publication, China itself seemed to provide an answer, which might be summed up by the phrase "You haven't seen anything yet," including, of course, destabilizing financial upheaval worldwide.

History bequeathed China the most complicated geopolitical situation of any major country, bar none. For starters, this means fourteen thousand miles of land borders and twenty adjacent countries, including seven of the fifteen largest countries in the world, from peer rivals including Russia and India to smaller but historically difficult neighbors, among them Korea, Vietnam and Myanmar (Burma). Add to that nine thousand miles of sea frontiers, across which China faces off against a number of rival territorial claimants, including a wealthy and heavily armed major historical antagonist, Japan, and

---

*In early 2016, the Laos government committed to the construction by China of a high-speed railway linking Kunming, in southern China, to Vientiane. It is the first stage of a vast scheme that will extend all the way south through Thailand and Malaysia to Singapore, with parallel wings envisioned that will also converge on Kunming. One of them will run north-south the length of Myanmar, the other through Cambodia from Bangkok and northward up the entire length of the Vietnamese coast.

the Philippines, both of which enjoy defense treaties with the United States. Beyond formal defense alliances like these, as Andrew Nathan and Andrew Scobell write in their book *China's Search for Security,* China is ringed by countries that belong to six different intricate regional diplomatic and economic systems, including Northeast Asia, Oceania, continental Southeast Asia, maritime Southeast Asia, South Asia and Central Asia, and Beijing "faces the U.S. presence in all of them."

China, therefore, although newly powerful, still feels tightly boxed in, and is determined to win space for itself, beginning with the pacification of its periphery. This it will seek to do first with economic strength, but as it grows stronger it will not shrink from using its newfound and growing military strength as the need arises. There is urgency in all of this too, for the fundamentals of the country's demographics and the uncertainties linked to its economic expansion, already decades old and slowing, showing more and more signs of imbalance, make the next decade or at most two the period of its greatest relative strength, and hence its moment of greatest opportunity. Current trends, which do not look amenable to dramatic improvement, suggest that by 2040 the Chinese population will be more skewed in favor of old people than Japan, the "grayest" major country in the world today.

How will the coming China-driven world look? The history that we have dwelled upon at length here so far is no idle lesson. One can only speculate about the future, but history offers the best foundation for anticipating and understanding China's motivations and behavior in shaping the world to come.

CHAPTER FIVE

Sons of Heaven, Setting Suns

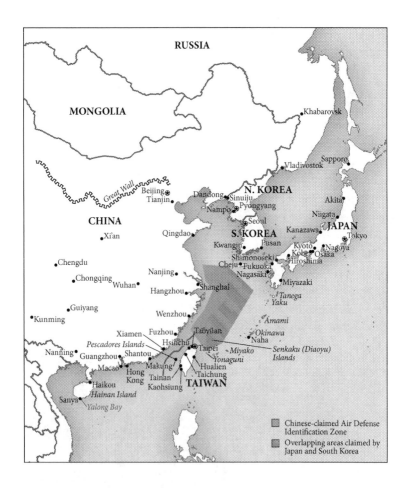

The human mind finds it hard to resist organizing history into discrete periods, but a sense of the transitions from one era to another usually only takes firm root with the distance of time. Nonetheless, events in Asia in recent years make it very tempting to declare that a new era is upon us.

One could take as its starting point the moment in 2010 when China surpassed Japan as the world's second-largest economy. Or one could just as easily go back a couple of years earlier, to the onset of a global financial crisis centered in American markets but that quickly spread throughout the West. China's response at the time included notes of triumphalism and outright schadenfreude, as commentators in state media crowed about the debility of Western democratic capitalism and the inevitability of China's rise to preeminence, premised explicitly or implicitly, as the case may be, on the presumed superiority of China's political economy. In the post-Mao era, that was certainly new, and what followed was a period filled with other examples of unaccustomed Chinese assertiveness, acts that seemed to mark a sharp break from the guiding axiom of Deng Xiaoping, which called upon China to hide its capabilities and bide its time.

The single most salient political event of all, though, was the assumption of power of Xi Jinping, a man who confounded analysts who had widely predicted a lengthy transitional period of consensual, collegial rule, in much the same vein as the two leaders who preceded him, before Xi could be expected to consolidate strong executive power—if ever—and put any firm personal stamp on affairs of state.

As significant as any of this was Beijing's launching of the Asian Infrastructure Investment Bank (AIIB) and the cascading adhesion of almost every traditional American ally, starting with Britain, in spite of Washington's strenuous attempts to dissuade them from joining, or at least to slow the stampede. The AIIB deserves this kind of historical significance not because it constitutes a threat to the United States in any traditional or immediate sense, but because it represents more fully than anything else China's will to emerge, its bold coming-out and a demonstration of its resolve to become a powerful, across-the-board geopolitical actor.

In the months before the bank's launch, Barack Obama had begun heavily promoting a major regional trade and investment agreement of his own called the Trans-Pacific Partnership (TPP), which figured to include twelve founding members—Australia, Brunei, Canada, Chile, Japan, Malaysia, Mexico, New Zealand, Peru, Singapore and the United States. By design, China was not among the founding countries, despite having recently risen to become the biggest trading nation in the world. What is more, the language that Obama employed to promote the pact, which not only covers trade in goods but also carries important intellectual property, financial services and labor provisions, laid bare American anxieties over being able to compete in Asia with China. Speaking before both domestic and foreign audiences, Obama has said things like, "We have to make sure the United States—and not countries like China—is the one writing this century's rules for the world's economy." If this wasn't enough to define the stakes for China, Ashton B. Carter, the last of Obama's succession of defense secretaries, made a highly unusual statement for someone whose job as head of the Pentagon is traditionally driven to a large extent by procurement issues. "In terms of our rebalance in the broadest sense, passing TPP is as important to me as another aircraft carrier," Carter said.

"Rebalance" was of course the more delicate phrasing the Obama team had come to favor after initially speaking more clumsily of a "pivot" to Asia earlier in his presidency. This policy had initially been heavily focused on military and security issues, and despite diplomatic denials, it bore all the hallmarks of an attempt by Washington to step up efforts to effectively counteract China's expansion, which had begun as far back as the 1990s. In the preferred wording of many independent observers, and indeed to Beijing, for all of the wordplay and denials, this amounted to nothing less than an attempt to contain China.

The years between the 1997 Asian financial crisis and the serious push to gain congressional approval for the TPP, beginning in early 2015, had been clearly marked by a new Chinese muscularity. This began quietly but ominously enough in 2009 with Beijing's petition to the United Nations claiming rights to virtually the entire South China Sea. To review: For this purpose, as we have seen, China resurrected its so-called nine-dash line to define Beijing's view of its territorial rights in the region. This cartographer's line, which was first published by China's Nationalist government in 1947, is also sometimes called the "Cow's Tongue" for the way that it lollingly droops more than nine hundred miles from the mainland to corral roughly 90 percent of the South China Sea. In doing so, it encompasses the near-coastal waters of a number of Asian countries, including Vietnam, Malaysia, Taiwan and Brunei. In the case of the Philippines, it draws up as close as to within twenty-five miles of the coast of Palawan, one of that country's major islands. China's most determined rival claimants are Vietnam and the Philippines. In the case of some of the Spratly Islands, which are claimed by both of those countries, in addition to China, most of the islands lie seven hundred or more miles away from Hainan Island, the nearest Chinese territory by any conventional reckoning. The shores of Vietnam and the Philippines, by comparison, are both several times closer. Beijing claims nonetheless that China discovered these islands, and frequently says, as we have seen, that its ownership and control of them dates from "time immemorial." And perhaps just to make sure that no one harbors doubts about its determination to impose its will in the matter, Chinese passports issued from 2009 onward have carried a map of the South China Sea complete with a nine-dash line map.

After laying down this marker with its Southeast Asian neighbors, China then initiated a showdown with Japan for control of a cluster of disputed islands lying between the two countries that are known as the Senkakus to the Japanese and Diaoyu to the Chinese (henceforth the Senkakus, for convenience). Excepting for a period of postwar occupation by the United States, the Senkakus had been under Japanese control since their annexation in 1895. After Taiwan had officially staked a claim to the islands in April 1971, China did the same that December. Early the following year, the Japanese government responded by saying that when it took over the Senkakus in 1895, the islands were uninhabited and not under the control of imperial China. According to Tokyo, the cession to it by China of Taiwan and the Pescadores Islands, which followed, coming as a result of Japan's victory in the Sino-Japanese War, in no way involved the already annexed Senkakus, meaning that these islands were not a spoil of war, and therefore not subject to claim by China.

In the 1970s, as we've seen, China's relations with Japan were originally driven by a desire to balance against the Soviet Union, and by the second half of that decade by the search for technology and financing needed to jump-start China's economic modernization. With these priorities in mind, during a visit to Japan, Deng Xiaoping famously suggested to his hosts that the two neighbors put aside their dispute over the islands. "It is true that the two sides maintain different views on this question. It doesn't matter if this question is shelved for some time, say, ten years," said Deng. "Our generation is not wise enough to find common language on this question. Our next generation will certainly be wiser. They will certainly find a solution acceptable to all."

Deng, in fact, was plenty wise. Although the Senkakus issue flared up again briefly as the two countries pushed to conclude negotiations on their 1978 Treaty of Peace and Friendship, it otherwise remained well in the background, allowing a poor and still relatively weak China to attract badly needed investment and technology. As a result, Japan quickly emerged as the leading foreign investor in China and a strong and early cheerleader for the country's reconstruction following the economic devastation of the Cultural Revolution. On a visit to China in 1975, Japanese prime minister Masayoshi Ohira went so far as to express his "heartfelt wish that [Japan's economic assistance] would provide the foundation for building the China of the twenty-first century." By the 1990s, Tokyo's aid to China accounted for between 10 and 15 percent of Japan's global overseas development assistance. Japan remained the number one provider of foreign aid to China until 2007, and by that point it had provided between 50 and 60 percent of China's total economic aid for over two decades.

As noted, Japan was the rare Asian country to directly criticize China over the June 4, 1989, Beijing massacre during the military crackdown on student demonstrations at Tiananmen Square. Its response was mild by the standards of the West, though, and its decision to suspend development lending was only reached after much tortured debate about the dangers of isolating China and about the two countries' large and growing shared economic interests. After the massacre, Beijing wooed Tokyo assiduously, and in ways that calculatedly played to a strong latent Japanese desire to put the tragic history of its twentieth-century invasion of China definitively behind it. Shortly before the crackdown on the demonstrations, Li Peng, a leading advocate in favor of adopting a hard line against the students' democracy movement, reached out to Japan with a feeler about hosting a visit by Emperor Akihito, who had freshly ascended to the throne earlier that year. Remarkably, in its long imperial history, no Japanese emperor had ever visited China. Adding considerable drama to the invitation was the fact that Akihito's father, Hirohito, as everyone knew, had presided over Japan's devastating invasion of China decades earlier.

Beijing's reaching out on Akihito strengthened the hand of the Japanese politicians who had argued against imposing sanctions on China, and in November 1990, Japan announced a resumption of lending to its neighbor. The following year, China stepped up its efforts to get Japan to consent to a visit by Akihito, and emphasized the importance of establishing a rhythm of visits at the highest strata between the two countries, which Beijing claimed would help take their relations to a "new level." This sparked an intense debate in Japan, where many were perplexed by the Chinese diplomatic initiative, with some conservatives regarding it as a trap to humiliate Japan over its imperial history or to extract new forms of apology. This obliged Japan's foreign ministry spokesman to publicly insist the emperor "is not on a mission to make an apology," as David Sanger quoted him in the *New York Times*. Other officials emphasized that the matter of Japan's responsibility for the war had been definitively settled twenty years earlier, when Tokyo and Beijing resumed diplomatic relations and China formally waived claims for reparations.

As it turned out, when the new Japanese emperor paid his visit in 1992, he showed little hesitation in speaking about the history that had so bitterly divided the two countries. At a state dinner, where he was hosted in the Great Hall of the People by China's president, Yang Shangkun, Akihito invoked a long history of Japanese admiration and respect for China, going back to the first exchange of emissaries between the two countries in the eighth century. Then he came to more difficult matters: "In the long history of the relationship between our two countries, there was an unfortunate period in which my country inflicted great sufferings on the people of China. I deeply deplore this."

The early 1990s were proving to be a time of repeated Japanese declarations of remorse over its past aggression, with some of the statements of senior government officials breaking fresh ground in terms of new details and degrees of forthrightness. In early 1992, Prime Minister Kiichi Miyazawa, for example, spoke repeatedly about the so-called comfort women, or females forced into sex slavery in order to service the Imperial Japanese Army. In 1993, speaking in his inaugural news conference, Prime Minister Morihiro Hosokawa declared that Japan had pursued "a war of aggression, a war that was wrong." The momentum created by successive apologies like these culminated with an eponymous statement in 1995 by the socialist Prime Minister Tomiichi Murayama on the occasion of the fiftieth anniversary of the end of the war, which remained the official position of the government of Japan until 2015 under Shinzo Abe:

> The world has seen fifty years elapse since the war came to an end. Now, when I remember the many people both at home and abroad who fell victim to war, my heart is overwhelmed by a flood of emotions.
>
> The peace and prosperity of today were built as Japan overcame great difficulty to arise from a devastated land after defeat in the war. That achievement is something of which we are proud, and let me herein express my heartfelt admiration for the wisdom and untiring effort of each and every one of our citizens. Let me also express once again my profound gratitude for the indispensable support and assistance extended to Japan by the countries of the world, beginning with the United States of America. I am also delighted that we have been able to build the friendly relations which we enjoy today with the neighboring countries of the Asia-Pacific region, the United States and the countries of Europe.

Now that Japan has come to enjoy peace and abundance, we tend to overlook the pricelessness and blessings of peace. Our task is to convey to younger generations the horrors of war, so that we never repeat the errors in our history. I believe that, as we join hands, especially with the peoples of neighboring countries, to ensure true peace in the Asia-Pacific region—indeed, in the entire world—it is necessary, more than anything else, that we foster relations with all countries based on deep understanding and trust. Guided by this conviction, the Government has launched the Peace, Friendship and Exchange Initiative, which consists of two parts promoting: support for historical research into relations in the modern era between Japan and the neighboring countries of Asia and elsewhere; and rapid expansion of exchanges with those countries. Furthermore, I will continue in all sincerity to do my utmost in efforts being made on the issues arisen from the war, in order to further strengthen the relations of trust between Japan and those countries.

Now, upon this historic occasion of the 50th anniversary of the war's end, we should bear in mind that we must look into the past to learn from the lessons of history, and ensure that we do not stray from the path to the peace and prosperity of human society in the future.

During a certain period in the not too distant past, Japan, following a mistaken national policy, advanced along the road to war, only to ensnare the Japanese people in a fateful crisis, and, through its colonial rule and aggression, caused tremendous damage and suffering to the people of many countries, particularly to those of Asian nations. In the hope that no such mistake be made in the future, I regard, in a spirit of humility, these irrefutable facts of history, and express here once again my feelings of deep remorse and state my heartfelt apology. Allow me also to express my feelings of profound mourning for all victims, both at home and abroad, of that history.

Building from our deep remorse on this occasion of the 50th anniversary of the end of the war, Japan must eliminate

self-righteous nationalism, promote international coordina-
tion as a responsible member of the international community
and, thereby, advance the principles of peace and democracy.
At the same time, as the only country to have experienced the
devastation of atomic bombing, Japan, with a view to the ultimate elimination of nuclear weapons, must actively strive to
further global disarmament in areas such as the strengthening
of the nuclear non-proliferation regime. It is my conviction
that in this way alone can Japan atone for its past and lay to
rest the spirits of those who perished.

It is said that one can rely on good faith. And so, at this
time of remembrance, I declare to the people of Japan and
abroad my intention to make good faith the foundation of our
Government policy, and this is my vow.

Despite having held out the enticing prospect of sustained high-
level visits between neighbors, it would take China a full six years
before it reciprocated the Akihito trip with the visit of a top-level
official to Japan, and when it came, it reflected little of the spirit of
reconciliation that Akihito had sought to promote. In part this was
because in the meantime China had gotten most of what it wanted
from Japan. The Japanese had successfully lobbied the United States
and others to ease China back in from the cold following their
Tiananmen-related sanctions. Beijing had also received a string of
apologies from Tokyo, placing Japan in the historically desired position of supplicant. And of course there was the large-scale lending
and investment in strategic, technology-intensive industries, like
automobiles. Equally important, by this time the rest of the world
was beating at China's doors in order to do business there and the
Chinese economy had firmly embarked on its historic takeoff.

In other words, by 1998, six years after Akihito's groundbreaking
trip to Beijing, Japan was simply no longer so important to China
as to require deference, or even ordinary diplomatic niceties, and
the first Chinese head of state to make his way to Japan did little to
hide this fact. In the lead-up to Jiang Zemin's 1998 visit, China had
pushed hard for a written apology from Japan over its wartime past,

citing a recent written apology that Japan had made to South Korea. Tokyo resisted this idea, citing the emperor's public apology and the Murayama Statement, among numerous other official statements of remorse. Japanese diplomats said privately that they would only entertain the idea of a written apology if China would firmly commit to not employing the history issue in future dealings between the two countries, something China flatly rejected. As a result, throughout his five-day visit, Jiang carried himself like someone who bore a chip on his shoulder. At one stop after another on his official schedule, he browbeat audiences about Japan's historical guilt for its aggression against China and showed little inclination toward forgiveness. At a state banquet in Tokyo in the presence of both Emperor Akihito and Prime Minister Keizo Obuchi, for example, Jiang lectured that "Japanese militarism tread the wrong path of invasion and expansion and caused great suffering to the people of China and other nations." At another Tokyo event, Jiang stated flatly, "I am opposed to the opinion that the problem of history [between Japan and China] has been sufficiently discussed."

At the conclusion of Jiang's visit, the final bilateral communiqué was delayed by six hours, and ultimately went unsigned, a rarity in such high-level bilateral diplomacy. Jiang, a normally wily politician who has been frequently underestimated—usually to the peril of others—had badly overplayed China's hand, not just by demanding that Japan deliver to him what it had so recently granted Korea but also by apparently drawing excessive confidence from a highly successful summit with Bill Clinton just a few months earlier. This seems to have fueled an exaggerated sense of his own power and of China's. For the Japanese public, the effect of Jiang's negative theatrics was as if a mask had fallen. Senior politicians of the ruling Liberal Democratic Party (LDP) readily understood that any major concessions to the Chinese would fatally cripple the government, and so Tokyo did what it felt it had to under the circumstances—it pushed back.

Here there are significant echoes of the long and complex history that links the two countries, or, more often than not, has divided them, and of a record that shows that whenever China has demanded Japanese submission, it has usually been stubbornly rebuffed. Examples of this begin in the year 600 CE, when emissaries from a Japanese kingdom known as Wa arrived in China on a diplomatic mission to the Sui dynasty. The Japanese delegation bore a letter referring to the ruler of Wa (even though it was a woman, Empress Suiko) as "son of heaven in the land of the rising sun," and to the Sui emperor, Yangdi, as "son of heaven in the land of the setting sun." With this simple wording, Japan seemed to signify that although it cherished its relationship with China, it had already begun to think of itself somewhat differently, as something substantially more than a run-of-the-mill vassal. Yangdi, or perhaps merely his court, because it is unclear whether a message that breached protocol so dramatically would have been read to the emperor, was outraged by the apparent Japanese claim to equal footing and simply refused to reply.

Early in the Tang dynasty, which followed immediately upon the Sui, Yamato Japan began to request that China change the name it used to refer to it, urging it to switch from Wa (倭), which could be variously read as "bent," "tortuous," or "throw away," and was therefore thought of as inelegant, to Nihon (日本, meaning "origin of the sun"). This was not just fussiness over semantics, but rather an act of growing self-assurance. Japan's sense of rightful autonomy continued to grow during the Song dynasty, which began in 960. The Song era was a period of tremendous wealth and cultural prestige for China, albeit one of relative military weakness and security challenges that proliferated from multiple directions. During the fourteenth century, at the start of the Ming dynasty, and less than a century after the twin failed naval invasions of Japan from China by the Mongols, which followed on demands that Japan pay tribute to China, the Ming again sent emissaries to insist that Japan submit. In 1369, one of them threatened an attack—"pay tribute or train your troops and strengthen yourselves." In one of Japan's most noteworthy rebuffs to China, its Prince Kanenaga replied to the Ming court, writing, "Now the world is the world's world; it does not belong to a single ruler. . . . I heard that China has troops able to fight a war, but my small country also has plans of defense. . . . How could we kneel down and acknowledge Chinese overlordship?"

In the one major exception to this pattern, in 1404, the Ashikaga ruler, Yoshimitsu, accepted the title "king of Japan" from the Ming as a means of opening lucrative trade with the mainland. Just as his predecessors had, though, later shoguns rejected Chinese superiority out of hand. Indeed, by the late sixteenth century, as we have seen, it was Japan's turn for the first time to try to impose itself on China militarily as the superior Asian power. In 1587, Toyotomi Hideyoshi, who had just unified the country after a period of intense civil war, wrote to his wife, "It is my lifelong goal to annex China into our territory." The increasingly megalomaniacal Hideyoshi twice attempted a feat that the Mongols had twice tried before him, a maritime conquest across the waters of East Asia. And twice he was defeated, by a combination of resistance by Koreans, through whose territory he passed, and by the marshaling of Ming armies to turn back his attacks.

The circumstances of the second invasion have much to tell us about the relationship between Japan and China. During the negotiations that followed the blunting of Hideyoshi's first bid, the Ming court mistakenly convinced itself that the Japanese daimyo had accepted investiture as a vassal, which was China's bottom-line condition for peace. This was because "the Chinese negotiator, Shen Weijing, was so fearful for his life that he did not report to the Ming court what the Japanese had really demanded," wrote the scholar of China Yuan-kang Wang in his 2010 book *Harmony and War: Confucian Culture and Chinese Power Politics.* Hideyoshi's original goal, in fact, had been the polar opposite of the Chinese demand: establishing the capital of his expanding Japanese empire in Beijing. When his first invasion stalled, what he demanded instead was "that the Chinese court provide a consort for the Japanese emperor, reopen licensed trade with Japan, and that four provinces of Korea be ceded to Japan," historian Marius B. Jansen wrote. When these conditions were not met, Hideyoshi dispatched a second expeditionary force, of 140,000 men, to attempt once again to subjugate the Ming.

Hideyoshi died in the midst of that campaign, and was soon followed in power by Tokugawa Ieyasu, the founder of the feudal regime that became known as the Tokugawa shogunate. Successive Tokugawa leaders reached out to the Ming to restore relations with

China, but neither side was willing to compromise on essentials. Japan wanted access to rich Chinese markets, while an understandably distrustful China insisted, as in the past, on the prerequisite that the Japanese first submit. Among other things, this would have meant that the shogun would have to call himself a subject of the Chinese emperor, adopting the title "king," as Yoshimitsu had briefly done, and employ other ritualized deferential language in bilateral correspondence. It would have also required adopting the Chinese calendar, another form of debasement. By the early 1640s, the security of the Ming had come under stout attack from the Manchus, who would soon overwhelm them, and this produced an unusual Chinese appeal to Japan for help. To this, a Japanese daimyo, or vassal of the shogun, scoffed that the Chinese "won't allow Japanese ships to approach their shores. . . . Therefore it is hardly proper for them to come, now that their country has fallen into civil war and say, 'We are having some trouble, so could you please send some troops?'"

These stories make clear that questions of hierarchy have been a recurrent source of serious friction in the relationship between China and Japan, and occasionally of outright crisis and war. For China, the idea that surrounding peoples, and most particularly peoples of the Sinic world, who had borrowed so heavily from its culture, should submit to it amounted to a bedrock element of its worldview, an essential article of faith. Japan's persistent failure to do so was an insult to China's self-image, a wound whose pain and irritation waxed and waned, but always commanded attention, and, when China was particularly strong, action. Yet for several reasons, the ability to do something decisive about it had always hovered just beyond China's reach.

Until recently, geography had provided Japan, unlike, say, Vietnam or Korea, all the benefits of proximity to China with few liabilities—sitting off of the mainland, in the medium distance, protected by rough seas. However massive and even awe-inspiring its continental neighbor was, once Japan came together as a coherent state governing extensive island territories in the early centuries of the Common Era, China could never quite muster the power, nor did it ever have the technological means, to capture its smaller neighbor and retain it within its orbit for any length of time, as it had so many of its other neighbors. Yet now and again down through the centuries it could not desist from trying.

The first decade of the twenty-first century saw a clear resumption of the time-honored testing between the two countries. What was different now and of profound significance was that the recent industrialization of the Chinese economy, and the construction of a powerful and rapidly modernizing People's Liberation Army (and PLA Navy), had vastly reduced the impediment of distance that for military purposes had long kept Japan securely beyond the practical reach of its neighbor. Nowadays, as China experiences a recurrence of the urge to bring to heel the island nation that so annoyingly contradicts its sense of proper hierarchical order in the region, it increasingly has the means to do so. As a consequence, Japan is facing a struggle to transform itself, in the words of a 2013 government report called the Basic Ocean Plan, from "a country protected by the ocean to one that defends the ocean."

The first serious augur of this new reality would come in October 2003, when Japan detected a Chinese ship conducting echo surveys of the ocean floor topography in Japan's inner coastal waters without giving the two months' prior notice that the two countries had recently agreed to. The survey incident briefly raised alarms in Japan about defense readiness and about the trustworthiness of its neighbor, but given the booming economic ties between the two states, there was no sense of crisis. Bilateral trade soared to $130 billion a year in 2003, a 30 percent increase over the preceding year, and there was a prevailing sense of shared economic interests. Few suspected at the time that the surveys would be the harbinger of much bigger tests to come, opening a decade of increasingly tense jockeying between East Asia's two great powers.

A broad awareness that times had changed came thirteen months later, though, when a fully submerged Chinese *Han*-class nuclear-powered submarine was discovered transiting Okinawa's Miyako Strait, near the island of Ishigaki. This was not just an ostensible lapse in prior notification, like the survey ship incident had been made out to be. Submarine maneuvers conducted beneath the surface in the territorial waters of another country are widely considered to consti-tute hostile intent under international law, and the discovery of the submerged boat caused Japan to put its maritime forces on a state of alert for only the second time since the end of the Second World War. For the next several days, the incident became the subject of almost nonstop television coverage in Japan, making a deep impres-sion upon public opinion. For a time, commentators competed with each other in stating the urgency the country faced in needing to roll out a new maritime security policy. The Japanese government was able to defuse the crisis by saying it had received an apology of sorts from Beijing, which it said had explained that the incursion was an accident and privately expressed its regrets. (Publicly, the Chinese foreign ministry declined to provide any information.)

The submarine incident took place against the backdrop of heightened political tensions between China and Japan during the nearly six-year tenure of the popular prime minister Junichiro Koi-zumi, a notably long period in office by modern Japanese standards, where the prime minister's office has been something of a revolving door. Koizumi, a self-assured and charismatic conservative, battled to revive the long-stagnant Japanese economy through privatization of the postal savings system and by shaking up the country's power-ful bureaucracy. At the same time, he pursued a frankly unapologetic nationalism, urging the Japanese to take more pride in their past, instead of being perennially apologetic, or as it was sometimes put, "masochistic." This was an astute reading of the national mood. As a Japanese analyst would tell the International Crisis Group a few years later, the people of his country wanted to "stop floating like a ghost in the sea of perpetual apologies for the Asia-Pacific War of 70 years ago."

His most symbolically important and controversial gesture in this regard consisted of regular visits to Yasukuni, the famed Meiji-era shrine to Japan's war dead, which honors the souls of those fallen in modern conflicts. Not incidentally, this category included fourteen people who were named by the International Military Tribunal for the Far East following Japan's surrender as Class-A war criminals, for their important roles in organizing Japan's aggression against China and other Asian nations. The most famous of the fourteen was the Imperial Japanese Army general Hideki Tojo, who was prime minister during most of World War II and who presided over the attack against Pearl Harbor. Although the Liberal Democratic Party, Koizumi's party and long Japan's dominant ruling party, had always been a strongly conservative force, with roots that lay deeply in the country's wartime past, the nationalist bent in Japanese politics in the early 2000s was in some measure a predictable response to the constant needling over war guilt from Chinese leaders like Jiang Zemin, and to the introduction of increasingly nationalist curricula under the so-called patriotic education campaign Jiang pushed after the 1989 Beijing massacre. It was, in other words, at least in part a manifestation of the negative feedback loop that persists between the two countries' nationalisms, which in turn, as we have seen, has deep roots.

After the June 4 massacre and the swift demise of communism in the Soviet Union and Eastern Europe, the Chinese Communist Party desperately needed time and political space, along with the expected fruits of rapid economic growth, to renew its ideological credibility with its own population, especially in the big, relatively prosperous cities of the country's east. Toward this end, Jiang's patriotic education campaign, which was introduced in 1991, sought to focus the

Okinawa cemetery from World War II

attention of his nation, and especially the youth, on the humiliations of the century that preceded Communist rule. And right from the start, Japan was given pride of place among the chosen villains.

Prior to this campaign, both modern history education and propaganda in China had largely followed narrative lines laid down by Mao, with heavy emphasis placed on victory over the Nationalists in the Chinese Civil War, leading to the "liberation" of the country and the triumph of socialism, which, it was long promised, would allow the country to overtake its rivals in both the East and West. Beyond these themes, Mao's personality cult and his obsession with continual class struggle consumed all the remaining oxygen. Mao (and Deng Xiaoping) had had little use for the story line of triumph over the Japanese, in part because, as we have seen, China under Mao had hopes of enlisting Japan in an effort to balance against the Soviet Union in Asia, while under Deng, China appreciated Japanese investment and technology. Additionally, vilifying Japan would not serve to glorify Communist China. It was the blood of Chiang Kai-shek's Kuomintang (KMT), plus the firepower of the Americans, culminating with the dropping of two atomic bombs, that had defeated Japan, with the PLA doing relatively little. Mao hardly wanted to emphasize such things, so the chosen emphasis became liberation.

On the most famous Japanese atrocity of the war, which has featured heavily in Chinese education and propaganda ever since Jiang, Ian Buruma wrote:

> Little was made in the People's Republic of the Nanking Massacre because there were no Communist heroes in the Nationalist capital in 1937. Indeed there had been no Communists there at all. Many of those who died in Nanking or Shanghai, or anywhere in southern China, were soldiers in Chiang Kai-shek's army. Survivors with the wrong class or political backgrounds had enough difficulty surviving Maoist purges to worry about what happened under the Japanese.

Unbeknownst to almost all Chinese nowadays, Mao virtually dismissed the idea that Japan should continually express contrition and remorse over the war of conquest it fought in China. Meeting with Japanese prime minister Kakuei Tanaka on September 27, 1972, at the time of normalization of their relations, after Tanaka expounded in his coy and abstract fashion that "by invading China, Japan created a lot of trouble for China," Mao replied in a way that blended irony with surprising candor. "We must express our gratitude to Japan," he said. "If Japan didn't invade China, we could have never achieved the cooperation between the KMT and the Communist Party. We could have never developed and eventually taken political power for ourselves. It is due to Japan's help that we are able to meet here in Beijing."

Junichiro Koizumi's reinforcement of Japanese nationalism, along with his visits to Yasukuni Shrine, occurred at just the moment when China was introducing a new predominant emphasis on victimization, which blamed outside forces for China's misfortunes, and for these purposes Japan now became an eminently useful foil. The Chinese press regularly excoriated Koizumi over his views of the war, and Beijing responded by restricting bilateral cooperation with Japan and, except for routine business, freezing the island nation out of the picture in every way it could. For six years, summits between the neighbors were completely suspended. In April 2005, when Japan announced revisions to its national education curriculum, watering down accounts of Japanese aggression against China in the twentieth century, and especially diluting details of its atrocities, things took a sharp turn for the worse. A major wave of anti-Japanese demonstrations kicked off around the country. On their first day, I followed tens of thousands of mostly young protesters in Shanghai as they walked from the historic riverfront district known as the Bund several miles to a commercial area called Hongqiao, blocking traffic along the entire route. Since Tiananmen, the Chinese authorities have been quick to put down any large protest that hasn't somehow been sponsored or supported by the state. The official imprimatur on this march was implicit for its having been allowed to disrupt business in the center of the city, as well as its high level of organization, replete with ushers, who kept everything orderly. When the demonstrators reached Hongqiao, however, where many Japanese

Anti-Japanese demonstration

companies maintain their offices in the city, tempers suddenly flared, as young men screamed anti-Japanese slogans and threw rocks and bottles at the Japanese consulate and at a number of Japanese businesses. I watched this scene for more than an hour, impressed most of all by the fact that throughout that time no police whatsoever were summoned to the scene to restore order.

From this nadir, the mood shifted quickly once Koizumi left office, in 2006, with both countries sensing a chance to mend ties and each seizing the moment. One of the biggest problems looming between them, the territorial dispute over the East China Sea, seemed to present the most immediate prospect of mutual gain. Rather than focus on the nettlesome question of sovereignty over the Senkakus, a problem that Deng had urged be left to a future generation, they turned to the idea of joint exploitation of underwater deposits of hydrocarbons in the East China Sea, which each believed held immense potential. This mutual interest was greatly reinforced by the results of a 1968 multinational survey conducted for the United Nations Economic Commission for Asia and the Far East, which tantalizingly concluded, "A high probability exists that the continental shelf between

Taiwan and Japan may be one of the most prolific oil reservoirs in the world." In 1971, a then-secret analysis by the CIA about the dispute over the Senkakus reaffirmed this judgment, stating that "many American geologists feel the area could be one of the ten largest oil deposits in the world." And most recently, the U.S. Energy Information Administration has estimated that "the entire East China Sea has between 60 and 100 million barrels of oil and between one and two trillion cubic feet of natural gas in proven and unproven reserves."

The UN survey also said, with considerable understatement, that the reservoir was to be found on "one of the few large continental shelves of the world that has remained untested by the drill, owing to military and political factors."

As China emerged from the economic chaos of the Cultural Revolution and began to grow rapidly in the early 1980s, the possibility that huge energy reserves existed offshore became an important driver of its diplomacy toward Japan. China was still far from being able to match the technological sophistication of its rich neighbor, and so it sought to find a way to set aside the Senkaku dispute temporarily and promote the notion of joint exploration and development of the suspected underwater oil fields. The first such Chinese proposal was made to a visiting delegation in 1980 by the deputy premier, Yao Yilin. Yao even suggested that the United States could be brought into any exploitation agreement, presumably because it had the most advanced offshore oil production technology at the time. Deng Xiaoping made a second proposal to Japan in 1984, calling for the joint development of energy resources before the two countries discussed questions of sovereignty involving the Senkaku Islands. Beijing launched yet another proposal of this kind in 1996. In each case, Tokyo demanded a settlement of its maritime border with China, or recognition from Beijing of its claim to the Senkakus, before any other business could be done together in the waters surrounding the islands.

In April 2007, amid the sudden post-Koizumi thaw in their relations, the notion of shared exploitation was put forward officially yet again, but this time by Japan. Prime Minister Shinzo Abe made the proposal during a visit to Japan by his Chinese counterpart, Wen

Jiabao, in which Wen, known in China for his warm, unusually avuncular persona for a top Chinese leader, applied all his charms with Japanese audiences. This meant going so far as to publicly acknowledge Japan's past apologies over past wars, a sharp departure from the approach of the previous Chinese president, Jiang Zemin. "The Japanese Government and leaders have on many occasions stated their position on the historical issue, admitted that Japan had committed aggression and expressed deep remorse and apology to the victimized countries," Wen said in a speech to the Japanese Diet. "The Chinese Government and people appreciate the position you have taken."

The ubiquitous slogan in Beijing at the time, under President Hu Jintao, was "harmonious society" (*hexie shihui*), which was usually taken to mean that China should get its domestic house in order, building a more livable, less conflict-ridden country. This slogan had a counterpart in foreign policy as well, albeit invoked somewhat less, called "harmonious world" (*hexie shijie*), which was itself a spin-off of an earlier slogan under Hu, since dropped, that invoked China's "peaceful rise." Talk of building a harmonious world was meant, among other things, to disarm China's neighbors, and most particularly Japan, which during Abe's first tenure as prime minister (September 2006 to September 2007) had begun trying to boost regional alliances and laying the groundwork for legal and constitutional changes that would allow Japan to become a "normal" country again, meaning giving it the right to field an army and use force for the purpose of collective self-defense.

It probably also helped that at the time China was barely a year away from hosting the 2008 Olympics, which it was treating as a historic coming-out party and a chance to ceremonially reintroduce itself to the world as a confident, modern and unthreatening rising great power. For Beijing, conveying a feeling of win-win harmony in its neighborhood was crucial to projecting the image it desired. Against that backdrop, negotiators from the two countries worked hard at completing a draft agreement on joint exploration of the undersea oil and gas resources in time for a visit to Japan by Hu Jintao in May 2008. It called for the two countries to cooperate in a

2,600-square-kilometer area that straddled the median line separating them (significantly employing the demarcation as drawn up by Japan, not China) and allowing companies from each nation to work in the other's adjacent maritime territory. The potential impact of this promising advance in bilateral diplomacy was greatly weakened, however, by the unusual way that the news was handled by both countries, via separate press conferences. Because of its censorship, China was able to manage news of the deal to make it appear it had compromised little. Abe's government initially came under harsh domestic criticism for supposedly capitulating to China.

Soon, this all became moot, leaving behind an unfulfilled moment that managed simultaneously to reveal both the tantalizingly rich promise of cooperation between the region's two most powerful countries on matters of vital common interest and the supreme difficulty they usually face in overcoming their shared past, along with the perpetual anxiety that divides them over relative status. In May 2008, China was struck by the Great Sichuan earthquake. In broad swaths of mountainous Sichuan Province, nearly everything was reduced to rubble. Japan, with its own long experience of tragic earthquakes, provided some of the earliest and most helpful emergency aid, generating an air of considerable goodwill between the countries and leading some to believe that relations could be sustained on an upward trajectory. China, though, was consumed well into the following year with its reconstruction efforts, and little energy was expended on bilateral relations with Japan.

Then, in the fall of 2009, the LDP surprisingly lost power in parliamentary elections to the Democratic Party of Japan (DPJ) before work on an implementation agreement between China and Japan over the maritime oil and gas exploration treaty could be completed. When the new DPJ prime minister, Yukio Hatoyama, met Hu Jintao at the UN that September, he expressed hope that the two countries could turn the East China Sea into a "sea of fraternity instead of a sea of dispute." In ideological terms, the inexperienced DPJ was a bit of a hodgepodge, but its policy priorities clearly consisted of rapprochement and closer relations with China and less dependence on the United States.

Japan's new governing party's policies were suddenly aligning in an almost undreamed-of fashion with one of the most deeply held and enduring goals of Chinese geopolitics: weakening the American alliance architecture in the region, with the ultimate aim of peeling Japan away from the United States. Nothing could go further toward allowing Beijing to replace Washington as the custodian of security in East Asia. But this moment, so full of historic opportunity and potential for China, slipped away ignominiously, as the result of an incident that could have been treated as a mere blip in bilateral relations but was instead blown out of proportion by Chinese leaders who seemed captive to the very angry nationalism they had themselves only recently fueled.

Naoto Kan, the DPJ leader who succeeded Hatoyama—who lasted less than nine months—was in office for all of three months when the events that would fundamentally derail relations with China occurred. (Kan won power because of the continuing decline of the economy and the perception that the government had caved in to the United States over a controversial troop-basing arrangement in Okinawa.) They centered on the refusal by the captain of a Chinese fishing trawler to allow his boat to be inspected by the Japanese coast guard after he was discovered on September 7, 2010, near the Senkaku Islands, fishing within Japan's twelve-mile territorial waters. The Chinese captain, Zhan Qixiong, reportedly first attempted to flee, and then proceeded to ram two coast guard vessels with his ship, the *Minjinyu 5179*, resulting in the seizure of his boat. The other members of the fifteen-man crew were promptly released, but Zhan was taken into custody.

The new Kan cabinet seemed both unsure of itself and strikingly lacking in confidence, fearing the consequences of appearing too lenient, given the DPJ's reputation for being pro-China. The cabinet began making preparations to prosecute Zhan under Japanese domestic law for obstruction of the coast guard, rather than simply expelling him. China responded with fury, summoning the Japanese ambassador in Beijing to demand the captain's release, and subsequently engaging in rapid escalation. In the space of a few days, a new wave of anti-Japanese protests was unleashed in Chinese cities, all, once again, seeming to have received an official imprimatur. Beijing announced it was suspending the East China Sea Agreement negotiations.

Two weeks after the crisis began, the Japanese trade minister announced that Japanese companies had suddenly become unable to procure shipments of vital rare earth minerals from China, which controlled some 90 percent of world supply, suggesting an orchestrated but officially unannounced industrial embargo. (A few weeks later, China would announce a decision to reduce exports of rare earth minerals by 30 percent, in order to "protect overexploitation.") At about the same time, on September 20, China arrested four Japanese employees of the Fujita Corporation in Hebei Province, where they were accused of entering into a restricted area. The four were working in China under the terms of a bilateral agreement whereby Japan was cleaning up chemical weapons sites employed during the war by the Imperial Japanese Army.

As these events were unfolding, Wen Jiabao was in New York on the eve of the UN General Assembly. While he was there, in a regular daily news briefing, the Chinese foreign ministry spokesman announced that "the time is not proper for a meeting between Chinese Premier Wen Jiabao and Japanese leaders at the United Nations." The next day, the kindly man known as gentle Uncle Wen warned in a speech that China would take "further actions," and added that "all the consequences should be borne by the Japanese side."

To be sure, Japan's own handling of the crisis under the DPJ was unusually clumsy. The Japanese coast guard, for example, possessed footage that left no doubt about the recklessness of the Chinese trawler captain, who gave every appearance of having deliberately rammed the Japanese vessels, and who may well have been drunk. Early release of the video would have solidified world opinion and made it difficult for China to work itself into such a public lather over the incident. But without solid countervailing information, China's state media completely misrepresented matters, telling domestic audiences that it was the Japanese coast guard that had provoked things. Clinging to narrow technicalities, the Japanese government insisted, meanwhile, that confidentiality rules applied to evidence in a civil legal matter like this, and during the critical early days of the crisis this continued to hold up release of the footage.

A great deal of additional procedural and political mismanagement ensured that the matter dragged out over the course of weeks, becoming a political football instead of being handled expeditiously. In speaking before the Diet on twenty-five occasions between September and November, for example, Japan's foreign minister, Seiji Maehara, a relative hawk within the DPJ, either explicitly denied that there had ever been a gentlemen's agreement to shelve the Senkaku dispute with China or, more broadly still, simply denied that there existed a territorial dispute with China over the islands. The contrast with other, recent LDP-led Japanese governments could not have been sharper. In dealing with Chinese incursions into the waters near the Senkakus, under Prime Minister Koizumi discretion was the norm; a fishing boat skipper who was apprehended would immediately be sent back to China. In this way, Koizumi managed to stand up for Japan's sovereignty claims without making a public issue of it. Koizumi was following long-standing precedent for Japanese governments vis-à-vis inflaming China over the Senkakus. This traditional policy was captured in a well-known Japanese saying, which held that "disturbing a bush only lets the snake out." Said in a more familiar American idiom, it is better to let sleeping dogs lie.

What is most remarkable in China's response is how quickly the "harmonious world" approach went out the window, as nationalist voices both in the broad public and in the senior ranks of the Communist Party constrained President Hu and Prime Minister Wen to toe a hard line. Henceforth, one could readily detect all of the hallmarks of the Central Kingdom's traditional *tian xia,* in terms of both rhetorical voice and gestures. Beijing was quick to find ways to ensure that the inferior neighbor would be made to pay for testing its forbearance, restricting access to China's markets and denying an audience with its leaders, as had been done to those who failed to pay proper tribute in days of old. The trawler crisis produced one measure by China, though, that stands out as an important shift in tactics, and an ominous portent for the future. In late October, Beijing ordered the continuous deployment of large Fisheries Patrol (a maritime service separate from the coast guard) vessels to the waters of the Senkakus. In practice, this meant that numerous thousand-ton Chinese ships, boats as big as many of Japan's coast guard patrol vessels, would assume a permanent presence near the islands, well inside Japan's claimed EEZ. To emphasize China's new assertiveness, these were accompanied by the deployment of the *Yuzheng 310,* a new, high-speed, 2,580-ton ship, equipped with two helicopters. There could be no more denial of a crisis.

In other respects, China's handling of the trawler collision crisis was not effective. It lost a potential windfall in East China Sea undersea oil and gas production. Rattled and exasperated, Japan eventually released the captain without finalizing an indictment of him. But even while it was making arrangements to do so, it was reaching out to the United States for new security reassurances, which were not long in coming. In New York, shortly after Wen Jiabao had refused to meet the Japanese foreign minister, Seiji Maehara, Maehara was able to secure a significant new public commitment about the islands from Secretary of State Hillary Clinton. Washington took no position on the question of ultimate sovereignty, she said, but added that "the Senkaku islands are under Japanese jurisdiction . . . covered by the U.S.-Japan security treaty."

It is far from certain that Tokyo and Beijing would have been able to come to terms on joint exploitation of the East China Sea hydrocarbon reserves. Just as the Japanese government had come under public criticism for offering a compromise, the Chinese government was subjected to fierce pressure from opponents within the Chinese political system to abandon the agreement. The first signs of this arose in December 2008, when two Chinese Marine Surveillance agency vessels conspicuously parked themselves for nine hours off the Senkakus in waters long controlled by Japan. This was an unprecedented action at the time, shocking Japanese public opinion anew, which seems to be exactly what was intended. It occurred on the very eve of an inaugural Japan–China–South Korea trilateral summit, hosted in Fukuoka, Japan, causing great embarrassment to Prime Minister Wen, who represented China at the meeting. The provocation was almost certainly the work of hawkish elements in the Chinese government and military who were opposed to conceding anything to Japan.

The most plausible reasons for their angry opposition, it would seem, were feelings that China had given away too much by accepting Japan's definition of maritime boundaries for the purpose of joint oil exploration. In the region where their disputed maritime boundaries lie, continental China and Japan are never separated by more than four hundred nautical miles. Since the United Nations Convention on the Law of the Sea (UNCLOS) took effect, in 1996, Japan has argued that the boundary should be set at the "geometrical median line" between the two countries in the East China Sea. China, however, has resorted to another argument, which states that its rights at sea should be determined by the continental shelf, which by Beijing's definition extends to the Okinawan Trench, some of the deepest water in the Pacific Ocean, and well beyond the geometrical median. Unhelpfully, both arguments might be allowed under UNCLOS. Internal dissent broke out over this question almost immediately following the 2008 draft agreement, with the Chinese foreign minister insisting that Beijing had not recognized Japan's median line.

Other opponents to the agreement invoked the long-standing Chinese complaint that Japan still declined to acknowledge even the existence of a territorial dispute with China over the Senkakus. Working in the shadowy recesses of government where high-level policy matters often get decided, significant parts of the bureaucracy started coalescing against the deal from its very inception on this basis. An online campaign even emerged against it, which is something the authorities would surely have suppressed if a strong political consensus existed behind it. In the end, though, not enough people could be brought together at a sufficiently high political level for whom expending political capital in the interest of mutually beneficial relations with Japan was deemed worthwhile. In retrospect, in fact, this seems clear even from the unusual way the agreement was announced, not in a joint event, but via concurrent press releases in two languages involving documents that lacked signatures or even dates. By proceeding in this way, China had all but declared that doing business involving questions of history or national sovereignty with Japan obliged it to hold its nose.

For the time being, though, conducting other sorts of business between the two nations was still not a problem. The East China Sea began to fade as an issue during the Naoto Kan cabinet (2010–11), as economic relations with China were booming once again, with bilateral trade hitting a new high of $345 billion in 2011. That same year saw investment soar by 50 percent, reaching $6.3 billion. Kan's tenure in the prime minister's office lasted nearly fifteen months, which was long by the standards of the post-Koizumi era in Japanese politics, but nonetheless represented a continuation of the revolving door pattern in national leadership. Kan's popularity was sharply weakened by a proposed doubling of the national sales tax, and regard for the government tumbled further with the perceived mishandling of the devastating March 2011 earthquake and tsunami that hit Japan, with three meltdowns dangerously crippling the Fukushima I Nuclear Power Plant. Ironically, for the second time, a major earthquake had contributed to a brief uptick in bilateral relations. For all of Kan's domestic woes, the Chinese public expressed unexpectedly widespread sympathy and admiration for Japan's highly orderly response to the disaster.

Kan was succeeded in office by Yoshihiko Noda, who managed to eke out another fifteen months at the helm for the DPJ, starting in September 2011. Noda continued along the path established by Kan, seeking to firm up relations with the United States after the abrupt distancing experienced under Hatoyama. Indeed, in one of his very first acts, Noda announced that Japan would negotiate entry into the U.S.-proposed Trans-Pacific Partnership, a twelve-nation trade pact that has been widely perceived as a bid by Washington to counterbalance China's growing economic influence in Asia, as mentioned earlier.

The weakness of this succession of DPJ governments had begun to embolden conservative forces in Japan, though, and in particular it energized prominent populist nationalists, like the far-right independent governor of Tokyo, the veteran politician Shintaro Ishihara.

As an LDP lawmaker, and leader of a group called the Seirankai, or Blue Storm Group, Ishihara had been a leader in peddling the Senkaku sovereignty issue as a nationalist cause ever since the era of normalization of relations with China in the 1970s, when he loudly criticized Prime Minister Kakuei Tanaka for setting aside the dispute. Other conservatives within the then-ruling LDP who demanded that Japan publicly assert what they believed to be its rightful sovereignty at the time notably included one Shintaro Abe, the late lawmaker who was the son-in-law of the former prime minister Nobusuke Kishi, onetime controversial wartime administrator in Japanese-occupied Manchuria. Shintaro Abe was the father of the prime-minister-to-be Shinzo Abe. Sensing the continuing political potency of a red-meat issue like this, Abe, who was already plotting his return to the prime minister's office, responded to Ishihara's demagoguery by organizing a group within the LDP that began making demands of its own. Abe and his allies called for demonstrating Japan's "effective control" (*jikko sihai*) over the Senkakus. Practically, this would mean, among other things, stationing government personnel on the islands, something that had been avoided in the past.

Seven months into Noda's tenure, Governor Ishihara launched a fund-raising campaign whose proclaimed goal was to purchase from their private owners the three Senkaku islands Japan did not yet own, on the premise that Tokyo wasn't doing enough to prevent them from falling into Chinese hands. For dramatic effect, the announcement of this drive was made at the headquarters of the conservative Heritage Foundation, in Washington, D.C. Here, Ishihara's misguided aspiration seems to have been drawing support from the American defense and foreign policy establishment in his provocation of Beijing. With characteristically inflammatory language, the Tokyo mayor and his associates in this campaign vowed to undertake the construction of lighthouses, harbors and other structures on the islands.

From its start in April to September of the same year, Ishihara's movement to take over the Senkakus far exceeded expectations, raking in $18 million in contributions from more than 100,000 individual Japanese donors, alarming the Noda cabinet. On September 11, with little public forewarning, the Japanese government announced the islands' purchase, effective immediately, for the sum of 2.05 billion yen. In Noda's unfortunate phrasing, Japan was nationalizing them, which, given China's well-known sensitivity over sovereignty, implied far greater significance than necessary. Beijing responded by immediately expressing its opposition to the move, triggering what has come to be known as the so-called Senkaku Shock, the second crisis with China in two years involving the disputed islands and their surrounding waters. This time, unlike the last, however, while the Japanese once again fumbled about in seeming surprise over the hostile reaction, China's thunderous response showed considerable premeditation.

The Noda government's motive in "nationalizing" the Senkakus seems to have been to defuse what it saw as a far more provocative outcome by preventing nationalist demagogues, led by Ishihara, from taking them over and provoking what it feared might become a far greater crisis. From Tokyo's point of view, the purchase by the government did nothing to affect the status of the islands' sovereignty, which Beijing, of course, had officially claimed since 1971; they had all along been Japanese, and were implicitly recognized as such even when some of them were leased by the United States for use as a firing range during the years of the American occupation of Japan.

In the timing of their announcement of the nationalization, the Japanese government was clearly responding to events, but it also imagined itself as displaying considerable sensitivity to Chinese political realities. Beijing was in the midst of a leadership transition at the time, immediately prior to the takeover by Xi Jinping from Hu Jintao, and disposing of tense business like this when it did, rather than hesitating further, not only preempted more trouble from Japan's nationalists, it avoided presenting China's incoming head of state with the possible loss of face. The Chinese didn't see things that way. Japanese officials had been briefing their Chinese counterparts since June on measures they were taking to prevent trouble over the Senkakus, and had publicly evoked the need for a government takeover of the islands throughout this time. Beijing nonetheless took the announcement of the nationalization as a challenge designed to take advantage of their country's transition and to weaken the new leader,

Xi, complicate his situation, or take advantage of possible distraction in Beijing early in the new administration.

In early September, Prime Minister Noda had sent a secret envoy to Beijing to brief senior Chinese officials on developments. There is no account of what transpired that is accepted by both sides, but the Chinese somehow came away from these discussions persuaded that Japan was open to abandoning the idea of nationalization, or at least to coming up with some other way forward that would preserve Chinese face. On this basis, Hu Jintao agreed to meet with Noda at a regional summit in Vladivostok. "Japanese officials had been surprised by the Chinese side's acceptance of the request for the meeting and interpreted it as a good sign," wrote the International Crisis Group in a report. "They assumed that President Hu had been made fully aware of Japan's intentions to finalize the purchase the following day." The September 11 announcement of the nationalization came just a week before the commemoration of the Mukden Incident, the staging by Japanese troops of a mock dynamite attack on a Japanese railroad in Manchuria, which created the pretext used by Tokyo for its invasion of northern China in 1931. In denouncing the Japanese moves, some invoked the proximity to this war anniversary to claim a deliberate provocation. It has often been said that history is a form of religion in Chinese civilization, but here again, as we have seen before, it is frequently wielded as a formidable weapon.

For all of our era's robust modern national security bureaucracies and instantaneous communications, a misunderstanding of this magnitude harkens back to the sixteenth-century misadventures of Hideyoshi, when China wrongly imagined that the daimyo who ruled Japan was preparing in his defeat to accept vassal status whereas in reality Hideyoshi was already steeling for a second war. He, on the other hand, mistakenly imagined that the Chinese were offering to cede to him suzerainty over the Korean Peninsula in order to avoid another invasion.

A war did not ensue over the Senkakus, but the misunderstanding and subsequent collapse of diplomacy sparked what soon became the greatest crisis in postwar relations between China and Japan— one that has altered the way the two countries deal with each other over the disputed sea that separates them and introduced sharply increased risks and growing instability. As the crisis unfolded, once again Chinese officials readily lapsed into their old imperial style with Japan, granting an audience out of the mistaken belief that the subordinate neighbor would come to duly acknowledge its place under heaven. Perhaps equally impressive is the similar way that Japan read the dynamics of the encounter, even amid such fundamental misunderstanding. The Noda government in its surprise thought, incorrectly, that Beijing was in good humor.

China responded immediately and with calculated fury to the announcement of the Japanese nationalization, aiming to inflict "multiple blows" against Japan, in the words of the International Crisis Group, its moves carefully worked out in advance:

> Top leaders delivered harsh rebukes of Japan, with the then–Premier Wen Jiabao vowing "never to yield an inch" and then–Vice President Xi Jinping calling the island purchase "a farce." The foreign ministry thundered that the purchase was "illegal and invalid, and changed nothing about the historical fact that Japan had invaded and occupied Chinese territories." Defense minister Liang Guanglie said China's military "reserves the right to take further actions." The commerce ministry warned that Japan's actions "will inevitably affect and damage the normal development of Sino-Japanese economic and trade relations." Chinese provincial- and central-level officials were also ordered to cancel visits to Japan and meetings with Japanese counterparts.

At the same time, anti-Japanese protests were staged in more than a hundred Chinese cities, with Japanese stores, restaurants, automobiles and even factories coming under widespread attack. Japanese goods were boycotted, and car sales were hit particularly hard amid the anti-Japanese fever. Japanese banks reportedly came under concerted attack by Chinese hackers, and street protesters in dozens of cities brandished slogans that seemed to up the ante, urging their countrymen to "Destroy Japan and retrieve Okinawa."

The most consequential measure by far, though, was Beijing's immediate announcement of territorial baselines, or precise geographic coordinates, covering the Senkakus and their surrounding waters. This amounted to a formal declaration that China would henceforth treat the entire area as its inherent territory, with both the land and water subject to its sole jurisdiction. Japan had of course controlled the Senkakus since it incorporated them on January 14, 1895, as *terra nullius,* albeit without making a public announcement of this move at the time, and it had occupied or administered the islands without interruption, save for the aforementioned American occupation, ever since.

As we've seen, in the post-Deng era, Japan had moved away from treating its differences with China over the Senkakus as a shelved dispute, denying instead with increasing firmness that there was any dispute at all. This shift began in 1992, when China passed something it called its Law on Territorial Sea and the Contiguous Zone, which explicitly included the Senkakus in Chinese territory, prompting Japanese politicians to flatly deny that there had been any private agreement to shelve the issue. Now, with the start of the island nationalization crisis, China announced its resolve to give vivid and continuous demonstration of the existence of a dispute, sending its ships and aviation into the area and treating Japan's long-established presence as illegal. In this, Beijing's behavior was conforming strongly to a recent trend: When provoked by an adversary, press fast-forward.

The most recent examples of this had come not with Japan, but on two occasions in 2012 in the South China Sea. The first of these involved the Philippines, which because it was so poorly equipped chose to employ a secondhand American frigate, the 1960s-vintage BRP *Gregorio del Pilar,* that April to arrest Chinese who it said were fishing illegally at Scarborough Shoal. This triangular chain of guano-covered reefs, which encloses a shallow 58-square-mile lagoon, lies 123 miles west of Subic Bay and, in Manila's view, well within the Philippines' 200-mile exclusive economic zone. By comparison, China's closest territory, Hainan Island, lies 550 miles to the northwest. China responded quickly, deploying its own civilian maritime vessels to counter the Philippines', which in turn dispatched a coast

Subic Bay, Philippines

guard vessel to replace the warship at the scene of what became a weeks-long face-off. The United States helped broker a seeming resolution of the dispute that called for a climbdown by both sides—the withdrawal of their ships from the area. Once this was accomplished that June, however, Chinese Marine Surveillance and Fisheries Patrol vessels soon returned to the shoal, where they roped off the entrance to the lagoon. China now maintains a permanent presence at the shoal where none had existed before.

The second event that June that reflected what has been called China's "reactive assertive" approach to pressing its territorial claims in moments of crisis in the region involved Vietnam. Hanoi passed a new maritime law that covered both the Spratly and Paracel island groups and imposed new rules of navigation through each. China's State Council, or cabinet, responded swiftly by announcing the incorporation of a new municipality called Sansha City, which it said would administer two million square miles of maritime territory covering all of what China calls the Xisha (Paracel Islands), Zhongsha (Scarborough Shoal and the Macclesfield Bank) and Nansha (Spratly) Islands. Given their history of maritime confrontations, Hanoi should have prepared itself for immediate Chinese counter-measures. As we have seen, Beijing had already responded forcefully to an attempted change of status quo by the Republic of Vietnam (Saigon), which made an all-encompassing claim to the Spratly Islands in September 1973. The following January, China deployed five hundred troops to take complete control of the Paracel Islands, the other major South China Sea group, evicting the South Vietnamese troops after a brief showdown.

In 2012, no force was used. In its place, this brand-new, supposedly prefectural-level city was founded on a five-square-mile coral reef, where China had recently conducted large-scale land reclamation. With only a few hundred residents, it was the most lightly populated city of this rank in the country, and yet by jurisdiction it controlled a surface area one-quarter the size of continental China. In announcing the move, China's ministry of civil affairs said that the new prefectural "capital" would help improve administrative management of the three chains of tiny islands Beijing claimed in the South China Sea. Perhaps the most important fact was given far less emphasis: China would immediately establish a division-sized military garrison there.

In its riposte against Japan, China's tactics were no less audacious. It hoped to impose on its neighbor a test of endurance and to initiate a game of chicken, premised on the idea that Japan's growing economic dependence on China, together with its military dependence on the United States, would constrain it, ultimately forcing Tokyo and not Beijing to step back from the brink. This new era of testing began to take shape almost immediately, with the dispatch of vessels from China's State Oceanic Administration into the waters around the Senkakus. That September, China sent 81 ships into nearby waters, including 13 that entered within Japan's claimed twelve-mile territorial waters around the disputed island group. The next month saw 122 Chinese ships enter the Senkaku waters, including 19 that entered Japan's claimed territorial waters. The pattern seen in the following months suggested this would be the new norm.

In December 2012, a Chinese surveillance aircraft flew through airspace near the Senkakus for the first time, triggering an alert by the Japanese Air Self-Defense Force, which scrambled F-15s from

Okinawa in response. Before the end of the year, China had begun dispatching surveillance flights whose small propeller aircraft were frequently escorted by Chinese jet fighters. In January 2013 came yet another turn of the ratchet, when a Chinese frigate locked its fire-control radar on the *Yudaichi*, a Japanese destroyer, in what is normally considered a signaling of hostilities. A suite of other calculated provocations would follow throughout that year, including the deployment of Chinese Marine Surveillance ships near the Senkakus that February to the circumnavigation of Japan for the first time by Chinese warships in July. On Thanksgiving weekend, China announced, perfectly legally, although without warning or prior consultation the establishment of an "air defense identification zone" (ADIZ) covering most of the East China Sea, including the entire airspace over the Senkakus, requiring foreign aircraft to file their flight plans with Chinese aviation authorities or, in theory at least, risk being shot down.

Something fundamental had changed in the meantime in Japan as well, since the nationalization of the Senkakus. Shinzo Abe, a deeply conservative politician whose publicly proclaimed dream was to create a Japan that "once again shines on the world's center stage," assumed office as prime minister for the second time on December 26, 2012, following his Liberal Democratic Party's rout of the DPJ. With both his career and his family background alike steeped in nationalist causes and defense hawkishness, Abe immediately made a show of standing up to China. During his early months in office, for example, he was photographed smiling and giving the thumbs-up sign from the cockpit of a jet fighter trainer. The numbers "731" stenciled boldly on the white fuselage stood out next to the imperial sun just beneath Abe. As even a casual student of Japan's wartime history would know, 731 was the name of the notorious biological warfare unit that performed experiments on live prisoners in occupied Manchuria.

For years, Abe had spoken proudly of his ancestry, and in particular of being the grandson of Nobusuke Kishi, a man with fascist tendencies who had helped administer Manchuria under imperial rule in the 1930s and then became a senior member of General Tojo's cabinet, as minister of munitions, before spending three years in prison under the American occupation for suspicion—he was never indicted—of war crimes. Abe enjoyed recounting memories of sitting on his grandfather's knee in the prime minister's office as they listened to the sounds of protests against Kishi's controversial moves to revise the security treaty with the United States in 1957 (approved in 1960). This was ostensibly in order to give Japan more scope for foreign policy independence from Washington (but also obligating Japan's Self-Defense Force to aid the United States in case of a war with another East Asian country, such as China), but Kishi's moves notably included successful efforts to gain the release of Class-B and Class-C class war criminals, who were still imprisoned for such crimes as torture, rape and murder. Kishi also hoped to revise the constitution so as to modify Articles 1 and 9, the first so that the status of head of state could be restored to the emperor, and the second to nullify Japan's constitutional abandonment of war. Knowing that these measures would generate strong opposition, Kishi first introduced a bill to strengthen the powers of the police. This galvanized strong opposition against his government and sparked a huge wave of protests. Kishi was able to force through his vote, but only by sending five hundred policemen into the House of Representatives for a session conducted under lockdown. Tactics like these injected yet more energy into the opposition, leading to what remain the biggest demonstrations in Japanese history and forcing the cancellation of a scheduled visit by President Dwight D. Eisenhower. Years later, in a 2006 book, Abe, many of whose policies would eerily resemble those of his grandfather, wrote that growing up amid criticism of Kishi as a "war criminal" and the "embodiment of reactionary conservativism" may have had "the opposite effect of making me embrace conservativism."

Unlike recent past Japanese governments, which had vacillated or caved in when faced with strong Chinese pressure, the Abe cabinet seemed to revel in the game of chicken with Beijing. For someone whose lifetime mission in politics had been to allow his country to field a national army, and to have it participate more assertively in Japan's self-defense, engaging with Xi Jinping perfectly suited his long-term purposes, and Abe proved adept at it. Before leaving office, the DPJ leadership had conciliatorily altered the rules of engagement at sea, ordering Japanese vessels to increase their minimum distance from Chinese ships from three miles to five. But after the *Yudaichi* radar incident, Abe rescinded this measure in an unmistakable signal that Japan would not be backing down in the future.

The mood was much the same in political circles under the new government, which mounted a huge diplomatic offensive to place Japan, after a long period of deference in international affairs, back in the global spotlight. Japan began opening embassies in forgotten corners of the world, including South Sudan, Bhutan and Iceland. Abe visited forty-nine countries by September 2014, a record for a sitting Japanese prime minister. His first stop was not the traditional choice of Washington, but rather Southeast Asia, a region where he sought to play up a sense of shared interest in pushing back against an increasingly assertive China. Before long, he had visited almost every country in the area. In the Philippines and Vietnam, Japan offered generous help with expanding and modernizing coast guards and improving marine surveillance. Abe pushed hard to strengthen relations with India and Australia, a revival of an idea he had initially broached during his first term in office, of building what he, pretty much alone for the time being, fancied as a diamond-shaped alliance of democracies around China's periphery. The Japanese undertook (ultimately unsuccessful) negotiations to sell Australia its most sophisticated diesel submarine technology, a vivid symbol as Tokyo broke with the past, reviving the country's armaments industry and freeing it in one fell swoop from legal restraints that had long prevented weapons exports.

During his first year in power, Abe engineered a major reorientation of national defense policy projecting forward ten years. This was done via a first-of-its-kind document called the National Security Strategy, which was an attempt to unify the country's foreign policy and defense visions. Its animating spirit was concern over the implications of China's rise. The strategy paper bluntly denounced Beijing's "challenges to the status quo by force," in both the East and South China seas, as "incompatible with the international order," and warned that China's increasingly frequent intrusions into Japanese waters and airspace "could cause unexpected situations," which in the softened and euphemistic tradition of language around Japanese defense matters is about as close to suggesting violent confrontation as is imaginable.

The new government also made waves with the first of what would eventually become several consecutive budget increases for Japan's Self-Defense Force. Each yearly increase was a mere 0.8 percent; that so much was made of it spoke volumes about the state of inertia that had hung over Japan's defense sector for years. China immediately rose to the bait, predictably warning about the remilitarization of its neighbor, hoping apparently to drive anxiety about Japan in other Asian nations. Besides South Korea, though, a country whose relations with Tokyo had been deteriorating in parallel with China's, no Asian countries displayed any concern about Japan. This was due in part to three factors: (1) Abe had raised Japan's profile as a development lender to most of the Southeast Asian nations he had visited, in a bid to compete for soft power against Beijing; (2) most of the region was quietly yearning for some other power to balance against China's growing preponderance; and (3) it was a common-sense reading of reality.

Japanese defense spending had been declining slowly for a decade prior to Abe, shrinking 5 percent overall during that time. During the same period, China's defense budget increased by 270 percent. In 2000, Japan's defense budget was 63 percent larger than China's. By 2012, though, it was spending barely a third of what China did. Newspaper headlines focused on flashy hardware, like the planned acquisition of five MV-22 Osprey tilt-rotor transport planes that would be required in any scenario to airlift troops to defend the Senkakus, six of the United States' top-end F-35A stealth fighters, thirty amphibious landing vehicles and an E-2D Hawkeye AWACS-style early warning aircraft (all of which were included by the time of Abe's third annual budget). But anyone looking beyond those headlines understood that Japan was a country of increasingly precarious prosperity struggling to increase its defense outlays.

During the past generation, Japan had quietly become one of the most heavily indebted countries in the world, with debt-to-GDP ratios not far from those seen in the most crisis-stricken countries of southern Europe, like Greece. For the Self-Defense Force, the twin crises of aging and population decline have created an expensive additional problem. Exorbitant personnel costs, related to both a shrinking workforce and an aversion to layoffs, have been consuming more and more of the SDF budget, squeezing the funds available for the acquisition of new weapons systems needed to keep pace with China. Philippe de Koning and Phillip Y. Lipscy wrote in *Foreign Policy,* "Because of declining procurement budgets and higher unit costs, Japan now acquires hardware at a much slower rate: one destroyer and five fighter jets per year compared to about three destroyers and eighteen fighter jets per year in the 1990s. In the coming decade, Japan's fleet of destroyers stands to be reduced by thirty percent." In certain ways, Abe was running a sophisticated but deeply uncertain bluff.

In December 2013, Abe created a National Security Council inspired by the American body of the same name. This was an important move in an overall effort both to speed up decision making and to concentrate national security powers under the authority of the prime minister. To strengthen that historically weak office, Abe was pushing other important changes that lay at the heart of his agenda, all of which recalled the spirit and program of his grandfather. The first of these was a new security law that vastly increased the power of the state in enforcing official secrecy. By extending classification and increasing punishment for violators, Abe was throwing a thick cloak of opacity over his entire national security program. At the same time, he endeavored to impose greater political conformity on the powerful state broadcaster, NHK, while mounting a campaign of intimidation against independent media that criticized his agenda. Then, less than a year into his prime ministership, with the press more restrained, he pushed for a major reinterpretation of the constitution that sought, much in his grandfather's mold, to ease its strong restrictions against collective self-defense, via its famous Article 9, which states that the Japanese people "forever renounce war as a sovereign right of the nation or the threat or use of force as means of settling international disputes." Sensing that popular support probably did not exist for outright revision of the constitution's most famous and, for many Japanese, most distinctive and cherished element, Abe undertook what would become a politically laborious process of circumventing the article altogether via the rewriting of a number of related security laws. The aim was to create a legal framework that would allow the use of force "not only when an armed attack against Japan occurs, but also when an armed attack against a foreign country that is in a close relationship with Japan occurs." Under pressure from the LDP's major alliance partner, the Buddhist New Komeito Party, however, the government was obliged to attach a number of conditions to this language, saying, for example, that such force could only be used where an impending attack "threatens Japan's survival."

Even after agreeing to these and other limitations, however, Abe's work to gain passage of the new laws remained hindered. In an extraordinary moment of testimony before the Diet, a legal scholar called upon to defend the bills by Abe's own government unexpectedly attacked them instead. The expert, Yasuo Hasebe, of Waseda University, warned that if governments were free to pick and choose from the constitution in security matters according to the desires of the moment, the document's capacity to limit political power "would almost evaporate." At a news conference later, he added, "any interpretation of any constitutional clause now seems up for grabs."*

On his first anniversary in office, in a clear act of symbolic defiance toward China, at the end of 2013 Abe paid a visit to Yasukuni Shrine, the controversial Shinto repository of the souls of Japan's modern war heroes. Abe likened the gesture to an American leader visiting Arlington National Cemetery. The prime minister's office issued a statement by Abe that day expressing "severe remorse" for the past and adding, "It is not my intention to hurt the feelings of

---

*With a victory in the July 10, 2016, elections for the upper house of Japan's Diet, Abe and his governing Liberal Democratic Party and allied parties secured the two-thirds majority in both houses of the legislature required to propose constitutional amendments via popular referendum.

the Chinese and Korean people. It is my wish to respect each other's character, protect freedom and democracy, and build friendship with China and Korea with respect, as did all the previous Prime Ministers who visited Yasukuni Shrine." This posture won over few of Abe's critics, and drew an unanticipated sharp rebuke from Washington. A few months later, in April 2014, the prime minister sent a written message to an annual memorial ceremony that explicitly honors Class-A and other war criminals, praising those executed by the Allied powers after their conviction as the "foundation of their nation." The note went on to say, "I want to establish the existence of a new Japan that would not be an embarrassment to the spirit of the war dead." His specific attachment to the Class-A war criminals included not only Hideki Tojo, but Iwane Matsui, the commanding officer responsible for the Nanjing Massacre. This confirmed that his lineal descent from revanchists like Kishi was every bit as much ideological as it was genealogical.

On the fortieth anniversary of Japan's defeat in World War II, in 1985, Prime Minister Yasuhiro Nakasone visited Yasukuni Shrine. Afterward, he said, "I did not go to pray for Tojo. My younger brother died during the war and his spirit lies there. I went to meet my brother." Twenty-one years later, after the last of his annual visits to the shrine, Prime Minister Junichiro Koizumi, Abe's boss at the time, explicitly stated, "I do not go to Yasukuni Shrine to pay my respects to Class-A war criminals. Class-A war criminals were punished, taking responsibility for the war." Fresh off of his election, in 2001, Koizumi had been warned against visiting Yasukuni by his foreign minister, Makiko Tanaka, following her meeting with the Chinese ambassador to Japan, but he reportedly told Tanaka, "I don't take orders from anyone." Even in defiance of what may have sounded to him like an imperial-style directive from Beijing, Koizumi had sought ways to soften the impact of his shrine commemoration, unlike Abe, whose statement about Japan's commitment to "never wage war again" was by comparison merely pro forma. Abe knew that Koizumi's actions enraged China.

China responded to Abe's snub with a diplomatic offensive of its own. "The Chinese people cannot be insulted, nor can the people of

Asia and the world be humiliated. Abe must own up to his wrongdoing, correct the mistake, and take concrete measures to remove its egregious effects," said Yang Jiechi, who by now had become China's state councilor for foreign affairs, a promotion from his previous position as foreign minister. "We urge Abe to give up his illusions and mend his ways, otherwise he will further discredit himself before Japan's neighbors and the international community."

Not content to condemn the Japanese leader in all the predictable places domestically, via the routine commentary of its leaders and in domestic press coverage, China instructed its ambassadors posted all around the world to speak up against Japan in press interviews and in public forums, including the World Economic Forum in Davos. This strategy produced diminishing returns, however, in part because the zeal brought to the endeavor veered too sharply from ordinary diplomatic decorum. China's ambassador to Great Britain, Liu Xiaoming, for example, contributed an op-ed to the *Telegraph* in which he likened Abe to the most nefarious villain in contemporary children's fiction. "In the Harry Potter story, the dark wizard Voldemort dies hard because the seven horcruxes, which contain parts of his soul, have been destroyed," Liu wrote. "If militarism is like the haunting Voldemort of Japan, the Yasukuni Shrine in Tokyo is a kind of horcrux, representing the darkest parts of that nation's soul." Liu's words drew a sharp rebuttal a week later from Japan's ambassador in London, Keiichi Hayashi, which was published in the rival British daily the *Guardian.* Hayashi emphasized that it was not Japan's maritime forces that "harass neighbors on the high seas," and then said, "Although China has so far refused to enable dialogue between our leaders, I sincerely hope that it will come forward, rather than invoking the ghost of militarism of seven decades ago, which no longer exists."

Voldemort was a new image, but demonization of Japan in China is standard fare in the country's daily life. As the China scholar William A. Callahan noted:

China's patriotic education campaign has made dehumanized images of Japanese as barbarians the stock-in-trade of the

PRC's mediascape. In 2012, for instance, sixty percent of the films and television shows made at China's premier Hengdian World Studios were about the Anti-Japanese War (1937–'45), and around 700 million Japanese were killed in all Chinese films that year. (For a sense of proportion, the total population of Japan was 127 million in 2012.) This is no mere unintended consequence of a Chinese censorship regime that makes more contemporary topics off-limits for filmmakers. Especially since Xi Jinping came to power, painting Japan as a barbaric militarist state has become a key soft power objective.

The following month, Xi Jinping was rebuffed in his efforts to turn his upcoming visit to Germany into an occasion to attack Tokyo. Xi's aides had sought for him to visit the Holocaust Museum or the country's Memorial to the Victims of Fascism and Militarism, together with Angela Merkel, with the obvious hope of drawing parallels between the Nazis and the Japan of Abe. "The Holocaust is a no-go area," one official told Reuters in curt explanation of the German refusal. A foreign diplomat in Berlin added, "They [the Germans] don't like China constantly comparing them with Japan and going on about the war."

Abe's brand of public diplomacy, and the Yasukuni visit in particular, presented difficult challenges for the United States. The Obama administration worried that the Japanese leader was making trouble gratuitously in Northeast Asia, not just needlessly provoking China, but fueling enmity between Japan and South Korea as well. Washington's security strategy in the region, as well as the broader political aim of balancing against China's rise, was heavily premised on a strong working relationship between these two prosperous democratic American allies. Not incidentally, Japan's own security was also deeply intertwined with that of South Korea. This made the failure of a Japanese leader elected with a majority as comfortable as Abe's to commit some political capital to putting what is often called the "history issue" to rest even more irksome. Commenting on Abe's failure to eliminate this irritant, the prominent foreign policy thinker and strategist Edward N. Luttwak said it signaled that "Japan does not accept the discipline of strategy, that it is not a serious power."

Early in Abe's tenure, President Obama seemed to regard him as a loose and even dangerously unpredictable cannon, whose actions could potentially spark an unwanted conflict with China that would test the United States' treaty commitments with Japan. Washington had strongly signaled its disapproval of the idea of visiting Yasukuni well in advance of Abe's calculated provocation, but its counsel was ignored. In an unusually strong statement of public criticism in the context of this alliance, the United States embassy in Tokyo promptly slammed the visit, expressing "disappointment that Japan's leadership has taken action that will exacerbate tensions with Japan's neighbors." Washington was obliged by circumstances to engage in a process of careful calibration. This could be seen most clearly four months later, during Obama's April 2014 visit to Japan. Standing next to Abe at a joint press conference, the president reaffirmed American treaty commitments toward Japan in relation to its dispute in the East China Sea, calling them "absolute." Other American officials had been saying more or less the same thing for months, but although Obama was coy about what exactly the United States would do, to have the American president stand at his side on Japanese soil and commit the United States to backing Japan in any territorial clash with China over the Senkakus represented a substantial victory for Abe. In virtually the next breath, however, Obama pointedly cautioned Abe about the "importance of resolving this issue peacefully—not escalating the situation, keeping the rhetoric low, not taking provocative actions."

Obama's uneasy two-step reflected an awareness that Tokyo and Washington were deeply dependent upon each other for support in balancing against a rising China in East Asia, a task that each understood would only become more difficult in the years ahead. The two longtime allies were also insecure about each other for reasons that displayed a peculiar and distinctive symmetry. The Obama administration was interested in balancing against China, but not in provoking it, and was certainly not interested in being drawn into conflict with Beijing, least of all to fulfill its alliance obligations over something of such little immediate strategic value (and of little apparent importance to the American people) as the Senkaku Islands. Abe, on the other hand, was worried about what he perceived as the flagging nature of the American defense commitment in East Asia, as he believed was borne out by declining Pentagon budgets and by America's inability to extricate itself from a long series of quagmires in the Muslim world. Japan and China, each for their own reasons, were both obsessively watching for signs that the United States was in fact becoming a paper tiger in their neighborhood, in spite of all the talk about a pivot to Asia. For Abe's purposes, the tension and vague menace that hung over the East China Sea helped create a welcome sense of urgency that he hoped would not only let him hammer away at changing the pacifist attitudes of Japanese voters, and thereby somehow generate eventual support for constitutional change, but also keep the Americans' feet to the fire.

Whatever the American reservations about Abe's public posture toward China, or his unwillingness to distance himself from odious behavior in Japan's imperial past, at a more fundamental level the United States was strongly in favor of Abe's security-related reforms. For decades, Washington had nudged Tokyo about doing more "burden sharing," and now there was finally the prospect of having a major ally in East Asia that would commit more plainly not just to its own defense in the skies over Japan and in nearby seas, a first in itself, but also contribute to American-led operations much farther afield. Indeed, according to the so-called Guidelines for Japan-U.S. Defense Cooperation, which Washington and Tokyo concluded in April 2015, "The Alliance will respond to situations that will have an important influence on Japan's peace and security. Such situations cannot be defined geographically." From Washington's perspective, this meant Japan's legal and constitutional reforms were in America's interest. In strictly military terms, the idea of having Japan step up its role in antisubmarine or anti–ballistic missile defense in the East China Sea, or in helping sustain air and signals superiority in the skies overhead, considerably strengthened America's hand in countering growing Chinese military power. This was reflected in the revised alliance guidelines. "The Self-Defense Forces and the United States

Armed Forces will provide mutual protection of each other's assets, as appropriate, if engaged in activities that contribute to the defense of Japan in a cooperative manner."

Having Japan create its own marine corps, complete with fast airlift capacity via the MV-22 Osprey tilt-rotor aircraft, and light, helicopter-bearing aircraft carriers like the brand-new *Izumo,* offered a more credible deterrent against any Chinese attempt to grab the Senkakus in a fit of "reactive assertion" than any American president's reaffirmation of his country's treaty obligations could ever do alone. In gaming conflict scenarios, credibility is seen to correlate strongly with measurements of skin in the game, and hitherto, for different reasons, neither Japan nor the United States had invested enough of it. This was the case for Japan because its leaders had taken refuge for so long in the constitutional bar on self-defense, almost entirely free-riding on American protection under the alliance, and it was true for the United States because in a moment of crisis Chinese leaders would find it difficult to imagine Washington risking terribly much for a set of rocks theoretically controlled by an ally that had itself historically proven willing to risk so little.

The meeting with Obama strengthened Abe's hand politically just as the behind-the-scenes updating of alliance guidelines had strengthened Japan's position militarily. In terms of global opinion, both Beijing and Tokyo understood the stakes in case of any direct confrontation between the two countries. The party that appeared in the public's eyes to be the aggressor might or might not win in any hard power showdown, but it would almost certainly suffer a catastrophic blow to its soft power. Abe understood this aspect of the contest better than did Beijing, however. After his Yasukuni visit, he grasped, furthermore, that between himself and President Xi, he must never be outflanked in offering conciliation. For this reason, the Japanese prime minister made a virtual ritual of stating whenever the occasion arose that he was willing to meet Xi at any time, without preconditions and in a spirit of "forward-looking" neighborliness and mutual respect.

Beyond the stakes of global public opinion, Abe knew that his security policies unsettled his own people, who remain largely opposed to changes to the "peace constitution." They cannot shake a lingering suspicion that their assertive prime minister might lead the country once again into a disastrous war. By late 2013 there had been signs of trouble for Abe in terms of public sentiment. Polls showed deep disapproval for the secrecy law passed then, along with the law creating a National Security Council. Further signs of public anxiousness and disapproval came in mid-2014 with discussions about reinterpreting the constitution, and by 2015, with Abe's legal reforms bogged down in Diet discussions, poll after poll was showing "little appetite for responding to the rising military capability of China with even greater Japanese military capability."

One might say that Abe had an unlikely tactical ally, albeit an inadvertent one, in the Chinese leadership, which for months after the Yasukuni visit haughtily rebuffed Japanese offers to meet, treating the very idea as anathema. The Japanese side would have to own up to its history before any meeting could even be contemplated, China said. On other occasions, it was often suggested that Tokyo would also be required to acknowledge the existence of a dispute over the Senkakus. This would seem to have played into Abe's hand, both in coloring relations with the initially wary Obama and with his country's broader public image, by showing that the Japanese leader's policies alone were not to blame for the lack of progress in ties with China. Finally, just shy of two years after Abe came to power, perhaps sensing that it was making others in the region nervous while gaining no ground against Japan, China agreed to an encounter between Abe and Xi in Beijing. This was decided after a November 7, 2014, meeting between foreign ministers of the two countries on the eve of an Asia-Pacific Economic Cooperation (APEC) summit in which they reached a four-point agreement on measures to manage bilateral tensions. Even in ostensible agreement, though, the language of the two sides was redolent of the fraught historical ties between the two countries and of their posturing around the question of China's presumed centrality and moral superiority.

As with their failed diplomacy several years earlier over the sharing of hydrocarbons beneath the East China Sea, Japan and China issued separate announcements of the breakthrough, rather than an identical joint communiqué. The Chinese statement said the two sides "acknowledged that different positions exist between them regarding the tensions" over the Senkakus, a wording implying very strongly that Japan had at last recognized the existence of a dispute. The Japanese statement, meanwhile, said only that Tokyo had "recognized that [Japan and China] had different views as to the emergence of tense situations." Predictably, this led to a bout of furious competitive spinning. China's nationalist *Global Times* newspaper wrote, for example, "Now that Japan has agreed to sit down with China to talk about crisis management, it is equal to admitting that the disputes over the Diaoyu [Senkaku] Islands' sovereignty have become the new reality." China's foreign minister, Wang Yi, drew on a trope dating from the fifteenth century, when rival kingdoms in Sumatra clamored to obtain audiences in the court of the Central Kingdom, virtually abasing themselves in the process. Beijing, he said, "attaches importance to the aspirations raised by Japan [for a meeting with Xi] many times." Then in true *tian xia* fashion, he made clear that the onus for improving the relationship rested entirely upon Japan. "We hope that the Japanese side will treat this consensus seriously, faithfully implement its commitment and create the necessary favorable atmosphere for a meeting between the two leaders." Wang's language was in keeping with China's oldest diplomatic practice. As the Australian historian Martin Stuart-Fox wrote, "because China stood at the center of the world, and because the emperor enjoyed the mandate of Heaven, any friction that arose in foreign relations was necessarily due to the failure of vassal kingdoms to act in accordance with Chinese expectations."

The Japanese government worked just as hard to dispel the idea that it had compromised on anything fundamental. Speaking on Japanese television the day the agreement was released, Abe said, "[Japan's] posture has not changed. We have secured effective control over the islands." A senior foreign ministry official insisted, "It is certainly not the case that Japan's position has retreated or been eroded." In truth, the agreement designed to pave the way for Xi and Abe to meet was deliberately crafted to give each side enough wiggle room to preserve face. Even with this tactical finessing of the differences between the two countries, however, when the meeting between their leaders took place the following week, China managed to squander most of the potential benefit. In China's staging of the encounter, Xi played to the nationalist sentiment that gripped his country, which the state itself had done so much recently to build up, and in doing so, whether consciously or not, he cloaked himself in high imperial style with the visible disdain that shone on his face and the failure to utter a single word of greeting in public for his guest.

China has one of the world's most rigid and carefully choreographed protocols for meetings on its soil with foreign leaders, and its stylization, with its *tian xia* trappings, descends directly from the kowtow of ancient court tradition. "When foreign dignitaries come calling to Beijing, the receptions—whether at the airport, Tiananmen Square, Great Hall of the People, Diaoyutai State Guest House, or Zhongnanhai leadership compound next to the Forbidden City—are all carefully scripted to show the foreigner following time-honored solicitous practices," wrote David Shambaugh in *China Goes Global*:

> For example, photographs of [the president] are always staged to show him standing in a statesmanlike welcoming pose to the foreign leader's left, right hand and arm outstretched, while the foreigner is forced into a less comfortable stance with the right hand awkwardly crossing the body to shake [the Chinese president's] hand. As a result, the Chinese leader always appears relaxed and confident, whereas the foreigner often seems physically uncomfortable. When receiving a foreign leader, the Chinese official always waits behind closed doors until they are opened and the foreigner is ushered in and walks up to the stationary, standing Chinese official—a practice reminiscent of approaching the emperor's throne.

In this case, however, it was a heavily stressed-looking Abe who was strangely made to loiter alone in the ceremonial greeting space before a thick blue curtain. He looked unsure if something was amiss until Xi entered the scene from the other direction a few moments later, awkwardly stopping a bit short of his guest. Abe took another

Xi-Abe meeting in Beijing

step forward, extending his hand, a gesture that an unsmiling Xi, his face resembling that of a man who had detected a bad odor, barely reciprocated. Then, still seeking to break the ice, Abe hurriedly uttered several phrases, but Xi, who nodded ever so faintly, let the encounter end without saying a word in reply. Afterward, in the official Chinese press virtually nothing was made of the twenty-five-minute private meeting the two leaders had held, which had broken the long spell in bilateral encounters.

Japan seems to have conceded nothing more than a vague and deniable recognition of a dispute. China, for its part, had consented to a temporary easing of their confrontation. It had concluded for the time being that facing off with Japan served little purpose in the region, and had become counterproductive in terms of the reinforcement of Tokyo's security relationship with Washington. It would be wrong to interpret this as China's abandonment of the cause of asserting its complete ascendancy over Japan; it was a mere tactical retreat. China is counting on becoming stronger in the meantime, while Japan continues to age rapidly and the United States supposedly becomes weaker.

CHAPTER SIX

Claims and Markers

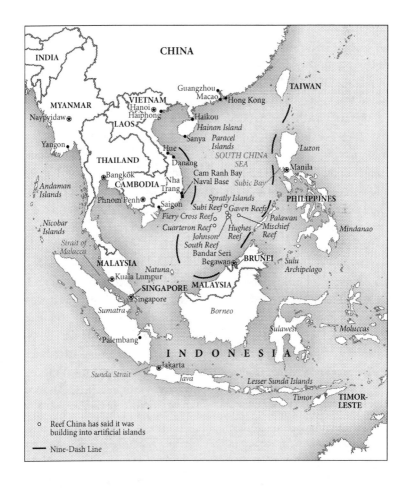

○   Reef China has said it was
    building into artificial islands

—   Nine-Dash Line

Having faced unexpectedly strong resistance from Japan, China shifted its priority to the strategic waters that lay to the south, and to the task, separate but related to that of restoring hierarchical relations with Japan in East Asia, of imposing its will on the collection of far smaller, far weaker states that ring the South China Sea. The first serious intimations of this came in the 2012 showdown with the Philippines over Scarborough Shoal. To most at the time it looked like little more than narrow opportunism, a chance to cow a neighbor that happened to be a conspicuously weak irritant. China's sealing off of this atoll, however, represented only the first sally in a broad and sustained push to claim maritime territory throughout the region.

Beijing's southward push began to take on a different coloration in the beginning of May 2014 with the sudden deployment of China's first domestically built deepwater oil drilling platform in disputed waters near the southwesternmost point in the Paracel island group, well within what would traditionally be considered Vietnam's exclusive economic zone. According to one description, the billion-dollar deep-sea exploration rig, which bore the name *Haiyang Shiyou (Ocean Petroleum) 981*, was "as big as a football field and as tall as a forty-story building." The rig was accompanied by eighty-six naval, coast guard and other vessels, including numerous fishing boats, which ringed it for protection. Several days of intense jousting ensued between the Chinese flotilla and Vietnamese vessels sent to harass it and hopefully to force its withdrawal from the disputed seas. Not only was the Chinese side better equipped numerically and in the relative displacement of its largest ships, but it was also armed with a special weapon that allowed it to bring devastating force to bear with no munitions fire and a low risk of casualties. The weapons it employed were powerful water cannons that forced the Vietnamese boats back whenever they drew close, or during bouts of determined ramming, a tactic employed by both sides. International public opinion quickly sized up the bullying Chinese action for what it was, earning Beijing widespread criticism and condemnation, as well as galvanizing most members of ASEAN out of shared concern over China's big-power tactics.

As the *New York Times* reported, in the two years prior to the

Confrontation with Vietnam over Chinese deep-sea oil rig deployment

rig's deployment, China had twice signaled its intention to explore the disputed waters around the Paracels, only to reverse course after strenuous Vietnamese protests. Just six months before *Haiyang Shiyou 981* was tugged into place off the Vietnamese coast, the two sides had announced that they would pursue joint development of undersea hydrocarbons in the area, much as China and Japan had once planned to do. Suddenly, with Xi Jinping at the helm in Beijing, though, China had changed its mind, and a state oil company official vividly captured the new prevailing sense of boldness and entitlement by calling the country's deep-sea platform China's "mobile national territory." When Vietnamese leaders first detected the rig, they apparently thought it was merely moving through the disputed waters, not setting up shop there. Once it anchored, they immediately attempted to activate the hotline that exists between Hanoi and Beijing connecting senior leaders of the two countries, but the Chinese side in effect refused to take the call. Next, Vietnam proposed dispatching a special envoy, and then asked for a bilateral meeting of representatives at the senior party level. All of these offers were snubbed.

In what was fast becoming the worst crisis between China and Vietnam since the end of the Cold War, the four days of active jousting at sea and international calls for China to desist from provocative actions failed to bring about a change of course in Beijing. To the contrary, the China National Offshore Oil Corporation (CNOOC), which owned the mobile platform, let it be known that its rig deployment was scheduled to last until August 15, a full four months. Widespread protests against the Chinese action, peaceful at first, broke out across Vietnam. Then, on May 13–14, 2014, things turned ugly, with a wave of arson and deadly riots targeting Chinese factories and businesses in Binh Duong, Dong Nai and Ha Tinh provinces. The crisis was quickly acquiring a more overt political tone, with pointed criticism by protesting Vietnamese about how their government, and implicitly how the ruling Communist Party, handled relations with China. Demonstrators began to clamor for *"thoát Trung,"* meaning an end to the loose but durable alignment with China it had sustained since the countries reconciled in the early 1990s. Some went further still and urged the strengthening of political and security ties with the United States.

This put the Vietnamese Communist Party in an uncomfortable position, its legitimacy teetering between the demands of an increasingly vociferous nationalism, once again using its domineering neighbor as a foil, as it had throughout its history, and the abiding need for fraternal relations with one of the few other ruling Communist parties in the world, which sat atop a country with which Vietnam sustained substantial ties across an unusually broad range of issues. Even while struggling to bring the protests under control and condemning anti-Chinese rhetoric, however, the Vietnamese deftly sought to leverage this sentiment. Members of the national legislature used previously unheard-of language, flatly labeling their neighbor as an adversary. In the midst of the crisis, Hanoi publicly revived memories of its most recent war with China, the 1979 conflict, a topic that had been all but banned for the last two decades. Going a step further, the Vietnamese government commemorated border clashes with China that occurred in 1984–85 but whose history had been largely suppressed ever since. President Truong Tan Sang praised the patriotism of those who defended Vietnamese territory. At the same time, Vietnam began to openly mull the idea of joining in legal action against China's maritime claims, following in the footsteps of the Philippines.

For Vietnam, with no end to the crisis in sight, activating a rapprochement strategy with the United States was beginning to look like a realistic step—and a powerful and carefully hoarded last card. Hanoi conveyed this impression through its diplomacy by suddenly initiating a telephone conversation between Foreign Affairs Minister Pham Binh Minh and Secretary of State John Kerry on May 21 to propose "implementing concrete measures to further develop the concrete partnership between the two countries." Kerry responded by inviting Minh to Washington for face-to-face consultations to be hastily convened in June. These developments raised sufficient alarm in Beijing to prompt the search for a way to climb down without losing face or making any material concessions. China's state councilor for foreign affairs, Yang Jiechi, was due in Hanoi in mid-June for a long-scheduled bilateral meeting, and managed to convince his Vietnamese counterparts to postpone a visit with Kerry until after his visit.

In all likelihood, Yang began his discussions by warning the Vietnamese that China would regard any broadening of the legal moves against it as an action so hostile as to rupture their relations. For the time being China had successfully isolated the Philippines by painting its behavior as somehow violating the supposedly consensual Asian norms of the region and acting as a pawn for an outside troublemaker, namely the United States. Even as concerns about Chinese behavior grew, most of the ASEAN states were loath to provoke Beijing, but if Vietnam, the most Sinicized country in the region, were to adopt the same approach as the Philippines, China's position would have crumbled.

According to published reports, China's opening bid to Vietnam was a four-point package for ending their standoff. First, Hanoi would have to stop "harassing" Chinese rigs and vessels; second, Vietnam would not contest China's ownership of the Paracel Islands; third, Vietnam would not pursue legal claims against China over maritime territories; fourth, with the United States certainly foremost in mind, Vietnam would not involve third parties.

The question of conceding ownership of the Paracels was clearly a nonstarter for Hanoi. Indeed, to do so might have threatened the survival of the Vietnamese leadership. Instead, Hanoi nudged things forward by postponing the conversation about a "concrete partnership" with Washington and by dialing back swelling domestic expectations on this score. In lieu of filing a case against China before the arbitral tribunal of the United Nations Convention on the Law of the Sea or any other venue, it announced that it was merely studying legal options. This appears to have been enough for the two sides to commence a climbdown choreographed in tandem. On July 15, China announced that it was withdrawing the platform due to "weather," unconvincingly invoking the approach of Typhoon Rammasun. The heart of the matter was keeping the United States at bay and Vietnam, at least loosely speaking, in its pocket.

Several weeks later, in mid-September, the Chinese Xinhua news agency announced that *Haiyang Shiyou 981* had discovered an "ultra-deep gas field" and drilled a well that could theoretically produce 56.5 million cubic feet of gas per day, or the equivalent of 9,400 barrels of oil. The find was located not near the area that had produced the confrontation with Vietnam, which the U.S. Department of Energy had already estimated was unlikely to hold major reserves, but rather 150 kilometers south of Hainan. This provided some face-saving for China after its having beaten its chest in the Paracels. CNOOC officials could boast to the national broadcaster, CCTV, that China "is now technologically capable of drilling in any place in the South China Sea."

In light of subsequent events, this represented a kind of shot across the bow of the littoral states of the region. That is because construction was already well under way of three new Chinese deep-sea oil rigs, each at least as large as the *Haiyang Shiyou 981*. The first of them, already baptized *HS-982,* was designed by a Norwegian company and built in China to drill at depths of five thousand feet or more and "withstand rough seas and typhoons." Leaving no doubt about the implications of this new fleet for China's neighbors, Wang Yiling, the chairman of CNOOC, stated that his company was preparing for more exploration throughout the South China Sea.

All this followed the traditional Chinese strategic cycle of *fang shou*, squeezing and then relaxing. Over the years, as the International Crisis Group noted, this had often followed a seasonal pattern:

> The March to June period raises the potential for clashes, with weather conducive to fishing, exploration, law enforcement patrols and naval exercises; the Scarborough Shoal and HS981 incidents were during this period. Disagreements could be carried to high-level regional forums in May-June, but those sessions could also give opportunities for engagement. The typhoon season, roughly June to September, offers a window for de-escalation and diplomacy, and regional October-November summits—Asia-Pacific Economic Cooperation (APEC), ASEAN-China and East Asia—allow leaders to engage and reaffirm peaceful intentions.

Already that June, the Chinese premier, Li Keqiang, had begun to intimate that China would seek to soothe its neighbors and encourage them to lower their guard. Li tapped into one of the most venerated myths of *tian xia*, with its origins in idealized Confucian conceptions of the way the world should be ordered and of virtue and the use of force, saying that "expansionism is not in the Chinese DNA," while assuring neighbors that talks could ensure stability in the region. This kind of traditional cosmological bluster was given unusually clear exposition in a 2010 book by the prominent military commentator Liu Mingfu, entitled *The China Dream*, one of the most popular works in China on the country's changing place in the world in recent years.

"The Chinese Empire, at its peak, could have looked at the world in disdain, because there was no other nation strong enough to challenge it, and if China had had the desire to expand, no other nation could have resisted," Liu wrote. "However, the Chinese Empire made the choice not to impose its central authority on the ethnicities or territory of other nations. As we can see, China is a nation that does not invade smaller or weaker nations and does not threaten neighboring countries. . . . China was a major power for thousands of years, but the small countries bordering it, like Annam (Vietnam), Burma, Goryeo (Korea), and Siam, all maintained their independence."

A few pages later, Liu went on to explain how Chinese preeminence in the region gradually took shape:

> In East Asia's tribute system, China was the superior state, and many of its neighboring states were vassal states, and they maintained a relationship of tribute and rewards. This was a special regional system through which they maintained friendly relations and provided mutual aid. The appeal and influence of ancient China's political, economic and cultural advantages were such that smaller neighboring states naturally fell into orbit around China, and many of the small countries nominally attached to China's ruling dynasty sent regular tribute. . . . The universal spread of China's civilization and the variety of nations that sent emissaries to China were simply a reflection of the attractiveness of the central nation, and the admiration that neighboring countries had for China's civilization. The small nations bordering China gained more than material benefits from their tributary relationship with China. Their rulers were granted royal titles by the mighty central empire, which enhanced their legitimacy, giving them political benefits, as well.

Premier Li's foray into regional diplomacy was followed up in November 2014 by a much remarked-upon speech by Xi Jinping to the Australian Parliament, in which China effectively announced its intention to take its place alongside the United States as a coequal great power. "A review of history shows that countries that attempted to pursue development with force invariably failed," he said. "This is what history teaches us. China is dedicated to upholding peace. Peace is precious and needs to be protected." Xi didn't say anything about upholding the present international system, which China, in a measured but deliberate fashion, was beginning to place under great strain. The opening salvo in China's announcement of its global ambitions, and the precursor to Xi's Australia speech, had come in

Obama-Xi summit at Sunnylands, California

a June 2013 summit meeting with President Obama in Sunnylands, California. During that meeting, the Chinese leader had told his American counterpart that Beijing sought to forge what he called a "new type of great power relations." This implied a measure of idealism in that Xi stressed the need for China and the United States to avoid the kinds of wars that have accompanied the rise of major new powers throughout history. For many it implied a kind of naïveté, or at least wishful thinking, insofar as Chinese explanations of Xi's cherished new formulation almost exclusively emphasized the need for the United States to surrender space and prerogatives in making way for its new peer rival.

Shortly after the Xi-Obama summit, Secretary of State John Kerry attempted to reframe the topic to include more of a sense of Chinese obligations to accompany any assumed new privileges, and in his remarks Kerry clearly had the Western Pacific foremost in mind.

"This constructive relationship, this 'new model' relationship of great powers, is not going to happen simply by talking about it," he said. "It's not going to happen by engaging in a slogan or pursuing a sphere of influence. It will be defined by more and better cooperation on shared challenges. And it will be defined by a mutual embrace of the rules, the norms, and institutions that have served both of our nations and the region so well." By the time of Xi's speech, though, President Obama himself had begun to explicitly warn of "disputes over territory—remote islands and rocky shoals—that threaten to spiral into confrontation," showing how far apart the visions of international order of the United States and China remained.

China's moves in the region—such as efforts to gain ground via occasional provocations—have often been likened to salami slicing, meaning that when they work well, they are calibrated so finely as to never draw direct involvement from the United States or galvanize its Southeast Asian neighbors to meaningfully coalesce in self-defense. When ASEAN concluded its annual summit on May 12, 2014, in the midst of the Chinese oil platform crisis, for example, the ten-country regional body failed even to mention Beijing involvement. ASEAN could only muster a statement expressing "serious concerns over the ongoing developments in the South China Sea," and a call to all parties to "exercise self-restraint, not to resort to threat(s) or the use of force." A previous ASEAN summit hosted by Cambodia in 2012 soon after China's takeover of Scarborough Shoal ended for the first time in the organization's forty-five-year history without a final communiqué. The vague, six-point statement issued in its place urged the implementation of a regional code of conduct, while failing to address China's takeover of the shoal from the Philippines, an ASEAN member. This was widely perceived to be the result of bandwagoning with China by Cambodia, which has been rewarded with lavish financial assistance by Beijing ever since, including $150 million in grants and $32 million in low-interest loans for infrastructure projects in 2014 alone. Beijing demonstrated its ability to cow and divide ASEAN once again in a June 2016 meeting held in China, when the body was pressured to retract a statement of criticism of recent Chinese actions in the South China Sea, causing tiny Laos, which held the rotating chair of the organization at the time, to object to the document. Whether in confusion or protest, Malaysia released the statement anyway. It had noted mildly, "we also cannot ignore what is happening in the South China Sea as it is an important

issue in the relations and cooperation between ASEAN and China."
According to Bloomberg, China's trade with Laos had risen twenty-
fold, to $2.7 billion in the ten years to 2015.

In fact, Southeast Asian societies have never shown much enthusiasm for banding together to balance against China. In his book *A
Short History of China and Southeast Asia: Tribute, Trade and Influence*, Martin Stuart-Fox resorted to the late-thirteenth-century invasion of Southeast Asia by the Mongols during the Yuan dynasty to
make this point. The region didn't lack powerful kingdoms and active
diplomacy among them, but, he writes, "successful defense of territory was no guarantee that another invasion [by China] would not
follow, as it did for the Vietnamese. The best way to avoid that was
to acknowledge Chinese suzerainty and the superiority of the Son of
Heaven. The way to ensure security, in short, was to send a tribute
mission. . . . For Southeast Asian rulers there was another, surer way
to ensure the security of their realms, and that was by acquiescing
in the Chinese world order, humiliating though this might occasionally be."

By this time, however, the *fang shou* cycles had begun to acceler-
ate, and when examined carefully in retrospect, the slices of salami
were also growing substantially thicker. No sooner had the region
begun to relax when Beijing entered a new phase that consisted of
the extraordinarily rapid construction of artificial islands in seven
disputed locations in the South China Sea where there had previously been only fully submerged reefs and what are called low-tide
formations, meaning clumps of rock and coral that only see the
light of day at low tide. This attracted little notice at first, most likely
because the initial moves were made at the height of the oil rig crisis
with Vietnam. China began at a place called Fiery Cross Reef, picking
up where it had left off in 1988.

While Vietnam spent the late 1970s consolidating its positions in
the Spratlys with the modest means at its disposal in those early post–
Vietnam War years, China was laying the groundwork for its own
big southward maritime push. As noted earlier, Beijing had forcefully evicted South Vietnamese troops from the Paracels in the waning months of the Republic of Vietnam. Possessing few of the naval

means that would have been required to press its claims on the distant islands and features in the southern reaches of the South China Sea, Beijing built up its positions in the Paracels instead. There, little noticed, it enlarged a harbor and built a runway on Woody Island, a two-kilometer-long, one-kilometer-wide islet lying about 350 kilometers south of China's island province, Hainan. For the time being, Beijing was perfectly content to bide its time; indeed, this had just become the official watchword of the Chinese Communist Party and of the state under Deng Xiaoping.

During the Mao years, and especially after the rupture with the Soviet Union, China had been ruled as a quasi-autarky. When Mao died in 1976, ending twenty-seven years of radical socialist management of the economy, the country's per capita GDP was a meager $163, barely nosing out Bangladesh ($140), whose name back then was a virtual synonym for misery. Deng's post-Mao reforms radically changed the nature of China's economic ties with the rest of the world, however, placing a heavy emphasis on international trade (including oil imports) and a consequent focus on protecting sea lanes and on the eventual need to project maritime force. The overhaul of the PLA Navy, both in its hardware and doctrine, fell to Admiral Liu Huaqing, whose strategy was called "active green-water defense." This meant gradually building up the capabilities of the navy to control the waters within the First Island Chain, so as to ward off attack from any hostile power on China's eastern coast, and to protect China's increasingly vital international trade routes. In the battles over resources within the Chinese bureaucracy, Liu also had other arguments in his favor: the suspected possibility of important oil and gas resources beneath the South China Sea, as well as food security, a perennial Chinese obsession. Specifically, that meant control over the region's vast fishing stocks.

Whatever the needs of the moment, the ideological foundations of China's move to take over its near seas were bound up in the concept of *tian xia*, namely that it was China's manifest destiny to once again reign preponderant over a wide sphere of Asia—the old "known world"—much as it supposedly had in a half-idealized, half-mythologized past. Only by doing so could the country realize its dreams; only in this way could its dignity be restored. This kind of thinking was shared not just by Deng and Mao, but by every modern Chinese national leader since Sun Yat-sen in the early twentieth century. Sun's successor, and Mao's greatest rival, the Nationalist leader Chiang Kai-shek, began keeping a diary in 1928 in which he created a daily entry under the heading *Xuechi,* meaning to avenge or wipe clean humiliation. It came to include everything from venting about the need to destroy the "dwarf pirates," as he commonly referred to the Japanese he was at war with, to the importance of creating textbooks that would inculcate his ideas about the people's duty to restore China's power and glory. Item three under this heading aimed to educate the people on the size of China. Though Chiang left that size unspecified, he mentioned four days earlier in his avenging humiliation column, "Recover Taiwan and Korea. Recover the land that was originally part of the Han and Tang dynasty. Then, as descendants of the Yellow Emperor, we will have no shame." Item four aimed to give a brief history, including the year and month, of the territory China had lost.

In 1983, China moved further toward realizing its manifest destiny in Southeast Asia when it undertook an extensive surveying exercise in the South China Sea, when two of its ships reached James Shoal, a "submerged coral reef over 1,500 kilometers from Hainan Island and just 100 kilometers from the Malaysian coast, but declared the 'southernmost point of Chinese territory'" under the framework of the nine-dash line, as Bill Hayton recounts in detail in *South China Sea.* In 1987, as Hayton writes, Beijing then sent survey ships into the Spratlys, taking advantage of a new mandate by UNESCO for countries to begin contributing to a study of the world's oceans. In May 1987, a month after the surveying had begun, China dispatched a navy ship to Fiery Cross Reef, where a single rock that emerges a meter from the sea is the sole above-water feature. The crew deposited a concrete block on it and declared the reef Chinese territory. "More surveys took place over the following months until, on 6 November 1987, the Beijing leadership invoked UNESCO in giving the green light for an 'ocean observation station' to be built on Fiery Cross Reef. Unusually, for a civilian research center, right from the start, the construction plans included a two-story barracks, a wharf, a helicopter hangar and a landing pad."

The following January, Chinese maritime construction crews showed up on Fiery Cross and began creating a sizable artificial island there. Vietnam, which for years had controlled almost all of the nearby land features, made a failed attempt in January 1988 to land troops on Fiery Cross, to which Beijing responded by occupying nearby Cuarteron Reef, the only feature of any consequence in the immediate vicinity that was not already under Vietnamese control. In what seemed like a game of geopolitical speed chess, the Vietnamese countered the Chinese move by moving to take control of Union Bank, the closest nearby feature, described by Hayton as a "large underwater mound, around 470 square kilometers in area, covered in coral reefs that stick out of the water in 31 places." On March 13, 1988, Vietnam's poorly equipped navy seized control of two features in Union Bank, Collins Reef and Landsdowne Reef, which remain under that country's control. Vietnamese troops also landed on another Union Bank feature named Johnson Reef, where they planted flags. There, however, Chinese troops confronted them, which was filmed from a Chinese ship and can be seen in a YouTube clip. It "shows the Vietnamese force standing knee deep in water as the tide rises over the reef, Hayton writes. "Huge spouts of water then erupt around the Vietnamese troops as the Chinese ships open fire. Within seconds the thin line of men has completely disappeared and 64 lie dead in the water: the machine guns are Chinese and the victims Vietnamese. The Chinese won the battle of Johnson Reef with a turkey shoot."

The story of China's push into the Spratlys resumed in August 2014. Soon afterward reports about Chinese land reclamation efforts in the area emerged. By the late spring of 2015, American officials and multiple other sources had publicly noted how Beijing, in well under a year, had pulled off a spree of island building unprecedented in scope, creating approximately 1.1 square miles of new "land" at seven different features in the Spratly archipelago that are also claimed by Vietnam and the Philippines. (By way of perspective, the naturally formed Spratly Islands, a collection of about 750 specks of assorted maritime features, including tiny cays, bits of protruding rock and coral heads, along with a few very small islands—spread out over an area as large as Iraq—collectively only measure about two square miles.) To achieve this feat, China deployed flotillas of heavy, sophisticated maritime dredging and trenching equipment—including the behemoth $130 million German-built dredger the *Tianjing Hao*— that worked day and night sucking up sand and rock from the ocean floor and hosing it onto submerged coral mounds, where it was consolidated.

Strategic domination of the region was Beijing's single-minded focus, and by early 2015 a growing collection of time-lapse photographs revealed that it had successfully built a combined air and naval base, complete with a harbor that is capable of docking the largest of China's warships, and a 3,300-meter-long airstrip, which can accommodate almost the entire range of the country's military aircraft. In the space of a few short months, Fiery Cross, which is located more than 600 miles from the Chinese coastline (and less than 250 miles from Vietnam, and about 300 miles from the Philippines, its rival claimants), had thus gone from being a one-meter-high rocky protrusion from the sea to becoming the linchpin of Beijing's push to assert its control over the entire maritime region located within the nine-dash line.

At neighboring Johnson Reef, which was seized from the Vietnamese in the 1988 turkey shoot, the Chinese are building what appear to be "radar towers, gun emplacements and a large multistory building with a footprint larger than 530 square meters" that is ten stories high, according to a satellite image assessment by the journalist Victor Robert Lee. Similar construction has also been carried out on Cuarteron Reef, and on several other Spratly features. In a sure indication of the importance of these works, the commander in chief of the PLA Navy, Admiral Wu Shengli, personally conducted an unannounced inspection visit to five of the island construction sites in September 2014, in effect consecrating the "active green-water defense" dream of his famous predecessor, Admiral Liu Huaqing, who had worked so closely with Deng Xiaoping.

China had first begun justifying its huge island-building push in

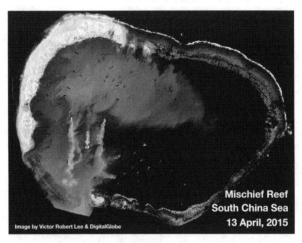

Mischief Reef
South China Sea
13 April, 2015

Image by Victor Robert Lee & DigitalGlobe

Dredging operations and island building in the South China Sea

the South China Sea by invoking the need to improve navigational and maritime safety in the region, a sort of public good that it was offering up benevolently in the interest of the region. In November 2014, just as the scale of the construction effort was becoming known, a senior air force official cited the difficulties encountered in rescue and recovery efforts following the failed search for the Malaysian airliner, Flight 370, that had disappeared while flying from Kuala Lumpur to Beijing the previous March. "There is a need for a base to support our radar system and intelligence-gathering activities," Jin Zhirui, a senior military officer, told a national security conference in Beijing. The search "made us realize we lacked sufficient air force capabilities in the South China Sea. There is a need for a base of operations in the South China Sea for state security and to protect national interests." Months later, Beijing would trot out the idea that its newly created islands could be used as places of shelter for fishermen from all nations in the region in times of dangerous typhoons.

In rhetorical style, this mirrored the events of 1987 when, as discussed above, China seized upon UNESCO's call for international ocean surveys as cover for building its first garrisoning facilities at Fiery Cross. Then, like now, the real interest in this locale was almost entirely military. China's new outposts sit at strikingly close proximity to those of its neighbors, particularly Vietnam, and because of China's vastly greater means, starting with a coast guard far larger than those of all of the other countries in the region combined, and a fast-growing navy that can easily overmatch any Southeast Asian rival, this will make it possible to quickly prevail over any local rival in a future conflict, and, more important perhaps, even intimidate them into silent acquiescence to Beijing's expansive claims. But there is a matter of even greater importance for China: its rivalry with the United States for primacy in the Western Pacific. Without that privileged position, China will not feel it has restored its place in the world.

It's possible that China favored Fiery Cross because the waters surrounding the reef quickly plunge to depths of over two thousand meters, making it an ideal jumping-off point or operational outpost for China's submarine fleet, the largest in the world and growing. Sea depths are important for both offensive and defensive evasiveness, which in submarine warfare are in any case tightly related. At present, the southern headquarters for China's nuclear submarine fleet is the Yulin Naval Base, located 580 miles to the north, at Yalong Bay on Hainan Island.

On an early winter afternoon in 2014, I stood at the edge of the bay, which to most Chinese is simply known as one of their country's best beaches, a long, undulating curve of white sand lined with resort hotels and condominiums, much like Honolulu. I had checked in to a Holiday Inn hotel at the very end of the resort zone and strolled down to the water's edge, where I had been told I could glimpse a view of the Yulin base. Sure enough, in the distance, just visible under an intense glare, sat an enormous late-model sea-gray Chinese frigate anchored at the end of a very long pier. The pier, I later learned, was built to accommodate nuclear submarines, which spend most of their time inside nearby caves. China's nuclear submarines are very insecure because the nearby waters are very shallow, and hence easy for the United States to monitor via acoustic and other means for the purposes of antisubmarine warfare. Because China's counterstrike capability partly depends on its submarine-based missiles, this renders the country's nuclear deterrence vulnerable. It also means that for the purpose of fighting a tactical war over Taiwan, or with Japan, or for the ultimate aim of challenging the United States in the Western Pacific, sortieing from the Yulin base in Hainan, China's submarines would be so closely tracked that they would be hard-pressed to mount stealthy attacks against the country's most formidable adversaries. As a fully operational secondary submarine station, Fiery Cross, by comparison, could conceivably allow Chinese boats to slip quietly into the depths, where they can better avoid detection, for deterrence purposes, and where they can prowl on the offensive in case of conflict, targeting enemy shipping well before it can reach China's inner coastal waters. Indeed, this thinking goes to the heart of the late Admiral Liu's doctrine of building a world-class Chinese navy that, step by step, could prevail in conflict, first inside the First Island Chain, then within the Second Island Chain (stretching from the central Pacific coast of Japan's main island, Honshu, southward through the Northern Marianas Islands, Guam, and down to New Guinea), and then finally, at some stage, presumably still decades off, in the wide-open Pacific and beyond.

China's rapid burst of island building has served one other important purpose, which has to do with a political feature of its dispute with its neighbors in its near seas. As we have seen, the arbitral tribunal of the United Nations Convention on the Law of the Sea was soon due to deliver a ruling on the Philippine complaint against China, which challenged the legal basis of its nine-dash line along with China's claims to rightful control of the waters surrounding all seven of the features that it has been building upon. China's crash construction program could be understood therefore as a kind of breakout strategy, intended to signal to the tribunal, and indeed to the world at large, that such legal technicalities as arguments about what constitutes an island versus a rock, or the exact contours of the Philippines' continental shelf or EEZ no longer matter in any practical or realistic sense, because China, as a "big country," in the words of the state counselor for foreign affairs, Yang Jiechi, could not be expected to cede its interests in the face of claims by small countries. As I have argued here, it amounted to a dare to the tribunal in The Hague not to rule against China, Beijing having already said that it would not be affected by the decision. Beijing clearly lost the dare, but even now it remains to be seen if it will play its ultimate card, of withdrawing from UNCLOS, inflicting a self wound, perhaps, but also a potentially grievous blow to the Convention's relevance.

By launching a crash island-building program, while simultaneously refusing to participate in the legal proceedings brought against it, China was pursuing a strategy that has been widely described as creating facts on the ground, or, better perhaps, creating facts at sea. It was the approach of a civilization with a very long-term perspective on time, a civilization that imagines itself as accustomed to gradually bringing smaller neighbors around to the idea of deferring to it in favor of their broader interests. In other words, it was very much a strategy that derives from the tradition of *tian xia*. As Alexander Vuving, a scholar of Southeast Asian relations at the Daniel K. Inouye Asia-Pacific Center for Security Studies in Honolulu, has said:

What China is doing right now is setting up various positions in the South China Sea and building them into robust points of control. Starting from this, China wants to create a situation that will lead people to look at the propensity of things and think that China would eventually win the game. They might see it as beneficial not to provoke China, to avoid a clash and give up. . . . This significantly increases the ability of China to control the South China Sea, even though they don't engage in a military clash, and it changes the calculus of the other claimants due to China's increasing dominance. Thereby, China is setting up the field so that it will psychologically change the strategic calculus of the nations in the region. If people look at the South China Sea ten years from now, what they will see is an area full of powerful Chinese bases, logistics hubs and points of control, [and] come up with the assessment that China is already the dominant force in the South China Sea. Meanwhile, the U.S. is far away.

That indeed has been China's aim all along.

In the early years of this century, the cycles of *fang* and *shou* squeezing and relaxing had observed a leisurely cadence. In the second decade, the rhythm had sped up so much as to become a blur. In fact by 2014, *fang* and *shou* were happening simultaneously. As China pushed for advantage against the small states on its Southeast Asian perimeter, it became increasingly important to have a powerful sweetener it could dangle at the same time to help offset the disquieting image of growing Chinese assertiveness and provide incentives for others to remain docile and play along. China's next big move was not rolled out in the South China Sea, at least not initially, but rather in the neglected inner reaches of Central Asia, where opportunity had long beckoned for any new partner with deep pockets, nice words to say about the local despots, and no pressure for political or economic reform.

No American president has ever visited Central Asia, thus deepening its appeal for Beijing, which had spent a decade pursuing a strategy in Africa of investing big where serious rivals were absent. So when Xi Jinping arrived in the region for a ten-day tour in September 2014, he came prepared to make a splash. In a ceremony in Turkmenistan, he launched production at Galkynysh, in the southeast of the country, which is slated to become the second-largest natural gas field in the world. In Kazakhstan (and then Russia), Xi also signed immense energy deals. But the real measure of China's ambitions was made clear in a political speech at the English-language Nazarbayev University, in Astana, which is largely run under the tutelage of a number of American and British partner universities. There, Xi proposed the launching of a "Silk Road Economic Belt," sometimes also called the Central Asian Silk Road, that would essentially lash all of Asia together, from China's rich, industrial eastern coast all the way to the Baltic Sea, with the dramatic build-out of new transportation links—including railways, highways and ports—that would promote trade and favor a greatly enhanced integration of regional markets. Much less widely noted than the infrastructure element of this scheme was its ambitious if still somewhat vague monetary component. Xi was simultaneously proposing that "all trade within the region be handled through intraregional local currency convertibility," which would in effect render the use of the dollar obsolete.

Xi followed up on his Central Asian foray with a visit to Indonesia the following month, where he announced the Southeast Asian counterpart to his big new initiative toward Central Asia, calling it the "Maritime Silk Road." Invoking the story of the fifteenth-century Chinese mariner Zheng He, Xi painted a picture of vastly enhanced trade links with China's neighbors in the South China Sea and beyond, with new ports, industrial parks, depots and processing centers, and fiber-optic-linked communications and data nodes to be created, wrapping around the southern flank of Asia and reaching into the Indian Ocean, connecting China to the Middle East, the East African coast and even Greece.

The two new Silk Roads were to be supported by a $40 billion fund that Xi would also later announce himself, as well as by a great deal of private and other public Chinese investment. These two initiatives, which were soon given the slightly ungainly name One Belt, One Road (OBOR), constituted a bid to create a new, China-centered economic order in Asia, and in the process outflank the United States and its proposal for a twelve-country Trans-Pacific Partnership, which had excluded China, at least at the outset.

By any measure, this was a remarkable turn of events, and one replete with its own sharp ironies. Less than a decade earlier, in 2005, American deputy secretary of state Robert Zoellick had publicly urged China almost patronizingly to become what he called "a responsible stakeholder" in the world. By this, he meant that with its fast-growing wealth and power, China should increasingly work toward undergirding the largely American-built and -sustained postwar international order; China should be a more willing burden sharer, which implied pulling the same set of institutional wagons that were hitched to the United States in tandem with it. Hillary Clinton, as secretary of state, in 2011 had proposed a "New Silk Road Initiative" that would boost Afghanistan's trade and transportation links with South and Central Asia. With its OBOR, China was effectively superseding both of these ideas.

By one estimate, China's new initiatives would encompass "4.4 billion people, 64 countries, and a combined economic output of $21 trillion—roughly twice the annual gross domestic product of China, or 29 percent of global GDP." On the strength of such numbers, Xi Jinping sounded almost boastful in proclaiming, "China has the capability and the will to provide more public goods to the Asia-Pacific and [to] the whole world." Although Beijing still remains careful not to speak of overturning the existing international order, it is becoming increasingly clear that the China Dream was about building something new and different that would sometimes, or perhaps even often, directly rival the century-old dream of the West. "One Belt One Road is an attempt and a pathway for China to change from being a regional power with worldwide influence to a world power with comprehensive power," wrote Xue Li, the director of the International Strategy Research Office of the World Politics and Economics Research Institute of the Chinese Academy of Social Sciences, the country's leading official think tank. Xue called the project "China's Marshall Plan."

The choice of Indonesia as a backdrop for the Maritime Silk Road announcement had a significance that went far beyond the historical symbolism reflected in the fact that Zheng He had made stops at Malacca. With its population of 250 million, Indonesia is the only country in Southeast Asia with the demographic heft to potentially serve as a counterweight to China in the region. As we have seen, this potential is enhanced by the dispersal of its many islands over an area broader than the continental United States—one that moreover sits astride perhaps the most strategic waters in the world. China's motivations in launching its new Central Asian Silk Road, with its heavy bias toward energy investments, can be seen as a hedge against a hostile power shutting down Chinese trade routes through the Strait of Malacca and thereby imperiling the Chinese economy.

There is little prospect of Indonesia becoming such an outright adversary of China, but Jakarta's interests and those of Beijing diverge over several matters of crucial importance to Indonesia. Jakarta sees itself as a natural leader of ASEAN, and that often means trying to herd its members back together when their unity fragments, especially on security issues, such as after the 2012 summit in Phnom Penh, which failed to produce a joint statement about Beijing's encroachments in the South China Sea despite the energetic lobbying of Vietnam and the Philippines. As an archipelagic state made up of thousands of islands, Indonesia takes the law of the sea particularly seriously, and managed to unite the organization in support of establishing a code of conduct in the South China Sea, and respect for UNCLOS. (China initially refused to cooperate on such a code, complaining that its ASEAN neighbors were ganging up against it.) Moreover, Indonesia has never hidden its deep skepticism about Beijing's nine-dash line. When China first filed notice with the UN staking claims based on this cartographic conceit, Jakarta immediately eschewed euphemism, saying that China's mapmaker's line "clearly lacks international legal basis."*

Xi Jinping not only announced the Maritime Silk Road idea in Jakarta, but he used the setting to launch a major charm offensive. Indonesia, he hinted, stood to benefit from big new Chinese investments in local infrastructure that were badly needed in order to bind the far-flung country more tightly together and to boost its economy. For ASEAN as a whole, the "sugarplum" loomed large indeed. As the Maritime Silk Road took shape, Chinese officials said they aimed to

---

*In March 2016, after an Indonesian patrol boat captured a Chinese fishing trawler operating in Indonesian waters near the Natuna Islands, two Chinese coast guard vessels appeared suddenly and towed the Chinese fishing vessel back into international waters, drawing strong condemnations in the Indonesian media. In late May 2016, when a similar event occurred, an Indonesian destroyer, the *Oswald Siahann-354*, was dispatched in time to block another attempted rescue of a Chinese trawler by the Chinese coast guard operating far from home. China says it does not claim the Natuna Islands under its nine-dash line, but has nonetheless invoked traditional rights to fishing in waters within Indonesia's 200-mile Exclusive Economic Zone. The following month, the Indonesian president, Joko Widodo, held a cabinet meeting aboard a warship off Natuna to demonstrate his country's resolve to protect its sovereignty over the area, and soon thereafter, Jakarta announced plans to build a naval base at Natuna.

double annual trade with the member countries to reach a level of $1 trillion in five years, an amount that dwarfs China's total bilateral trade with the United States.

The ambitions reflected in these cascading announcements stemmed from policy thinking that had begun in the earliest days of the Xi administration, when the new leadership sought ways of responding to what it regarded as American efforts to contain China via the Obama administration's rebalance. In October 2014, the Central Committee of the Chinese Communist Party convened an important meeting that it designated a "work forum on diplomacy toward the periphery." In this meeting, the need to respond vigorously to competition for influence in regions surrounding China was stressed repeatedly. The meeting focused in unusually detailed ways on "timelines, strategic objectives, and implementation plans" that would allow Beijing to take advantage of a period of what it saw as "major strategic opportunity" over the next decade and place itself on a path to realize the "complete rise of China" and become, by the middle of the century, the "defender of a Harmonious Asia-Pacific," which sounds very much like becoming principal architect and leader. In this forum, the Chinese leadership stressed the need to oblige the country's neighbors to accept China's "core interests" as a bottom-line condition for peace in the region, which amounted to terms for a new Pax Sinica. Such results were not to be obtained by simply enunciating demands and banging one's fist on the table, they said, but rather by applying "the whole of government pressure against neighboring powers."

Clearly, this would mean a rich blend of both carrots and sticks. Xi said that Beijing needed to find ways to "warm the hearts of others so that neighboring countries will become even friendlier," and said the goal must be having the region "identify more with us" and "render more support." This was an incentive-based approach to getting smaller neighbors to concede to China on points of vital interest. Others spoke, meanwhile, of finding ways to be harder on states that resist China, without allowing situations to degenerate into armed confrontation.

The rollout of China's twin Silk Road initiatives was followed a year later by the establishment of something arguably even bolder, the Asian Infrastructure Investment Bank (AIIB), which was announced in November 2014. With $100 billion in capital, this multilateral infrastructure bank was intended in part as a direct challenge to the existing Japanese-led and American-supported Asian Development Bank, and as an implicit rebuke to Washington and to the leading European nations for not having ceded more power to China within Western-dominated Bretton Woods organizations, such as the World Bank and the International Monetary Fund. The new bank's more important purpose, however, was to channel some of China's more than $3 trillion in reserves into loans that would finance big projects mostly led by Chinese companies in the realization of the twin Silk Road schemes. "Xi Jinping would like to see an early harvest from his One Belt, One Road project. The AIIB provides a conduit for that," explained Ju Jiejin, a professor at Fudan University's School of International Relations and Public Affairs, in Shanghai.

The rush of Britain and other old-line allies of the United States to join the Chinese bank quickly overwhelmed American objections and turned Washington's behind-the-scenes lobbying to slow down its progress into something of an embarrassment. The United States' public position was steadily walked back from barely concealed opposition to the bank to a denial that it had ever objected. At a news conference in Beijing in late 2014, Secretary of State John Kerry said Washington's concern was establishing rules and norms through multilateral institutions, "where all voices can be heard." But in the spring of 2015, during a joint news conference in Washington with Prime Minister Abe, President Obama personally denied American opposition. "Let me be very clear and dispel this notion that we were opposed or are opposed to other countries participating in the Asia Infrastructure Bank," Obama said. "That is simply not true." Contradicting this months later during an October 2015 visit by Xi Jinping to London, the *Financial Times* reported that the Obama administration had lambasted Britain for what it called its "constant accommodation" of China, after London announced it was joining the new bank. "The thing that upset us was that it was done in almost zero consultation with the US," a former U.S. official told the newspaper. "Britain didn't just undermine the US. It undermined the entire G7."

Chinese officials and diplomats were surprised by the ease with which they were able to gain the adhesion of so much of the world and get the new bank off the ground with fifty-seven prospective charter members. They had proclaimed into existence "the largest program of economic diplomacy since the US-led Marshall Plan for postwar reconstruction of Europe, covering dozens of countries with a total population of over three billion people," wrote the *Financial Times*. This created a new challenge of its own: how to explain the large-scale reengineering of the global architecture that Beijing had suddenly taken on so that no one is unduly threatened or disturbed.

The ideological and rhetorical lineaments for this, unsurprisingly, all derive from *tian xia*. One of the best assays that it has been given publicly so far was by China's vice minister for foreign affairs, a woman named Fu Ying. In a talk before the Asia Society in New York in 2014, she deftly explained that a key difference between the world's incumbent superpower and its only challenger was Washington's assiduous habit of maintaining alliances, which indeed constitute the very foundation of American power in Asia. "Military alliances are exclusive in nature," she said. "Where do non-members come in in its security vision? How do members balance their security interests and responsibilities with those of non-members? Second, where do alliances draw the line when it comes to principles? Do members always support their allies, be it right or wrong?" Without criticizing the United States by name, the Chinese vice minister was speaking completely in step with her president, who had expounded on a similar topic a year earlier, during the previously mentioned Central Committee "work forum" on diplomacy toward peripheral countries. On that occasion, Xi had spoken not only about the use of carrots and sticks with other countries, but also about the need to build the case for Chinese "righteousness" and to reinforce Beijing's moral authority in the world.

With the pursuit of ideas like this, China in the early twenty-first century is reaching back to its roots as the Central Kingdom, the world divided into China and non-China, a hierarchy between the two, with China, of course, at the summit. As we've seen, this hierarchy was violable only by Chinese setbacks, implicitly temporary, that stemmed from the failure of leaders to govern with virtue. The result was a loss of the mandate of heaven, bringing about defeat at war or subjugation by barbarians, and ultimately the collapse of dynasties. Other states were to be treated with impartiality, evenhandedly. Under such circumstances, formal, Western-style alliances make no sense whatsoever.

It is important never to lose sight of bedrock concepts like these, because they provide insights into how Xi Jinping imagines ordering the world of today and tomorrow. They help to understand the China Dream itself. This is not because China is about to proclaim the restoration of Confucianism, even if recent leaders, including Xi, have eagerly, if selectively, and perhaps even cynically, promoted some of its language and tenets. It is even less because Beijing is about to baldly proclaim its superiority to the world, even if it is not hard to track conversations in the country, including occasional official statements, about China's superior culture, or its superiority outright. Rather, it is because habits of mind and of statecraft are as deeply ingrained in China as they are in the West, if not far more so, given the longevity of China's political culture. This means that when Chinese leaders proclaim that the United States would be welcome in the AIIB, even after Washington had scornfully lobbied against it, they were not merely tweaking the Americans to score cheap propaganda points by demonstrating their own openness of spirit and equanimity, which of course they were. They were also making a show of their cultural self-confidence and belief that as China gradually but inevitably becomes number one, other countries including the United States will slowly come to appreciate that resistance is pointless and will petition for admission into the Chinese court.*

---

*These big new initiatives were almost immediately followed by a strong downturn in the Chinese economy, and a corresponding surge in international pessimism about China's medium-term growth prospects, along with signs of mounting anxiety among the Chinese leadership.

To say that Washington has been ill-prepared to deal with a China that strategizes in these terms would be a vast understatement. It has focused disproportionately on the hard elements of the power balance with China, where things of late have not gone so well for the United States. On the eve of a 2015 tour of Southeast Asia, the U.S. defense secretary, Ashton Carter, on his way to attend an annual Asian security conference in Singapore, sought to reassure friends and allies of American resolve, pointedly flying over the Strait of Malacca and presumably authorizing the overflight of Fiery Cross Reef, with a CNN crew aboard, by a P8-A Poseidon surveillance aircraft, one of the newest weapons systems in the Pentagon's arsenal that had been pressed into service in the Western Pacific as part of the American pivot. On the CNN broadcast of the P8-A overflight, Chinese soldiers below can be heard saying, "This is the Chinese navy. This is the Chinese navy. . . . Please leave immediately to avoid misunderstanding." After a few moments of being ignored, the radio operator on the ground then shouted the blunt and simple command, "You go!"

Carter vowed to frustrate any Chinese efforts to limit the movements of American vessels in the South China Sea. "The United States will fly, sail, and operate wherever international law allows, as we do all around the world," he pledged in Pearl Harbor. He also said, "We will remain the principal security power in the Asia-Pacific for decades to come."

It took less than a month for the tune in some precincts of the American national security establishment to change, but change it did. On June 26, 2015, Deputy Secretary of State Anthony Blinken decried China's continuing land reclamation projects in the South China Sea and called upon Beijing to freeze them. It was the analogy that he then drew, however, which was most telling: "In both the eastern Ukraine and the South China Sea, we're witnessing efforts to unilaterally and coercively change the status quo—transgressions that the United States and our allies and partners stand united against." And as with Russia in the Ukraine, there was scarcely anyone who believed that the American protests or overflights or whatever other gestures might be mustered could alter China's course.

Conclusion

An old era is passing, even if the contours of what is yet to come have not truly announced themselves. We cannot fully imagine them in part because of the sticky weight of the present. But even if the quotidian blinds us, an age of substantially redistributed global power is fast approaching.

A time when China will be able to keep the United States at bay is rapidly drawing nearer. A time when, by virtue of its new wealth and rapidly increasing military strength, it can hold at mortal peril the United States' most precious symbols of national power, military assets like the aircraft carrier, may already be upon us. Witness the installation of high-frequency radar towers on four of China's artificial islands in the Spratlys late in 2015, followed by the positioning of antiaircraft barriers and fighter aircraft in the Paracels early in 2016. The new radar capabilities appear designed to counter the stealth features of the most sophisticated U.S. Air Force platforms, such as the F-22, the B-2 bomber and even the newest American combat jet, the F-35 fighter. Commenting on the new radar stations, the Center for Strategic and International Studies warned that Beijing was on the verge of turning the South China Sea into a "Chinese lake." Admiral Harry B. Harris Jr., head of the U.S. Pacific Command, said one would "have to believe in a flat Earth" not to grasp that China's goal was to "achieve hegemony in East Asia."*

---

* Already, a decade earlier, in October 2006, in a demonstration of American vulnerability, a Chinese Song-class attack submarine surfaced within nine miles of the USS *Kitty*

The questions that preoccupy us cannot be given a definitive answer: What will China seek to do with its newfound power? Just how far can it take things? There are different schools of thought and analysis for assessing such matters—realism, liberalism, hegemonic transition and constructivism, along with narrower frameworks, such as power transition theory. To these I have added a cultural and historical view of China's approach to geostrategic power, and the very least it tells us is that China will wish to restore itself to the pinnacle of affairs in East Asia, and that it will seek to maximize its power and its space for maneuver. Along with this comes its expectation that at least in its own sphere, others, near and far, will eventually bow before its authority. This turn of events was anticipated a half century ago, when China was still a weakling by almost any measure except population, by the Singaporean scholar Wang Gungwu, who wrote in Fairbank's edited volume *The Chinese World Order: Traditional China's Foreign Relations*:

> In the nineteenth century China had to be forced "to enter into the family of nations." China joined an international system in which all members were equal, at least in theory; in fact, it was difficult for China not to feel that it had been admitted as a less-than-equal member. China's bending before superior force was a rational decision which the Western powers could approve of, but there has always been some doubt as to whether it was simply a decision of strategy and whether the Chinese ever believed that equality really existed in international relations. This doubt partly explains the current feat that, when given the chance, the Chinese may wish to go back to their long-hallowed tradition of treating foreign countries as all alike but unequal and inferior to China.

The open questions that flow from this thought concern the broader world as much as they do China and its own region. Is it plau-

---

Hawk aircraft carrier, having gone undetected as the *Kitty Hawk* sailed on a training exercise in the East China Sea, between Japan and Taiwan.

sible to think that this "emerging potential superpower," as described in one recent assessment, having secured broad preeminence in East Asia, would stop there? This isn't a matter of what the Chinese say today, nor even what they may privately believe. It is deducing that having gone very far and very fast over the space of a short few generations, China may very well not be inclined to stop there.

Thinking like this does not flow from any obsession with what many in the United States already fancy as a Chinese threat. In fact, what I've set out to do is to "normalize" China. Having said so much in this book to explain the particulars of its history, this is the place to deexceptionalize its attitudes toward strength and power. The prevailing impression, of a China in a great hurry, is what leads many people to think of it as a threat. But however great its apparent haste today, many of its seemingly outsized present-day energies may gradually diminish or even peter out in due time.

What will come in the near future, though, as China continues to grow in both power and assertiveness, will try the nerves and patience of many in the United States and elsewhere. Geopolitically, America will undoubtedly attempt to hold firm here and there, but the coming decades will also necessarily involve a certain amount of yielding to China. Deciding how to accomplish this as smartly as possible will require both cultivating a much finer understanding of America's aspiring peer rival and appreciating that even the best outcomes will often involve important departures from today's comfortable and familiar patterns of global power. After a crisis with China over Taiwan in 1996, when the United States deployed two aircraft carrier battle groups nearby, sailing one of them through the narrow strait separating the island from the mainland, Bill Clinton's defense secretary William Perry crowed, as if anyone could have missed the point, that "the strongest military power in the western Pacific is the United States." Although America will remain powerful in the region for the foreseeable future, unquestioned preeminence in the seas near China will be among the first things to go.

In a widely commented-upon 2015 essay entitled "Beyond American Predominance in the Western Pacific," Michael D. Swaine, a senior associate at the Carnegie Endowment for International Peace, writes,

"For both the United States and China, the primary future strategic challenge is to develop a mutually beneficial means of transitioning away from U.S. maritime predominance toward a stable, genuine balance of power in the Western Pacific in which neither nation has the clear capacity to prevail in an armed conflict. This will be difficult to achieve and potentially dangerous, but nonetheless necessary, given the existing and future trends shaping the region." Swaine said that, among other things, such an outcome would require new agreements between Beijing and Washington over fresh new dispensations for the Korean Peninsula, Taiwan and the entire South China Sea. In essence, he said, this would mean turning those places into effective "buffer zones" from which neither the United States nor China would be able to project power.

Whether or not this is realistic or politically achievable, best outcomes for the United States will often simply mean stopping China somewhere short of the maximal pursuit of its strategic goals. Already, regarding China's near seas, Washington is nudging Beijing to sign on to rules and processes that would allow other regional stakeholders to feel that their interests have been sufficiently acknowledged and that some measure of their rights is protected. A China that ignores these urgings will be a China that perversely assists the United States in maintaining its current place in the world. This is because the more China subjects others to its sharp elbows, the more others will naturally band together to defy it, as the last few years have already shown, while clamoring for the United States to stand with them. Edward N. Luttwak wrote about this predicament perceptively in his 2012 book *The Rise of China vs. the Logic of Strategy*:

Riders in a crowded elevator cabin into which an extremely fat Mr. China has just stepped in must react self-protectively if he is becoming fatter at a rapid rate, squeezing them against the walls—even if he is entirely unthreatening, and indeed affable. True, the crowded elevator cabin already contained an even fatter, louder, and frequently violent Mr. America, but simply because he had long been a fellow rider, almost everybody had over the decades come to a satisfactory accommodation with his noisy bulk, with the exceptions—Cuba, Iran, North Korea, Syria, Venezuela—themselves an advertisement for Mr. America's respectability. Most important, Mr. America is not rapidly becoming fatter, thereby undermining past accommodations and compromises, and it is also very helpful that no sudden threats are to be feared from him, because of his mostly very open democratic decision processes.

If China continues to puff itself up against a motley collection of smaller states that challenge it today, that will be nothing compared to the coalition that will await in the future. An increasingly wary India, for example, is already firming up relations with both Japan and Vietnam with an eye to China, while jockeying to avoid being outmaneuvered by Beijing in its own backyard in places including Sri Lanka and Nepal. Similarly, Japan is also rapidly strengthening its defense ties with the Philippines and Vietnam (and India), aiming to boost their ability to deter China. In April 2016, one of the largest destroyers in the Japanese fleet, the antisubmarine helicopter carrier *Ise,* made a port call at Subic Bay, in preparation for joint drills with the Philippine navy. "It is aimed at promoting friendly relations [with the Philippines], but it also includes a strong message to keep China in check," a senior Japanese defense ministry official told the *Yomiuri Shimbun.* After the eventual demise of Vladimir Putin, the Russians may awaken one day to their own special Chinese nightmare: the discovery that the West, with its rule-driven ideology, is not their country's main threat, as they have been told for the last two decades, but rather it is a resurgent, highly modernized and increasingly revisionist China that gives the greatest cause for worry. Its eastern neighbor is, after all, a country with historical grievances over territory, where the population of a single border province, say, Heilongjiang, far outweighs the dwindling number of people in the entire Russian Far East. Under circumstances like these, the agonizing question of how to keep Russia whole will shift from Europe to Asia, and it will not be easily answered.

For all of the potential for radical change that the future seems to hold out for us, the most important lesson to retain may well be that contrary to superficial impressions, the urgency that sometimes gives China the appearance of a juggernaut is driven more by a sense of precariousness and self-doubt than by any clearly reasoned belief in its inevitable triumph. The history of Chinese dynasties has always been written by their successors, and a primary factor in their judgment has been whether under the outgoing regime the imperial realm shrank or expanded. It is in this light, ultimately, that Xi Jinping's China Dream must be seen, along with all of the talk about his country's "sacred" mission to recover territory supposedly lost to others throughout history. Xi and his fellow leaders appreciate that China's window of opportunity to transform the geopolitics of the world of *tian xia*, and perhaps of the world itself, has never been opened wider, and very possibly will never open this wide again.

The reasons for insecurity on this point are multiple. Most obviously, the historical era of miracle growth in the Chinese economy is finally coming to an end, a fact that brings with it the possibility of widespread disaffection, unrest and a variety of other threats to the legitimacy of the Chinese Communist Party. Likeliest of all in this regard is a nerve-racking struggle to escape what is known as the "middle income trap," a situation that has bedeviled many developing countries wherein they have risen fast during an initial ascent from poverty only to plateau or even stagnate before their citizens can attain anything like the levels of generalized prosperity enjoyed in wealthy Western societies.

On the military side, as elsewhere, China has benefited greatly so far from its position of playing catch-up. This has offered it all of the economies classically enjoyed by the late starter: exemption from the need to build its way expensively through generation after generation of costly weapons systems the way the United States has, say, since World War II. China has been able to make many strides simply via emulation, aided heavily by industrial theft and espionage. As a result, its first high-tech systems were built at comparatively low cost, facilitated even further by the availability of cheap labor and capital. As it catches up or potentially even surpasses the United States in a variety of economic measures, including perhaps in military budget, however, these sorts of savings will steadily diminish. In an article entitled "The Implications of Seapower," published in *World Politics Review*, Andrew S. Erickson, a close observer of China's military, wrote:

> One of China's greatest strengths in recent years has been its ability to allocate tremendous resources rapidly to programs for security, infrastructure and technology development. Many of these programs are seen as extremely inefficient. As competition for resources intensifies, the leadership's ability to allocate increasingly contested funds will face unprecedented tests. Domestic challenges may place increasing demands on, and fund claims by, China's internal security forces, whose official budget already exceeds the PLA's. This has a special significance for China's ability to continue developing its external military capabilities. Beijing has judged that it can sustain multiple overlapping advanced programs simultaneously. China's shipbuilding industry—which, aside from its missile, space and electronics industries, produces China's most advanced indigenous defense products—is producing multiple modern submarine and warship classes. But how long such dynamic investments can be sustained is unclear.
>
> The closer the PLA approaches leading-edge capabilities, the more expensive and difficult it will be for it to advance further, or even to keep up with the general increase in global capabilities. China's cost advantages decrease as military equipment becomes less labor-intensive and more technology- and materials-intensive. The more sophisticated and technology-intensive PLA systems become, the less relative benefit China can derive from acquiring and indigenizing foreign technologies, and the less cost advantage it will have in producing and maintaining them.

On September 3, 2015, Xi Jinping occupied the place of honor atop a reviewing stand in Beijing's Tiananmen Square for a nearly daylong ceremony honoring the country's armed forces. It was the materialization of a side of his political project that was less well known outside of the country than his China Dream—his so called Military Dream, which he had invoked on numerous occasions during his first two years in office, but only before domestic audiences. This dream was to turn China into a first-rank power during the normal span of his ten-year mandate as head of the Communist Party. On this day, the prized fruits of China's heaviest expenditures on military modernization were on full display. There were antiship cruise missiles and short-range ballistic missiles, as well as intercontinental ballistic missiles. On public view for the first time there were also the Dongfeng-21 and -26, the world's only antiship ballistic missiles, which China had recently developed with only one obvious adversary in mind, the United States. If their performance lives up to their billing, with their heavy payloads these weapons would be able to sink even the largest moving enemy ships. This was in accordance with a major new military policy document issued under Xi in 2015, which said that for China "the traditional mentality that land outweighs sea must be abandoned." Great importance, it said, must be attached to "strategic management of the ocean."

For all of the self-confidence that Xi radiated amid the heavy choreography, for Beijing the challenges that strew the path to his goals are enormous. Although China is the only conceivable potential challenger to American preeminence in the world today, according to some assessments the gulf separating the two countries in comprehensive power is larger than any that has separated the world's strongest countries in modern times, save for the immediate post–Cold War's so-called unipolar moment that lasted between 1991 and the early 2000s.

To be sure, China has already dramatically narrowed the GDP gap with the United States, but assessments like these suggest that such a crude traditional measure may conceal more than it illuminates. Despite its recent wealth, China lags badly in technological capacity and innovative technologies. Its scientific and engineering base, things that are only built up slowly through gradual, cumulative processes, is still nowhere near that of the United States. Even though it has become a manufacturing powerhouse, its industrial base remains critically weak in some respects in comparison. And it also lacks America's dense tissue of highly competitive multinational corporations, just to highlight a few of its disadvantages. In the area of defense, whether in the research, design and production of new advanced weaponry, sophisticated systems integration or less esoteric-seeming things like training, combat experience and flexibility of command, China lags even further still. As a result, in the recent estimate of one Chinese expert, the People's Liberation Army "is still more suited to fighting a Vietnam-era conflict than a 21st century engagement." One widely read review of the challenge China poses, "The Rise and Fall of the Great Powers in the Twenty-First Century: China's Rise and the Fate of America's Global Position," by Stephen G. Brooks and William C. Wohlforth, concluded that "the nature of technology itself has changed to make it even harder for entrants to match the military capabilities of the leading state. Ultimately, the military and technological hurdles [facing] China will remain formidably high for decades."

Cognizant of the many imposing barriers to challenging the United States in an across-the-board fashion, Beijing seems to have opted for a strategy of naval and maritime expansion, Xi's "management of the ocean," in other words. Even here, though, the road will be dauntingly steep. China, unlike the United States, is still in the very early phases of building a world-class navy. In his article on seapower, Erickson goes on to say that almost everywhere maritime weapons systems have been developed, the costs tend to increase substantially faster than inflation, typically at a clip of around 9 percent a year, which at some point in the near future would begin to present China with an astounding financial burden if things were to remain on this course. The challenge China will face in trying to develop and acquire advanced weapons affordably will be further compounded by the fact that, unlike the United States, which has defense pacts with sixty-eight countries, Beijing has no network of allies who can be counted upon to purchase these systems, thus reducing their unit cost through economies of scale and in some cases shared development costs. Right now the country is in a kind of sweet spot, where the economy is still growing fast, albeit hardly as fast as it once did, and defense expenditures are at a relatively modest level in relation to GDP. Many analysts expect that this window of opportunity will begin closing by the end of Xi's mandate, hence the urgency for the country to lock in as many gains as it can now.

Factors like these leave the United States, the incumbent super-power, with a raft of options that go well beyond any kind of direct confrontation with China. Prominent among them is a so-called denial strategy, a variation on the Michael Swaine notion of turning the South China Sea into a buffer zone—a region that neither power can decisively exploit. In their previously cited article, Brooks and Wohlforth write:

> [T]he premise of the denial strategy is that even if China is able to effectively deny U.S. surface ships and aircraft access to the area close to its coast, it can be prevented from using this geographic space as a launching pad for projecting mili-tary power in a conflict. In this view, the geographic area close to China's coast is not poised to flip from being a potential launching pad for the United States to use surface ships and aircraft to project power against China in a conflict to being a potential launching pad for China itself to use these military assets to project power. Instead, the zone close to China's coast is poised to turn into a "no man's land (or "no man's sea") in which neither state can effectively use surface ships or aircraft for force projection during a conflict. This change is notable but needs to be kept in perspective. The 1990s baseline had China, a putative great power, incapable of preventing the globe's leading military power from having essentially unfet-tered access to its airspace and ocean surface right up to its ter-ritorial border. That China has begun to reverse this unusual vulnerability after spending tens of billions of dollars over decades is hardly surprising.

History, in my estimate, would eventually come to regard this as a relatively small price to pay for both preserving peace between the United States and China and sustaining American support for regional allies and the favorable economic and institutional arrangements that come with this order.

It is in this light that one can begin to understand the Obama administration's rebalance to Asia, and not as a crude bid to contain China. A country of China's size cannot be contained, and any effort to do so would be strongly counterproductive. Rather than containment, what is going on is a process whereby Washington is steadily raising the costs for China by repositioning 60 percent of its naval assets to the neighborhood and upgrading military cooperation with its allies, Japan, the Philippines and others, while helping medium-sized powers like Vietnam. The United States is playing the role of facilitator, or matchmaker, encouraging all kinds of new or enhanced relationships among Chinese neighbors. The most salient U.S. goal, as I've written elsewhere, is "thickening the web among China's wary neighbors, who have a shared interest in keeping China from using force to upend the existing order. Japan excepted for the time being, none of these countries has any prospect of prevailing toe-to-toe with China, and some of them are frankly Lilliputian. In concert, however, even if not in outright alliance, they may be able to effectively tie down the giant and constrain it to a mutually acceptable set of international rules."

Although some argue that they are unwise, efforts like these by the United States to raise the costs for China in its bid to reign paramount in its region should not be understood as unusual. This is what great powers do as a matter of course, seeking to balance against real or potential rivals and trying to frustrate or complicate each other's moves, while avoiding direct confrontation. China routinely decries American behavior like this as an objectionable relic of what it calls Cold War thinking, but Washington's efforts are mirrored by an array of Chinese actions aimed at similarly raising costs for the United States or eroding its position in the region. These range from Chinese efforts to more tightly economically integrate its region through the One Belt, One Road program, for example, to developing what might be called military counter-encirclement positions in Pakistan and Djibouti, say, where China is building a major

Indian Ocean port and a distant military base, respectively. Even more pointedly, Beijing is heavily focusing its military resources and research and development on what is known as an Anti-Access/Area Denial (A2AD) weaponry, whose deployment will steadily make it harder (and more costly) for the United States to deploy naval assets, or even to render secure military bases on land in Japan, Guam and elsewhere in the Western Pacific. This is because China is steadily acquiring the capacity to rain relatively cheap long-range missiles on these installations from its mainland. Among other things, these weapons would destroy runways, making it much harder for the U.S. Air Force to employ manned long-distance bombers.

Then there is the matter of geography. With its One Belt, One Road scheme, Beijing is striving mightily to integrate on favorable terms its most broadly defined neighborhood, a space ultimately stretching from littoral Southeast Asia as far west as Europe, via immense new infrastructure projects and the business deals it will hopefully generate, but this changes nothing about the fundamentals of its physical disposition in the world, which seen objectively is chock-full of challenges. According to the Columbia University political scientist and China scholar Andrew J. Nathan, "China's immediate periphery has a good claim to be the most challenging geopolitical environment in the world for a major power." Seven of its neighbors rank among the twenty-five countries with the largest armies in the world, and although China has the largest army in the world, it suffers a net two-and-a-half-to-one disadvantage compared to the aggregate troop strength of the six largest armies among its immediate neighbors. As Andrew J. Nathan and Andrew Scobell wrote in *China's Search for Security*:

> Although no country is immune from external influences—
> via migration, smuggling, and disease—China is the most
> penetrated of the big countries, with an unparalleled number
> of foreign actors trying to influence its political, economic,
> and cultural evolution, often in ways that the political regime
> considers detrimental to its own survival. . . . No other coun-
> try except Russia has as many contiguous neighbors.

Numbers aside, China's immediate neighborhood is uniquely complex. The contiguous states include seven of the fifteen largest countries in the world (India, Pakistan, Russia, Japan, the Philippines, Indonesia, and Vietnam—each having a population greater than 89 million); five countries with which China has been at war at some point in the past seventy years (Russia, South Korea, Japan, Vietnam, and India); and at least nine countries with unstable regimes (including North Korea, the Philippines, Myanmar/Burma, Bhutan, Nepal, Pakistan, Afghanistan, Tajikistan, and Kyrgyzstan). China has had border disputes since 1949 with every one of its twenty immediate neighbors, although most have been settled by now.

Above and beyond all other constraints, though, it is China's demographics that will constitute the country's greatest challenge by far over the coming decades, and for the United States it is this same population factor that will provide its greatest buffer against a sustained challenge. Furthermore, the changing dynamics of the Chinese population more than anything else explain Beijing's apparent present haste. China has embarked on a process of aging that is due to proceed with almost unprecedented speed, soon placing the country in a situation unparalleled in world history: that of a newly and still very unevenly modernized country that must build a social welfare system on the backs of a rapidly declining workforce. In journalistic shorthand, China's new dilemma is known as the paradox of growing old before growing rich. What few understand is that the scope of this problem is so great that Chinese society would be stuck with this outcome even if the formidable economic growth of the last several decades could somehow be sustained.

Instead, China's economy has recently embarked on what most experts believe will be a protracted secular decline in growth rates, which even in many of the more optimistic scenarios will eventually slow the economy a tick faster than the rates familiar in more mature industrialized countries. Michael Pettis, an economist who has long resided in China, where he teaches at Peking University, has emerged as one of the most astute analysts of economic trends in the country. A recent assessment of his is characteristic of the spreading caution about China's medium- to longer-term growth potential among economists. It is based on a view that countries that experience "miracle growth" periods, such as China, or Japan before it, gradually become heavily overdependent on investment and run up ultimately unsustainable levels of debt. Few economies that have experienced this pattern have escaped prolonged periods of agonizing adjustment efforts and low growth. "Beijing will run around busily implementing or not implementing reforms," he wrote. "Growth will slow sharply, to below 3–4% on average before the end of Xi's administration, whether it is disruptive or non-disruptive. And so well before the end of the decade, today's bears will be saying 'Aha! See? China was unable to grow, just as we said.'" In other writings, Pettis speaks of 3–4 percent growth as China's upside potential.

Interestingly, some of the most incisive critical assessments of the initiatives of Xi Jinping to stave off an outcome like this come from Chinese, not Western analysts. Writing about One Belt, One Road, Xi's most ambitious program to date, Xue Li of the Chinese Academy of Social Sciences said:

> The Marshall Plan rebuilt the economies of the developed European countries. The One Belt One Road plan, however, promotes economic development in economically backward countries. More than sixty countries are involved and so its overall implementation will be much harder than the Marshall Plan. Speaking frankly, sparking economic development in all the states along the route is beyond the capabilities and responsibilities of any one country. China must consider the economic risk and the political risk inherent in the implementation of the One Belt One Road strategy.

Xue went on to say that, even taken together, the included states would be incapable of absorbing China's present overproduction of many industrial goods. To take one example, according to the *Economist*, China's excess capacity in steel exceeds the total steel output of the United States, Japan and Germany. "A very large economic entity,

China's economic problems can generally only be solved by making internal adjustments. We cannot pin our hopes on the undeveloped countries along the two routes."

History offers other reasons to temper expectations for China's economic future. As a German economist at a Bretton Woods institution in Washington remarked to me, there appears to be a correlation between efforts by rising powers to create ambitious new global or regional economic and political institutional arrangements as a way of "locking in their power and influence" and the rough peaking of those powers' economic strength in relation to the rest of the world. The United States led in the creation of the World Bank in 1944, for example, when its share of global GDP peaked at 36 percent. Japan created the Asian Development Bank in 1966 and Germany created the European Bank for Reconstruction and Development in 1991, following unification, each country close to or at its relative peak. In scale of ambition, Xi's two biggest foreign policy initiatives, One Belt, One Road and the associated Asian Infrastructure Investment Bank, certainly warrant comparison with these predecessors. No causation is being suggested here, but if this pattern holds, even loosely, China, which accounts for nearly 17 percent of the global economy, may also be approaching a plateau in terms of relative size at best.

As the aging problem worsens, toward the middle of the century and beyond, it will exacerbate things by exerting a serious drag of its own on the economy. A 2007 paper by Mark L. Haas, a Duquesne University political scientist, which asserted that global aging is "not only likely to extend U.S. hegemony (because the other major powers will lack the resources to overtake the United States' economic and military lead), but deepen it as these other states are likely to fall even farther behind the United States," raised many eyebrows, often out of skepticism or puzzlement. Among a blizzard of other data, the author noted that "China alone in 2050 will have more than 329 million people over 65, which is equal to the entire current populations of France, Germany, Japan and the United Kingdom combined." It went on to say that China will have one of the highest median-age populations in the world, and that its ratio of working-age people would shrink to be among the lowest.

Looking back, what is most striking about this forecast is how dramatically it falls short of taking the full measure of China's demographic crisis. Increasingly nowadays, even within China, the country's demographic situation is being spoken of in terms of a crisis. According to the *South China Morning Post*, "the authorities expected twenty million new births in 2014, but only 16.9 million babies were born. By May 2015, only 1.45 million couples—out of 11 million eligible ones—had applied to have a second child. The figures reflected a surprisingly low level of interest." In October 2015, after years of handwringing over deteriorating population trends, the Chinese government announced the lifting of its so-called One Child Policy; almost all parents were now allowed to have two children. Alas, the move is widely believed to be too late to make an important difference, coming at a time of massive urbanization and rising incomes, when (as in many wealthy countries) few parents yearn for the cost and bother of having larger families. "The government recognizes that the cohort born in the 1950s and '60s will move into old age, disability, and chronic disease very soon," Zheng Zhenzhen, a leading demographer at the Chinese Academy of Social Sciences, told me in Beijing shortly after the end of the One Child policy was announced. "It really doesn't matter what happens now with the fertility rate. The old people of tomorrow are already here."

The number of young males in the country has begun to decline, and between now and 2050 the number of men between twenty and twenty-five, that is, of prime military recruitment age, will fall by half.

The aforementioned expression "getting old before getting rich" has become a popular journalistic catchphrase about China, but even it fails to capture the full weight of the challenge that lies ahead for the country. Over the past thirty years, the total fertility rate, or the number of children born per woman, has fallen from a fairly robust 2.5 to 1.56, which is well below the replacement rate, and the UN Population Division predicts it will continue falling, reaching 1.51 by 2020. America's rate, by contrast, is 2.08, and rising. At this rate, as a consequence, China's population is set to fall below one billion by 2060. By that time, America's, by contrast, will have grown to over 450 million. "People say we can be two to three times the size of America's economy," Yi Fuxian, a Chinese demographer at the University of Wisconsin told the *New York Times*. "I say it's totally impossible. It will never overtake America's, because of the decrease in the labor force and the aging of the population."

China is indeed on pace to become one of the oldest large societies in the world. By 2050 the median age will be forty-nine, or nine years older than America's. This will produce an immense surge in the number of pensioners, and those retirees will be entering a system that is relatively new (launched only in 2000), covers fewer than 400 million people and is already severely underfunded. (According to the *Economist,* unfunded pension liabilities already amount to roughly 150 percent of gross domestic product.) What is worse, China's retirees will be flooding into the pension system at a time when the workforce is experiencing a massive contraction. The only way to compensate for this is to offset the decline in the number of workers by productivity increases, but even here there are mounting problems. In December 2015, Du Yang, an economist with the Chinese Academy of Social Sciences, told me that after years of rapid growth, China may have entered into a period of prolonged decline in productivity growth. "We've started shifting from the manufacturing to the service sector, but the productivity in services is even lower than in manufacturing," he said. "The reason countries fall into the middle-income trap is that they face decreasing productivity." What this means is that the need to fund China's ballooning social security costs, beginning in the near future, will create monumental new burdens for the society that will radically undermine most of today's straight-line assumptions about the country's future wealth and power.

One of the best-reasoned assessments of what this means for China comes again from Mark Haas. By 2040, he says, as expensive chronic diseases pervade the population, rapidly aging wealthy countries like France and Germany will have to spend more than five times on elderly care than they currently spend on defense. By roughly that same time, though, China's "median age will reach the levels of France, Germany, and Japan today, but at GDP per capita

levels significantly lower than these states currently possess. Consequently, when China's aging crisis hits with full force, it will, at best,
confront similar economic and fiscal constraints as France, Germany and Japan do today.... China's political leaders, beginning in
roughly 2020, will be faced with a difficult choice: allow growing levels of poverty within an exploding elderly population, or provide the
resources necessary to avoid this situation. To the extent that these
politicians succumb to the significant moral and political pressure
pushing for the latter decision, America's relative power position will
be benefitted."

Already, demand for nursing home beds, a relatively new and
poorly organized sector, is skyrocketing. Presently, nine million Chinese are estimated to suffer from dementia (more than twice the
figure in similarly-sized India, because of the higher ratio of older
people in China), and the prevalence of this condition is projected
to increase fourfold by 2050. Another recent study has found that
11.6 percent of Chinese suffer from diabetes, another costly chronic
disease that correlates with aging. Alarmingly, fully half of the population is estimated to be prediabetic. I believe factors like these help
explain why Xi has made his dramatic break with the famous Deng
Xiaoping strategy of biding one's time. Xi has decided that China
must seize whatever advantages it can now before its window of
opportunity slams shut within the next ten or, at best, twenty years.
This will make the immediate future a moment of maximum risk
between the United States and China.

It has already become tempting for many who look at snapshots
of these two countries to conclude that the United States has little
chance of holding its own against what is often perceived as a Chinese
juggernaut. Such pessimism is out of place. To be sure, the United
States must play its hand well, which is by no means guaranteed, even
if its advantages are many and varied in nature.

Driven in large part by immigration, the American population
stands to grow smartly during the remainder of this century, by
30 percent in the next forty years alone. China's will peak in 2025,
aging radically along the way. In the second half of this century, their
diverging demographic trajectories will shrink the enormous four-

to-one population size ratio that China enjoys over the United States today to something approaching two to one, and along the way there are strong reasons to believe that Americans will continue to enjoy a large lead over Chinese in terms of per capita gross domestic product.

As these numbers help reveal, while American politics, especially at presidential campaign time, often veer into delusional negativism over immigration, it has been and will remain one of this country's most important competitive assets, constantly replenishing the U.S. population with eager, energetic and ambitious people—especially young people—who will drive enterprise and innovation, along with economic demand, in the decades ahead, while flattening out the stark aging curves that will afflict China (and Japan and Europe). Ironically, a great many of these newcomers will be Chinese, who are already the third-largest source of immigration to the United States. The absorption of these newcomers is as key to the sustenance of the U.S. Social Security system as it is to the future of American economic growth, as well as to the staffing of what will remain a large, dynamic and technically advanced American military.

Beyond this powerful story of numbers, the United States has at least one other formidable asset that will provide it crucial ballast during the risky and uncertain two to three decades ahead: values. There is no mistaking that China is a nation on a civilizational march, one driven by its deep sense of its historical place in the world and the entitlement this brings it. As we have seen, this sense has only been augmented by the feelings of exclusion that China suffers from having been at its weakest point in terms of power during the very century when the rules and customs of our international system were laid down and put into practice and its many benefits locked in. It is important for Americans to understand this, and even to look upon China's predicament with sympathy. The only peaceful way forward, however, is to work even harder to draw China into the international system, making room for Beijing here and there as needed along the way. This need has been most painfully obvious with regard to the international financial system, including representation at the World Bank and International Monetary Fund, or in more generous and ready acceptance of Chinese initiatives like One Belt, One Road. But it is also needed just as much in international security matters, where China's voice should be welcomed more and heard.

The United States should undertake such things with serenity. China today is a country virtually without allies, whereas America has a globe-spanning network of formal alliance relationships and a set of fundamental values—based on participation, openness, democracy and human rights—that constitute a tremendous appeal for peoples all over the world, often including citizens of unfriendly states and outright foes. The liberal international order, which ended the two-millennia-long run of the old China-centered order in Asia and with the United States as its center became truly global, "is not just a collection of liberal democratic states but an international mutual-aid society—a sort of global political club that provides members with tools for economic and political advancement," wrote John G. Ikenberry in a 2011 essay. There is no prospect of China overmatching it anytime in the foreseeable future. China's political system operates out of an instinctive distrust of the people it admin-isters, and that distrust is mirrored by the people's feelings toward the system. China's soft power abroad, meanwhile, is largely limited to appeals to prosperity, and to the negative notion that relatively closed and authoritarian states should work together to prevent interference in their affairs by others, or even pollution by democratic values. As even Yan Xuetong, one of China's most well-known inter-national relations theorists and an unabashed advocate of his coun-try's pursuit of geopolitical preeminence, has written, "an increase in wealth can raise China's power status but it does not necessarily enable China to become a country respected by others, because a political superpower that puts wealth as its highest national interest may bring disaster rather than blessings to other countries."

A China that is treated as an equal with much to contribute to human betterment, but met with understated but resolute firm-ness when need be, is a China that will mellow as it advances in the decades ahead, and then most likely plateau. That is a China that will grow more secure in its greatness, a China we can live with.

Afterword to the Vintage Books Edition (2018)

The writing of this book was completed late in the summer of 2016, when that year's presidential election in the United States still loomed a few months in the future.

The American public was well aware that nothing was guaranteed, but a preponderance of opinion polls, together with the majority of analysts of both parties, predicted a victory by the centrist Democrat and former secretary of state Hillary Clinton. And from Clinton, furthermore, pretty much everyone in the American body politic—and indeed in the world at large—expected a high degree of continuity in the conduct of United States foreign policy.

Although the persistent closeness of the race late into that summer had already caused some commentators to speculate about the cost to America's standing in the world that a Trump victory might engender, eight months after the event I feel confident in writing that virtually no one publicly envisioned the full weight of the coming blow to America's power, prestige, and influence abroad.

Current events were never intended as the centerpiece of *Everything Under the Heavens*. This book's arguments derive principally from an effort to examine the long course of Chinese history and to draw lessons from it. As readers will know, its central focus is on certain striking patterns of behavior that have emerged over time in China's relations with its neighbors. And yet, the Trump victory now weighs so heavily upon any reasonable scenarios for the near and medium-term future, which I mostly touch upon in the conclusion, that I felt readers deserved an updated assessment.

Some of the factors that weigh on these scenarios were already known about Trump even as I completed this manuscript: his grudg-ing attitude toward alliances, including some of America's oldest and closest geopolitical partnerships; his hostility toward multilateral agreements, whether the Paris climate accord or the Trans-Pacific Partnership; his persistent, self-destructive attraction to Russia, a country whose meager economy is only roughly the size of Italy's; his loud hostility toward China on trade issues; and his racially charged opposition to immigration and antagonism toward Mexico, the United States' important neighbor to the south.

I argued herein that, given the monumental scale of the challenges that China now faces after more than a generation of extraordinary growth, a United States in relative but far from absolute decline should above all avoid the temptation to panic about its position in the world. On the contrary, it need "only" attend moderately well to its own problems, while avoiding committing big, gratuitous blun-ders.

The spirit of this take on things seems to find its reflection in Barack Obama's parting advice to Donald Trump, contained in a handwritten letter for his successor, left for Trump in the Oval Office in the drawer of the famous Resolute desk. "American leadership in this world really is indispensable," Obama wrote. "It's up to us, through action and example, to sustain the international order that's expanded steadily since the end of the Cold War, and upon which our own wealth and safety depend."

Even if not wholly unforeseen, in each of the areas I listed above, President Trump has wreaked significant damage on America's pros-pects in the decade or two ahead. Whether with NATO or with Japan and South Korea, the American alliance system is a major source of leverage for the United States, and a force multiplier, as much for American diplomacy and its economy as it is for its military. The current international system is not only largely of American design but is kept alive and vigorous by constructive American leadership and engagement.

Beyond these transoceanic alliances, at least since the earliest for-mulation of the Monroe Doctrine, which China itself in some ways is now attempting to emulate, American leaders have understood and embraced the important advantages their country derives from its position as the unquestionably paramount power of its own home region.

The increasingly complex markets and integrated production chains of the Americas constitute a major, albeit low-profile, pillar of prosperity for the United States. As argued at length in this book, immigration from the world in general, but from Mexico and the rest of Latin America in particular, constitutes a competitive boon for the United States at the precise moment when China stands on the precipice of an aging crisis and demographic crunch of unprecedented scope.

In less than a year, President Trump has attacked all these things, weakening the United States in ways that would be hard to surpass even if one set out with that objective in mind. During his first months in office, Trump pulled out of TPP while simultaneously calling NAFTA into question. Keenly aware of the undreamed-of gift it has received from Washington, China, meanwhile, has responded by enthusiastically pursuing a free trade agreement of its own with Mexico, while further strengthening its efforts to integrate Eurasia on favorable terms through its One Belt, One Road initiative. As it did so, China's foreign minister, Wang Yi, said that Beijing had begun to "innovate upon and transcend the past three hundred years of traditional Western international relations theory."

This writer believes that in the medium to longer term, the United States will recover its footing in many of these areas. Presidential mandates, after all, last a maximum of eight years, and although few foresaw the changes that Trump has brought to American politics, it is hard to imagine future leaders so willingly throwing away what have so long been inherent American advantages.

What may be of even greater long-term negative impact on the position of the United States than geopolitical considerations like these, however, is the crudeness of language and comportment that President Trump has brought to his office, his administration's casual disregard or abandonment of values that so many have for so long associated with American global leadership, even if in their frequent and sometime even grave breach.

I speak here of this society's vocal commitment to democracy, to openness in trade, and to human rights and human dignity. The United States' rhetorical attachment to such ideals and the deep civic creed that has built up around them have created strong ripples in societies in every corner of the globe, of belief in its positive example and of a better future for themselves.

The abandonment of all but the flimsiest attachment to virtue, which is the flip side of the Trump credo called America First, is an invitation to the rest of the world to reassess its attraction to the United States. The loss of this sort of power, which stems foremost from example, is the biggest gift to America's rivals and foes, and it will be the hardest to recover.

Acknowledgments

This book's earliest roots lie in my childhood, when I heard stories from my late father, stories told to him during the Great Depression by his father, a railway postal worker, about the great civilization found on the opposite side of the globe: China.

My grandfather, Joseph B. French, an Ohio native, never left the United States, but as an African American man beset by the stark racism of his era, he was deeply curious about China's history and its place in the world, and within his means he read everything he could about it.

One of the things that fascinated Joseph French most about China was the idea, vividly passed on to me by my father through these stories, that in a world of suffocating white supremacy, the Chinese somehow managed to sustain the belief that they were more civilized, and hence superior, to every other people. What this meant, I was told as a boy, was that to the Chinese the rest of the world, whites included, were to one degree or another mere barbarians.

In the segregated Washington, D.C., of the 1960s, where I grew up, this was an astounding thing to hear, and although it was not a guiding motivation in my research, this book project, along with much subsequent life experience, gave me a chance to explore for myself the tenacity as well as the limits of this enduring Chinese worldview.

I studied Chinese politics in college, in the immediate aftermath of the Cultural Revolution, even then never suspecting that I would end up working there, and yet sustaining a fascination that was driven in substantial part by memories of those childhood conversations. And for this, along with many other things, I thank my father, David M.

French, a surgeon and public health physician who brought stories back home from Asia in the 1970s after investigating the American bombing of Hanoi for the U.S. Senate, and the grandfather, Joseph, whom I scarcely knew.

Career-wise, I came to the topic of China only somewhat belatedly and by a most circuitous route. As a foreign correspondent for many years, I worked my way there step by step, through lengthy stints in Africa, jobs in Latin America and the Caribbean and then a posting in Japan, my first stop in Asia. It was in Tokyo, nearly two decades ago, that the first ideas that gradually set me on the precise path of this book began to percolate. The starting interrogation, an observation, really, was that Northeast Asia (China, Japan and the Koreas) shared at least as much in history, culture, religion and philosophy—a common "moral order" in the felicitous phrase of Benedict Anderson—as the leading countries of Western Europe (Germany, Britain and France). And yet while the Europeans had overcome centuries of calamitous warfare and persistent distrust, the Asians clearly had not. The starting question for me was, why? As readers will know, my focus changed with time, eventually leading me to study Chinese history, and in particular the ways in which China has interacted with its neighbors over time. The journalist in me brought this same preoccupation to today's world and has tempted me to try to see over the horizon and give a tentative sense of expectation, based on what I've learned, of what is to come.

Along the path toward the completion of this effort I have benefited hugely from the wisdom, generosity and encouragement of others who helped shepherd me during my long, veering mid-career turn toward China.

For years, Liu Hui, whom I first met in Tokyo, has been an important guide to both societies, Japan and China.

I have also been extremely fortunate to have always had wonderful language teachers, beginning with Japanese, studying under Janice Omura in Hawaii, and a pair of graduate students, Kyoko Matsuda and Yuko Yamamoto. During the five years I lived in Tokyo, I studied with the redoubtable Akiko Nagao, who coupled immense grace and unfailing rigor with great historical and political curiosity.

Moving to Shanghai in 2003, I worked with a coven of Chinese teachers who tag-teamed me for eight hours a day for six months before I took up my assignment there. Among them were Jiao Bei and Chen Yuyun. After moving back to New York in 2008, definitively bitten by the bug, I returned regularly to China, eventually meeting the Chinese teacher who would have the greatest impact on me of all, Wang Zhao (Alicia), who tutored me in Shanghai one summer, then moved to New York for graduate school and taught me there, but more important has now helped me with several books with Chinese-language transcriptions of interviews and many other vital matters.

Since initiating this project proper, I have learned a great deal from conversations and other exchanges with any number of generous colleagues, including historians of East Asia, diplomats and specialists in many related disciplines. Some of the people named here will be well aware of their importance to this work, others perhaps less so. For reasons of sensitivity and discretion, a number of people must go unnamed. To all of you, your thoughtful help with my queries, your encouragement or your example is truly appreciated. Having said this much, however, the usual disclaimers apply: The responsibility for any shortcomings or errors is of course entirely mine.

This very incomplete list begins with Wang Gungwu and Prasenjit Duara, both of whom generously made time for me in Singapore. I would also like to thank Rafael Alunan, Ian Buruma, Ying Chan, David Cowhig, Roger Des Forges, Mark Driscoll, Clayton Dube, Alexis Dudden, Yoichi Funabashi, Carol Gluck, Krizna Gomez, Douglas Howland, Hsin-Huang, Michael Hsiao, Bruce Jacobs, Joan A. Kaufman, Paul A. Kramer, Le Hong Hiep, Narushige Michishita, Nguyen Giang, Nguyen Hong Thao, Mark Selden, Shen Dingli, Shi Yinhong, Chito Santa Romana, Akio Takahara, Makiko Inoue, Keith Weller Taylor, Edith Terry, Tran Truong Thuy, Wu Shicun, Scott Snyder, Su Hao, Sun Yiting, Michael M. Tsai, Sebastian Veg, Yang Bojang, Marilyn Young and Zhang Ruizhang.

Jeffrey Wasserstrom, a University of California, Irvine, historian of China who seems to know everyone and to have read everything, has been a friend and valued interlocutor for years, and he provided many suggestions on the manuscript. My distinguished colleague at Columbia University, Andrew J. Nathan, also provided many helpful criticisms and insights. Edward Friedman, emeritus professor at the University of Wisconsin, Madison, also kindly read the book in manuscript and gave me many invaluable pointers. Jeffrey Kingston, a Temple University historian of Japan and of Asia, has done much the same, and on several occasions generously gave me the run of his homes in Japan. Joe Arden, another friend of long date, similarly allowed me to use his home in Bangkok during a critical phase of the writing.

More indirectly, I have drawn immense benefit from the community of scholars who are members of Chinapol, which I have followed closely now for well over a decade.

I would also like to thank the University of Hong Kong for hosting me as a visiting professor in 2013, during which time I made important progress in getting this project off the ground. Thanks also go to the libraries of Columbia University, which I have long reveled in. Without a resource like this, my work on this book would have been impossible and my life much impoverished.

Thanks go to the editors of *The Atlantic* magazine, and in particular Don Peck, for their sustained interest in my work and their support.

My sincere appreciation goes to Gloria Loomis, who has always been my literary agent, matching a sharp sense of humor with inexhaustible wisdom.

Notes

INTRODUCTION

6 "To control the barbarians": Lien-Sheng Yang, "Historical Notes on the Chinese World Order," in *The Chinese World Order: Traditional China's Foreign Relations*, ed. John K. Fairbank (Cambridge, MA: Harvard University Press, 1968), 23.

6 "When two emperors appear": Mark Mancall, quoting Kham-dinh Viet-su thong-giam cuong-muc, in "The Ch'ing Tribute System: An Interpretive Essay," in ibid., 64–66.

7 "Like any hegemonic": Takeshi Hamashita, "Tribute and Treaties: Maritime Asia and treaty port networks in the era of negotiations, 1800–1900," in *The Resurgence of East Asia: 500, 150 and 50 Year Perspectives*, ed. Giovanni Arrighi, Takeshi Hamashita and Mark Selden (London; New York: Routledge, 2003), 20.

7 Finally arriving in China: Alain Peyrefitte, *The Immobile Empire* (New York: Alfred A. Knopf, 1992), 88.

7 "Most dynasties collapsed": John King Fairbank, "A Preliminary Framework," from the oft-cited here *The Chinese World Order,* 3.

8 "Ever since the founding of 'New China'": Wang Jisi, "The 'Two Orders' and the Future of China-U.S. Relations," *ChinaFile,* July 9, 2015.

9 "Modern China's difficulty": Fairbank, *The Chinese World Order,* 4.

10 "awakened my country": Zheng Wang, *Never Forget National Humiliation: Historical Memory in Chinese Politics and Foreign Relations* (New York: Columbia University Press, 2012), 74.

11 "to give [China]": Shi Yinhong, "China's Complicated Foreign Policy," commentary published in *European Council on Foreign Relations,* March 31, 2015.

CHAPTER ONE: NATIONAL HUMILIATION

15 "a rope in the offing": George H. Kerr, *Okinawa: The History of an Island People* (Boston: Tuttle Publishing, 2000), 22.

18 Captain Fanell's comments: Geoff Dyer, "China Training for Short, Sharp War, Says Senior US Naval Officer," *Financial Times,* February 20, 2014.

19 "being able to fight": "Xi Steps Up Efforts to Shape a China-Centered Regional Order," *China Brief* 13, issue 22, Jamestown Foundation, November 7, 2013.

21 In marking Japan's defeat: "The Danger of China's 'Chosen Trauma,'" *ChinaFile,* September 2, 2014.

21 Meanwhile, to turn on the television in China: David Lague and Jane Lanhee Lee, "Why Chinese Directors Love to Hate Japan," Reuters, May 25, 2013.

22 On top of all these extraordinary measures: Gabriel Wildau, "China's Biggest State Banks Recruited into Stock Market Rescue," *Financial Times,* July 18, 2015.

25 "2,000 troops or up to 600 tons of weapons": Richard Fisher, "Osprey Versus Bison in the East China Sea," *Diplomat,* September 20, 2013.

25 There are few missions this hovercraft seems more suited to: "Zubr-Class LCAC Gives PLA Quick Access to Disputed Islands," *Want China Times,* January 2, 2014.

26 "has the ability to reach": "If China grabs Senkakus, U.S. military Would Snatch Them Back: Top Marine Commander," Kyodo News, April 12, 2014.

26 Privately, the two countries: Kuniichi Tanida, "SDF, U.S. Forces Worked Out Joint Operations Study Plan in 2012 to Combat Feared Senkaku Invasion," *Asahi Shimbun,* January 25, 2016.

28 There were 58,820: Jun Hongo, "Five Things to Know About Centenarians in Japan," *The Wall Street Journal,* September 12, 2014.

29 The Keidanren report: "Global Japan: 2050 Simulations and Strategies," Keidanren, April 16, 2012, 1.

31 Ōkōchi Teruna, a former feudal lord: D. R. Howland, *Borders of Chinese Civilization: Geography and History at Empire's End* (Durham, NC: Duke University Press, 1996), 43–44.

32 By 1870, Japan had already deeply imbibed: *Japan-China Joint History Research Report* (provisional translation), *Modern and Contemporary History,* vol. 1 (March 2011), 18.

32 The Chinese sometimes used particular insults: Howland, *Borders of Chinese Civilization,* 100.

33 "There was no tradition": Christopher Ford, *The Mind of Empire: China's*

History and Modern Foreign Relations (Lexington: University Press of Kentucky, 2010), 85.

33 Finally, in 1876: *Japan-China Joint History Research Report,* 20.

34 "The Qing envoys . . . were not favorably disposed": Ibid., 21.

35 Almost all the members: Howland, *Borders of Chinese Civilization,* 63.

37 He represented a country of 8 million subjects: Alain Peyrefitte, *The Immobile Empire* (New York: Alfred A. Knopf, 1992), xviii.

37 Qing China, a country of 350 million people: James L. Hevia, *Cherishing Men from Afar: Qing Guest Ritual and the Macartney Embassy of 1793* (Durham, NC: Duke University Press, 1995), 31.

38 Befitting a fast-industrializing nation: Stephen R. Platt, "New Domestic and Global Challenges, 1792–1860," in *The Oxford Illustrated History of Modern China,* ed. Jeffrey N. Wasserstrom (Oxford: Oxford University Press, 2016).

38 Contemporaneous Chinese accounts make no mention: Peyrefitte, *The Immobile Empire,* 206.

40 Far more important to the Chinese: Kerr, *Okinawa,* 67.

40 Worse, officials in the imperial court: Morris Rossabi, *China Among Equals: The Middle Kingdom and Its Neighbors, 10th–14th Centuries* (Los Angeles: University of California Press, 1983), 3.

40 Early in his mission to open relations: Peyrefitte, *The Immobile Empire,* 120, 236.

42 After visiting both Japan and China: *Japan-China Joint History Research Report,* 24.

43 The goal was to sustain plausible deniability: Kerr, *Okinawa,* 166.

43 The stark difference in Ryukyuan attitudes: Ta-tuan Ch'en, "Investiture of Liu-Ch'iu Kings in the Ch'ing Period," in *The Chinese World Order: Traditional China's Foreign Relations,* ed. John K. Fairbank (Cambridge, MA: Harvard University Press, 1968), 162.

43 The Japanese ordered them to simply comply: Ibid., 148.

44 "Letters were prepared": Kerr, *Okinawa,* 152.

44 "With the severing of diplomatic ties": Seo-Hyun Park, "Small States and the Search for Sovereignty in Sinocentric Asia: Japan and Korea in the Late Nineteenth Century," in *Negotiating Asymmetry: China's Place in Asia,* ed. Anthony Reid and Zheng Yangwen (Honolulu: University of Hawaii Press, 2009), 34.

46 "fed the growing sense of self-confidence": Joshua A. Fogel, *Articulating the Sinosphere: Sino-Japanese Relations in Space and Time* (Cambridge, MA: Harvard University Press, 2009), 24.

46 it disloyally ran the Ryukyus: Kerr, *Okinawa,* 164.

47 President Franklin Pierce rejected Perry's idea: Ibid., 4.

48 "that most superlative": Hevia, *Cherishing Men from Afar,* 26.

49 "The islands called the Lew Chew": Kerr, *Okinawa,* 85.

50 "By mid-century": Fogel, *Articulating the Sinosphere,* 49.

51 Shō Tai explained: Ibid., 384.

52 "China's internal order": Wang Gungwu and Zheng Yongnian, *China and the New International Order* (New York: Routledge, 2008), 5.

52 "lay at the center of the sphere": Fogel, *Articulating the Sinosphere,* 4.

53 "Cutting China": Ian Buruma, *Inventing Japan: 1853–1964* (New York: Modern Library, 2003), 50.

CHAPTER TWO: ISLAND BARBARIANS

57 It features a drooping, segmented line: Zhiguo Gao and Bing Bing Jia, "The Nine-Dash Line in the South China Sea: History, Status and Implication," *American Journal of International Law,* January 2013.

58 "The early history of Chinese use": Ibid.

59 "They will control the South China Sea": Prashanth Parameswaran, "US South China Sea FONOPs to Increase in Scope, Complexity: Commander," *Diplomat,* January 28, 2016.

60 Conventional interpretations of the international law of the sea: Sam LaGrone, "Chinese Warships Made 'Innocent Passage' Through U.S. Territorial Waters off Alaska," USNI News, September 3, 2015.

60 As one recently retired Chinese general said: Minnie Chan, "China Needs Third Runway in Spratly Islands to Break US Grip in South China Sea If Tensions Escalate, Experts Say," *South China Morning Post,* September 16, 2015.

63 The king was received by Li Hongzhang: Rebecca E. Karl, *Staging the World: Chinese Nationalism at the Turn of the Twentieth Century* (Durham, NC: Duke University Press, 2002), 58–59.

66 In a 1903 essay: Ibid., 64.

67 "Distance and oceans": Paul A. Kramer, *The Blood of Government: Race, Empire, the United States, & the Philippines* (Chapel Hill: University of North Carolina Press, 2006), x.

67 "How can this island": Karl, *Staging the World,* 88.

68 "The Philippine sea": Ibid., 93.

68 "Not only for Liang, but for many others": Ibid., 90.

70 "Japan is an island nation": Kawashima Shin, "China's Re-interpretation of the Chinese 'World Order' 1900–40s," in *Negotiating Asymmetry: China's Place in Asia,* ed. Anthony Reid and Zheng Yangwen (Honolulu: University of Hawaii Press, 2009), 146.

71 "when China was a great power": Ibid., 149.

71 In his March 1924 Principle of Nationalism: Ibid., 148.

72 Vietnam "had grown to understand China": Keith Weller Taylor, *The Birth of Vietnam* (Berkeley: University of California Press, 1991), xvii.

72 "the future of the East": Shin, "China's Re-interpretation of the Chinese 'World Order' 1900–40s," 148.

75 Obama's news conference: Michael D. Shear, "With China in Mind on a Visit to Manila, Obama Pledges Military Aid to Allies in Southeast Asia," *New York Times,* November 17, 2015.

75 So far, China has responded coolly: Yufan Huang, "Q+A: Yan Xuetong Urges China to Adopt a More Assertive Foreign Policy," *New York Times,* February 9, 2016.

75 In March 2016, the Philippines announced: Trefor Moss, "U.S. Set to Deploy Troops to Philippines in Rebalancing Act," *Wall Street Journal,* March 20, 2016.

77 "China's bottom line on joint exploration": Barry Wain, "ASEAN: Manila's Bungle in the South China Sea," *Far Eastern Economic Review,* January 18, 2008.

81 "although Chinese navigators": Press Release, The South China Sea Arbitration (*The Republic of Philippines v. The People's Republic of China*), The Permanent Court of Arbitration. July 12, 2016.

82 "The South China Sea arbitration": "Yang Jiechi Gives Interview to State Media on the So-called Award by the Arbitral Tribunal for the South China Sea Arbitration," Ministry of Foreign Affairs, People's Republic of China, July 15, 2016.

83 "Suppose the tribunal makes": Christina Mendez, "China Will Snub Int'l Tribunal Ruling on Sea Row with Philippines," *The Philippine Star,* September 25, 2014.

84 "We have this pact": "Philippines Looks Set to Move Away from the U.S., Its Longtime Security Ally," Reuters, May 31, 2016.

85 "This game will take time": Paterno Esmaquel II, "Game of Diplomats Begins in West Philippines Sea," *Rappler,* July 16, 2016.

87 "The world's largest aircraft carrier": Carl Thayer, "What If China Did Invade Pag-asa," *Diplomat,* January 16, 2014.

87 Many analysts claimed: One of the best examples of this analysis was by Xie Yanmei, "China Hardens Position on South China Sea," *Diplomat,* July 16, 2016.

CHAPTER THREE: THE GULLET OF THE WORLD

91 "The discovery of India": Felipe Fernández-Armesto, *Pathfinders: A Global History of Exploration* (New York: W. W. Norton, 2006), 177.

91 But with the aid of a Muslim pilot: Arturo Giráldez, *The Age of Trade: The Manila Galleons and the Dawn of the Global Economy* (Lanham, MD: Rowman & Littlefield, 2015), 41.

91 Despite the Indian ruler's striking a conciliatory stance: Bailey W. Diffie and George D. Winius, *Foundations of the Portuguese Empire, 1415–1850* (Minneapolis: University of Minnesota Press, 1977), 224.

91 "by 1487, El Mina": Martin Meredith, *The Fortunes of Africa: A 5,000-Year History of Wealth, Greed, and Endeavor* (New York: PublicAffairs, 2014), 98.

92 Just one year after laying out this strategic vision: Diffie and Winius, *Foundations of the Portuguese Empire,* 227.

92 By virtue of this position: Janet L. Abu-Lughod, *Before European Hegemony: The World System A.D. 1250–1350* (London: Oxford University Press, 1991), 311.

94 Portugal's claims to the Spice Islands: William Lytle Schurz, *The Manila Galleon* (Boston: E. P. Dutton, 1959), 16.

96 The best modern scholarship confirms: Edward L. Dreyer, *Zheng He and the Oceans in the Early Ming Dynasty, 1405–1433* (New York: Pearson Longman, 2007), 102.

96 Christopher Columbus's largest ship: F. W. Mote, *Imperial China, 900–1800* (Cambridge, MA: Harvard University Press, 1999), 614.

97 "In the language of a later era of navalism": Dreyer, *Zheng He and the Oceans in the Early Ming Dynasty,* 9.

97 "If the imperial kindness extended": O. W. Wolters, *The Fall of Srivijaya in Malay History* (Ithaca, NY: Cornell University Press, 1970), 30.

98 "These were thus friendly": Bill Hayton, *The South China Sea and the Struggle for Power in Asia* (New Haven, CT: Yale University Press, 2014), 24–25.

100 This time, in order to permanently secure: Sun Laichen, *Southeast Asia in the Fifteenth Century: The China Factor* (Singapore: NUS Press, 2010), 52.

101 "The goods and treasures without name": Dreyer, *Zheng He and the Oceans in the Early Ming Dynasty,* 34.

101 "When thousands of troops": Robert Finlay, "The Voyages of Zheng He: Ideology, State Power, and Maritime Trade in Ming China," *Journal of the Historical Society* 8, no. 3 (September 2008): 337.

102 Chinese history can be understood as: Sun Laichen, *Southeast Asia in the Fifteenth Century,* 44.

102 Such thinking clearly animated: Ibid., 57.

103 Ming archives record the killing: Geoff Wade, "Ming China and Southeast Asia in the 15th Century: A Reappraisal," Asia Research Institute Working Paper Series No. 28, National University of Singapore, July 2004, 14.

104 The fighting of land battles: Dreyer, *Zheng He and the Oceans in the Early Ming Dynasty,* 81.

105 "the first gunpowder empire": Sun Laichen, *Southeast Asia in the Fifteenth Century,* 61.

105 "The strength of our dynasty": Ibid., 58.

106 Some historians see this move: Finlay, "The Voyages of Zheng He," 338.

107 "The forceful aspect of Yongle's policy": Ibid.

107 "China should not stoop to fight": Louise Levathes, *When China Ruled the Seas: The Treasure Fleet of the Dragon Throne, 1405–1433* (New York: Simon & Schuster, 1994), 179.

108 Such a decision would have dramatically reduced: Bruce Swanson, *Eighth Voyage of the Dragon: A History of China's Quest for Seapower* (Annapolis, MD: Naval Institute Press, 1982), 40.

108 "A desire for contact with the outside world": Levathes, *When China Ruled the Seas,* 180.

108 Whatever the cause for the about-face: Freeman Dyson, "The Case for Blunders," *New York Review of Books,* March 6, 2014.

108 Beginning in the thirteenth century: Abu-Lughod, *Before European Hegemony,* 8.

108 "crew members were told by the natives": Diffie and Winius, *Foundations of the Portuguese Empire,* 381.

109 At the other end of the Eurasian landmass: Sun Laichen, *Southeast Asia in the Fifteenth Century,* 70.

109 "The 'Fall of the East' preceded the 'Rise of the West'": Abu-Lughod, *Before European Hegemony,* 361.

110 Once Spain had settled Manila: Benito Legarda Jr., "Two and a Half Centuries of the Galleon Trade," *Philippine Studies,* December 1955, 351.

111 "They had watched the great powers": Michael H. Hunt and Steven I. Levine, *Arc of Empire: America's Wars in Asia from the Philippines to Vietnam* (Chapel Hill: University of North Carolina Press, 2012), 124.

111 These Westerners finally shook the Chinese: Finlay, "The Voyages of Zheng He," 328.

111 As late as the Opium Wars: Swanson, *Eighth Voyage of the Dragon,* 71.

111 As a result, the British were able: Dreyer, *Zheng He and the Oceans in the Early Ming Dynasty,* 180.

112 Out of deference, Ricci drew another map: Finlay, "The Voyages of Zheng He," 327.

112 "Information of Chinese participation": Derek Heng, *Sino-Malay Trade and Diplomacy from the Tenth Through the Fourteenth Century* (Athens: University of Ohio Press, 2009), 30–31.

113 "It is not possible to say": Wang Gungwu, *The Nanhai Trade: Early Chinese*

Trade in the South China Sea (Singapore: Eastern Universities Press, 2003), 59–60.

113 "The countries of the barbarians": Wolters, *The Fall of Srivijaya in Malay History,* 22.

114 This created lucrative opportunities for ports: Abu-Lughod, *Before European Hegemony,* 33.

114 This traditional desire on the part of the Chinese state: Wang Gungwu, "Chinese Political Culture and Scholarship About the Malay World," in *Chinese Studies of the Malay World: A Comparative Approach,* ed. Ding Choo Ming and Ooi Kee Beng (Singapore: Eastern Universities Press, 2003), 14.

115 Conflict in the north of China: Finlay, "The Voyages of Zheng He," 331.

116 "The South China Sea [became] the main route": Wang, *The Nanhai Trade: Early Chinese Trade in the South China Sea,* xvii.

116 By 1017, the maharajas who ruled the Srivijaya: Wolters, *The Fall of Srivijaya in Malay History,* 1.

117 The Arabs called Palembang: Ibid., 39.

117 In substance and in ceremony: Ibid., 26.

119 Places like Palembang and Jambi: Ibid., 42.

119 A little more than a century later: Ibid., 14.

123 In January 2016, a website of the Chinese Public Security Ministry: http://www.mps.gov.cn/n16/n1237/n1342/n803715/4991897.html.

124 This was reflected in the surprise huge success: Alan Wong, "Imagining Hong Kong's Future, Under China's Tightening Grasp," *New York Times,* January 29, 2016.

124 The city's role, she wrote: Abu-Lughod, *Before European Hegemony,* 153.

126 When the Singapore delegate made a statement: John Pomfret, "U.S. Takes a Tougher Tone with China," *Washington Post,* July 30, 2010.

CHAPTER FOUR: A PACIFIED SOUTH

131 "On his coronation in 1802": Benedict Anderson, *Imagined Communities: Reflections on the Origin and Spread of Nationalism* (London: Verso, 1983), 157.

131 It wasn't until the Tang dynasty: Keith Weller Taylor, *The Birth of Vietnam* (Berkeley: University of California Press, 1991), xx.

132 His "success rested not only on his ability": Ibid., 24–25.

133 Que's pessimistic memorial raises the question: Ibid., 79.

134 Such inviting conditions redoubled China's determination: Nayan Chanda, *Brother Enemy: The War After the War* (New York: Collier, 1986), 113.

136 "Our command must be to cut up your corpses": Ibid., 112.

137 As many as seven million Vietnamese: Geoff Wade, "Ming China and

Southeast Asia in the 15th Century: A Reappraisal," Asia Research Institute Working Paper Series No. 28, National University of Singapore, July 2004, 7.

137 "Schools were permitted to teach only in Chinese": Joseph Buttinger, *A Dragon Defiant: A Short History of Vietnam* (New York: Praeger, 1972), 45.

138 Champa, which had itself only recently: Henry J. Kenny, *Shadow of the Dragon: Vietnam's Continuing Struggle with China and the Implications for U.S. Foreign Policy* (Washington, DC: Brassey's, 2002), 33.

139 This feeling was based: Alexander Eng Ann Ong, "Contextualizing the Book-Burning Episode During the Ming Invasion and Occupation of Vietnam," in *Southeast Asia in the Fifteenth Century: The China Factor,* ed. Geoff Wade and Sun Laichen (Singapore: NUS Press, 2010), 155.

139 "I called myself emperor": Marc Mancall, "The Ch'ing Tribute System: An Interpretive Essay," in *The Chinese World Order: Traditional China's Foreign Relations,* ed. John King Fairbank (Cambridge, MA: Harvard University Press, 1968), 67.

140 Proper protocol theoretically called for: Alexander L. Vuving, "Operated by World Views and Interfaced by World Orders: Traditional and Modern Sino-Vietnamese Relations," in *Negotiating Asymmetry: China's Place in Asia,* ed. Anthony Reid and Zheng Yangwen (Honolulu: University of Hawaii Press, 2009), 82.

140 One traditional approach to this problem: Ibid., 81.

141 "What developed from this was a kind of play-acting": Ibid., 79–80.

141 "In the present circumstances": Chanda, *Brother Enemy,* 115.

142 Not long afterward, as he prepared to push southward: Ibid., 116.

143 "The Vietnamese court employed": Vuving, "Operated by World Views and Interfaced by World Orders," 79.

143 "Vietnamese history has flowed across Indochina": Chanda, *Brother Enemy,* 49.

143 "Our troops built two walls": Mancall, "The Ch'ing Tribute System," 68.

144 Following an unsuccessful Thai attempt: Chanda, *Brother Enemy,* 51–52.

145 "The French made no bones": Anderson, *Imagined Communities,* 129.

145 "I was dumbfounded, stunned": Odd Arne Westad, *Restless Empire: China and the World Since 1750* (New York: Basic Books, 2012), 51.

146 "Here is a big mansion": John King Fairbank, *The Cambridge History of China,* vol. 10, *Late Ch'ing, 1800–1911, Part I* (Cambridge: Cambridge University Press, 1978), 6.

146 During the Ming dynasty, a Chinese envoy: Anthony Reid, "Introduction— Negotiating Asymmetry: Parents, Brothers, Friends and Enemies," in Reid and Zheng, eds., *Negotiating Asymmetry,* 13.

147 On the return voyage home: Ibid., 18.

147 "We are a tributary state": Westad, *Restless Empire,* 96.

148 "Fight to keep our hair long": Chanda, *Brother Enemy,* 120.

148 Now, though, rather than mobilizing: David G. Marr, *Vietnamese Antico-lonialism: 1885–1925* (Berkeley: University of California Press, 1971), 26.

151 In the face of strong initial Soviet skepticism: Nicholas Khoo, *Sino-Soviet Rivalry and the Termination of the Sino-Vietnamese Alliance* (New York: Columbia University Press, 2011), 62–63.

151 In the 1960s, in a distinct echo: Jung Chang, *Mao: The Unknown Story* (London: Jonathan Cape, 2005), 597.

151 Mao's first ambassador to Hanoi: Keith Weller Taylor, *A History of the Vietnamese* (Cambridge: Cambridge University Press, 2013), 567.

152 "Indochina is devoid of decisive military objectives": Joint Chiefs of Staff JCS Memorandum for the Secretary of Defense, May 1954, in Defense Department, *Pentagon Papers,* vol. 9, 487.

152 Chinese engineering crews: Odd Arne Westad and Sophie Quinn, eds., *The Third Indochina War: Conflict Between China, Vietnam and Cambodia, 1972–1979* (London: Routledge, 2006), 35.

153 "Your struggle is our struggle": Khoo, *Sino-Soviet Rivalry and the Termination of the Sino-Vietnamese Alliance,* 102.

153 Vietnam had begun to lean so much: Westad and Quinn, eds., *The Third Indochina War,* 5.

153 In early 1969, Mao himself grumbled: Khoo, *Sino-Soviet Rivalry and the Termination of the Sino-Vietnamese Alliance,* 148.

154 "The Chinese Maoist leadership": Westad and Quinn, eds., *The Third Indochina War,* 5.

154 "Why are you afraid": "Discussion Between Zhou Enlai, Deng Xiaoping, Kang Sheng, Le Duan and Nguyen Duy Trinh," Wilson Center Digital Archive, International History Declassified, April 13, 1966.

156 "The Soviet revisionists are claiming": Ibid., 13.

157 "It is for the sake of our two parties' relations": Ibid., 6.

158 Because China cherished its image: Ibid., 14.

159 After a second series of clashes: Michael Pillsbury, *The Hundred-Year Marathon: China's Secret Strategy to Replace America as the Global Superpower* (New York: Henry Holt, 2015), 54.

159 "Recently Kissinger visited China": Westad and Quinn, eds., *The Third Indochina War,* 54.

160 "Ho is getting too big for his britches": Kenny, *Shadow of the Dragon,* 42–43.

161 "We sincerely wish that the South Vietnamese people": Chanda, *Brother Enemy,* 28.

161 "One of the great ironies of history": Ibid., 22.

161 In August of that year: Andrew Mertha, *Brothers in Arms: Chinese Aid to the Khmer Rouge, 1975–1979* (Ithaca, NY: Cornell University Press, 2014), 5.

162 "You have achieved with one stroke": Chanda, *Brother Enemy,* 17.

162 As late as 1944, only five hundred Khmer students: Ben Kiernan, *How Pol Pot Came to Power: A History of Communism in Kampuchea, 1930–1975* (London: Verso, 1985), xiii.

163 "The rulers would call themselves": Chanda, *Brother Enemy,* 116–17.

164 "On this occasion . . . Mao was particularly effusive": Kiernan, *How Pol Pot Came to Power,* 223.

164 Later, speaking to a member: Westad and Quinn, eds., *The Third Indochina War,* 164.

165 The Khmer Rouge may have possessed: Ibid., 166.

166 By the late 1950s, Beijing was already: Kiernan, *How Pol Pot Came to Power,* 182.

167 From its tiny and relatively recent beginnings: Ibid., 345.

169 Beijing simultaneously pressures South Korea: "Chinese Envoy Warns THAAD Deployment Would 'Destroy' Ties," *Chosun Ilbo* (English), February 24, 2016.

171 Hayton's story continues: Bill Hayton, *The South China Sea: The Struggle for Power in Asia* (New Haven, CT: Yale University Press, 2014), 75.

171 This was a self-serving statement: Minxin Pei, "China's Asia?," *Project Syndicate,* December 3, 2014.

173 This action was taken: Khoo, *Sino-Soviet Rivalry and the Termination of the Sino-Vietnamese Alliance,* 127.

174 For the leaders of Vietnam: Kenny, *Shadow of the Dragon,* 99.

174 In its propaganda, Hanoi began: Tuong Vu, "The Evolution of Modern Korea and Vietnam," in *Asia's Middle Powers?: The Identity and Regional Policy of South Korea and Vietnam,* ed. Joon-Woo Park, Gi-Wook Shin, and Donald W. Keyser (Stanford, CA: Shorenstein Asia-Pacific Research Center, 2013), 161.

175 Its economy was so weak that in 1975: Odd Arne Westad et al., eds., *77 Conversations Between China and Foreign Leaders on the Wars in Indochina, 1964–1977* (Washington, DC: Woodrow Wilson Center for Scholars, 1998), 194.

177 "Remember after defeating": Kenny, *Shadow of the Dragon,* 105.

177 "If China succeeds in its reform": Kenny, *Shadow of the Dragon,* 105.

178 "Tributary states lived next to": Yuan-kang Wang, *Harmony and War: Confucian Culture and Chinese Power Politics* (New York: Columbia University Press, 2011), 150.

179 From the start, Subic Bay: Peter J. Rimmer, "US Western Pacific Geostrategy: Subic Bay Before and After Withdrawal," *Marine Policy,* July 1997, 3.

179 In addition to fulfilling the age-old Russian dream: Ibid., 6.

180 Other Asian countries: David Shambaugh, *China Goes Global: The Partial Power* (New York: Oxford University Press, 2013), 116.

181 China "acted responsibly and in a stabilizing way": Ibid., 96.

181 Perhaps most important, Beijing: Andrew J. Nathan and Andrew Scobell, *China's Search for Security* (New York: Columbia University Press, 2012), 16.

182 Beijing does not report: Jonathan Holslag, *China's Coming War with Asia* (Malden, MA: Polity Press, 2015), 114.

183 This was the first big step: Ibid., 109–10.

185 Beyond formal defense alliances like these: Andrew J. Nathan and Andrew Scobell, *China's Search for Security* (New York: Columbia University Press, 2012), 6.

CHAPTER FIVE: SONS OF HEAVEN, SETTING SUNS

188 "We have to make sure": Tanya Somanader, "President Obama: "Writing the Rules for 21st Century Trade," The White House, February 18, 2015.

188 "In terms of our rebalance": "Felicia Schwartz, "U.S. Defense Chief Heads East, Talking Tough on China," *Wall Street Journal*, April 6, 2015.

189 According to Tokyo: Sheila A. Smith, *Intimate Rivals: Japanese Domestic Politics and a Rising China* (New York: Columbia University Press, 2014), 109.

190 "It is true that the two sides": Ibid., 102.

190 Japan remained the number one provider: Ibid., 35.

191 This obliged Japan's foreign ministry spokesman: David E. Sanger, "China Party Chief Visits Japan Amid Tensions in Relations," *New York Times*, April 7, 1992.

192 Then he came to more difficult matters: Robert Benjamin, "Japanese Emperor Deplores War Pain RTC Monarch Avoids Apology to China," *Baltimore Sun*, October 24, 1992.

192 In 1993, speaking in his inaugural news conference: James Sterngold, "Tokyo Journal: Admitting Guilt for the War: An Outraged Dissent," *New York Times*, August 21, 1993.

192 "The world has seen fifty years elapse": "Statement by Prime Minister Tomiichi Murayama 'On the occasion of the 50th anniversary of the war's end' (15 August 1995)," Ministry of Foreign Affairs of Japan, http://www.mofa.go.jp/announce/press/pm/murayama/9508.html.

196 During the fourteenth century: Joshua A. Fogel, *Articulating the Sinosphere: Sino-Japanese Relations in Space and Time* (Cambridge, MA: Harvard University Press, 2009), 26.

196 "Now the world is the world's world": Yuan-kang Wang, *Harmony and*

War: Confucian Culture and Chinese Power Politics (New York: Columbia University Press, 2011), 149.

197 "It is my lifelong goal": Ibid., 174.

197 This was because "the Chinese negotiator, Shen Weijing": Ibid., 176.

197 When his first invasion stalled: Marius B. Jansen, *The Making of Modern Japan* (Cambridge, MA: Harvard University Press, 2000), 20.

198 To this, a Japanese daimyo: Ibid., 87.

199 As a consequence, Japan is facing: Smith, *Intimate Rivals*, 145.

200 As a Japanese analyst would tell: "Dangerous Waters: China-Japan Relations on the Rocks," International Crisis Group, April 8, 2013, 30.

202 "Little was made in the People's Republic": Ian Buruma, "The Joys and Perils of Victimhood," *New York Review of Books*, April 8, 1999.

203 Meeting with Japanese prime minister Kakuei Tanaka: Geremie R. Barmé, "Mirrors of History: On a Sino-Japanese Moment and Some Antecedents," *Japan Focus*, May 16, 2005.

205 In 1971, a then-secret analysis by the CIA: "The Senkaku Islands Dispute: Oil Under Troubled Waters," Central Intelligence Agency, Directorate of Intelligence, May 1971.

205 And most recently, the U.S. Energy Information Administration: "East China Sea," Analysis Brief, U.S. Energy Information Administration, September 2012.

205 The UN survey also said: "Geological Structure and Some Water Characteristics of the East China Sea and the Yellow Sea," Economic Commission for Asia and the Far East, 41.

205 In each case, Tokyo demanded a settlement: Reinhard Drifte, "The Senkaku/Diaoyu Islands Territorial Dispute Between Japan and China: Between the Materialization of the 'China Threat' and Japan 'Reversing the Outcome of World War II,'" *UNISCI Discussion Papers*, no. 32 (May 2013): 26.

207 When the new DPJ prime minister: "China's Hu, Japan's Hatoyama Agree to Extend Thaw in Relations," Bloomberg, September 22, 2009.

209 The next day, the kindly man: Smith, *Intimate Rivals*, 210.

210 In speaking before the Diet: Drifte, "The Senkaku/Diaoyu Islands Territorial Dispute," 34.

210 Said in a more familiar American idiom: Ibid., 20.

211 To emphasize China's new assertiveness: Kenji Minemura, "China to Establish Permanent Senkaku Patrols," *Asahi Shimbun*, December 20, 2010.

211 Washington took no position: Lachland Carmichael, "Clinton Urges Dialogue to Resolve China-Japan Row," Agence France-Presse, September 24, 2010.

211 The provocation was almost certainly the work: Giulio Pugliese, "Japan

Between a China Question and China Obsession," in *Asia Maior,* ed. Michelguglielmo Torri and Nicola Mocci, vol. 25, 2014 (Bologna: Emil di Odoya, 2015), 7.

212 Internal dissent broke out: Xinjun Zhang, "Why the 2008 Sino-Japanese Consensus on the East China Sea Has Stalled: Good Faith and Reciprocity Considerations in Interim Measures Pending a Maritime Boundary Delimitation," *Ocean Development and International Law* 42 (2011): 57.

213 That same year saw investment soar by 50 percent: Drifte, "The Senkaku/ Diaoyu Islands Territorial Dispute," 34.

214 Abe and his allies called for: Smith, *Intimate Rivals,* 241.

216 In early September, Prime Minister Noda: "Dangerous Waters: China-Japan Relations on the Rocks," 8.

216 "Japanese officials had been surprised": Ibid., 8.

217 "Top leaders delivered harsh rebukes": Ibid., 10.

217 Japanese banks reportedly came under: "Protests Flare in China on Contentious Anniversary. The Pretext for Invasion 81 Years Ago Fuels Rallies in 125 Cities," *Japan Times,* September 19, 2012.

218 This shift began in 1992: Pugliese, "Japan Between a China Question and China Obsession," 5.

220 The following January, China deployed: Paul H. B. Godwin and Alice L. Miller, "China's Forbearance Has Limits: Chinese Threat and Retaliation Signaling and Its Implications for a Sino-American Military Confrontation," Institute for National Strategic Studies, *China Strategic Perspectives,* no. 6 (April 2013).

220 In announcing the move: Teddy Ng, "New City to Run Disputed Island Chains," *South China Morning Post,* June 22, 2012.

221 Shinzo Abe, a deeply conservative politician: Alexis Dudden, "The Shape of Japan to Come," *New York Times,* January 16, 2015.

221 As even a casual student of Japan's wartime history: Max Fisher, "Japan's Leader Revives Dark Memories of Imperial-Era Biological Experiments in China," *Washington Post,* May 18, 2013.

221 For years, Abe had spoken proudly: Ian Buruma, "East Asia's Sins of the Fathers," *Project Syndicate,* December 15, 2013.

222 Tactics like these injected yet more energy: Herbert P. Bix, "Hirohito and the Making of Modern Japan," Japan Policy Research Institute, Occasional Paper No. 17, September 2000.

222 Years later, in a 2006 book: Yuka Hayashi, "For Japan's Shinzo Abe, Unfinished Family Business," *Wall Street Journal,* December 11, 2014.

224 In 2000, Japan's defense budget: Philippe de Koning and Phillip Y. Lipscy, "The Land of the Sinking Sun: Is Japan's Military Weakness Putting America in Danger?," *Foreign Policy,* August 5, 2013.

224 Newspaper headlines focused on flashy hardware: "Abe Seeking Record ¥4.98 Trillion in Defense Spending to Counter China," AFP-Jiji Press, January 14, 2015.

224 During the past generation: Clifton B. Parker: "Stanford Economist Warns of Japanese Fiscal Crisis," *Stanford News,* March 27, 2014.

225 "Because of declining procurement budgets": Koning and Lipscy, "The Land of the Sinking Sun."

226 The aim was to create a legal framework: Ministry of Foreign Affairs of Japan, "Cabinet Decision on Development of Seamless Security Legislation to Ensure Japan's Survival and Protect Its People," July 1, 2014.

226 At a news conference later: Toko Sekiguchi, "Japanese Legal Experts Criticize Abe's Defense Push," *Wall Street Journal,* June 15, 2012.

226 "It is not my intention to hurt the feelings": Statement by Prime Minister Abe—Pledge for Everlasting Peace, December 26, 2013.

227 "I want to establish the existence": "Abe Praised Class-A War Criminals for Being 'Foundation' of Japan's Prosperity," *Asahi Shimbun,* August 27, 2014.

227 "I do not go to Yasukuni Shrine": Jennifer Lind, "Beware of the Tomb of the Known Soldier," *Global Asia* 8, no. 1 (Spring 2013).

227 "I don't take orders from anyone": Wikileaks, "Daily Summary of Japanese Press 08/15/06," http://wikileaks.org/cable/2006/08/06TOKYO4629.html.

227 "The Chinese people cannot be insulted": "Outrage Still Festers over Abe Shrine Visit," *China Daily,* December 30, 2013.

228 "In the Harry Potter story": Liu Xiaoming, "China and Britain Won the War Together," *Telegraph,* January 1, 2014.

228 "Although China has so far refused to enable dialogue": Justin McCurry, "Japan Hits Back over Voldemort Comparison," *Guardian,* January 6, 2014.

228 "China's patriotic education campaign": William A. Callahan, "The Negative Soft Power of the China Dream—II," *Asan Forum,* March 2, 2015.

229 "The Holocaust is a no-go area": Ben Blanchard and Michael Martina, "China, Eyeing Japan, Seeks WWII Focus for Xi During Germany Visit," Reuters, February 23, 2014.

229 Commenting on Abe's failure: Edward N. Luttwak, "What Should Obama Say About China in Japan," *ChinaFile,* May 22, 2014.

230 In an unusually strong statement of public criticism: "The Legacy of Historical Revisionism," *Asan Forum,* Sept. 17, 2014.

230 In virtually the next breath, however: White House, Office of the Press Secretary, April 24, 2014.

231 "The Alliance will respond to situations": Ministry of Defense, "The Guidelines for Japan-U.S. Defense Cooperation," April 27, 2015, http://www.mod.go.jp/e/d_act/anpo/shishin_20150427e.html.

233 Further signs of public anxiousness and disapproval: Sheila A. Smith, "Defining Defense: Japan's Military Identity Crisis," *World Politics Review,* May 12, 2015.

234 Beijing, he said, "attaches importance": "China's Media Claims Victory After Japan 'Agreement' on Isle, Historical Issues," AFP-Jiji Press, November 8, 2014.

234 "We hope that the Japanese side": Christopher Bodeen, "Chinese, Japanese Foreign Ministers Meet at APEC," Associated Press, November 8, 2014.

234 As the Australian historian Martin Stuart-Fox wrote: Martin Stuart-Fox, *A Short History of China and Southeast Asia: Tribute, Trade and Influence* (Crows Nest, NSW: Allen & Unwin, 2003), 78.

234 "It is certainly not the case": "Japan, China Both Claim Advantage in Pre-Summit Document," *Asahi Shimbun,* November 8, 2014.

235 "When foreign dignitaries come calling": David Shambaugh, *China Goes Global: The Partial Power* (New York: Oxford University Press, 2013), 57.

CHAPTER SIX: CLAIMS AND MARKERS

238 According to one description: Jane Perlez and Keith Bradsher, "In High Seas, China Moves Unilaterally," *New York Times,* May 9, 2014.

238 The rig was accompanied: Minnie Chan, "PLA Navy Sends Two of Its Biggest Ships to Protect Oil Rig, Vietnamese Media Report," *South China Morning Post,* May 16, 2014.

239 Suddenly, with Xi Jinping at the helm in Beijing: Perlez and Bradsher, "In High Seas, China Moves Unilaterally."

239 All of these offers were snubbed: Carl Thayer, "Four Reasons China Removed Oil Rig HYSY-951 Sooner Than Planned," *Diplomat,* July 22, 2014.

240 Some went further still: Ibid.

240 President Truong Tan Sang praised: Alexander Vuving, "Did China Blink in the South China Sea?," *National Interest,* July 27, 2014.

241 China's state councilor for foreign affairs: Thayer, "Four Reasons China Removed Oil Rig HYSY-951 Sooner Than Planned."

241 According to published reports: Vuving, "Did China Blink in the South China Sea?"

242 CNOOC officials could boast: Shannon Tiezzi, "China Discovers Gas Field in the South China Sea," *Diplomat,* September 16, 2014.

242 Leaving no doubt about the implications: Ibid.

243 "The March to June period": "Stirring Up the South China Sea (III): A Fleeting Opportunity for Calm," International Crisis Group, May 7, 2015, 8.

243 Li tapped into one of the most venerated myths: David Tweed, "China Seeks Great Power Status After Sea Retreat," Bloomberg, July 3, 2014.

243 "The Chinese Empire, at its peak": Liu Mingfu, *The China Dream: Great Power Thinking and Strategic Posture in the Post-American Era* (New York: CN Times Books, 2015), 86–87.

244 "In East Asia's tribute system": Ibid., 100–101.

244 "A review of history shows": "China Will Never Use Force to Achieve Goals, Xi Vows," *South China Morning Post,* November 17, 2014.

246 By the time of Xi's speech, though: Ibid.

246 ASEAN could only muster a statement: "ASEAN Concerned over China's Sea Disputes," Agence France-Presse, May 13, 2014.

246 This was widely perceived to be: Stuart White, "China Gives $150 Million to Cambodia," *Phnom Penh Post,* May 21, 2104.

246 "we also cannot ignore": David Tweed and David Roman, "South China Sea Talks End in Disarray as China Lobbies Laos," Bloomberg, June 14, 2016.

247 In fact, Southeast Asian societies have never shown much enthusiasm: Stuart-Fox, *A Short History of China and Southeast Asia,* 67–68.

248 There, little noticed, it enlarged a harbor: Bill Hayton, *The South China Sea: The Struggle for Power in Asia* (New Haven, CT: Yale University Press, 2014), 79.

248 When Mao died in 1976: Andrew G. Walder, *China Under Mao: A Revolution Derailed* (Cambridge, MA: Harvard University Press, 2015), 324.

248 The overhaul of the PLA Navy: Hayton, *The South China Sea,* 80.

249 Item four aimed to give a brief history: Zheng Wang, *Never Forget National Humiliation: Historical Memory in Chinese Politics and Foreign Relations* (New York: Columbia University Press, 2012), 80–81.

249 Unusually, for a civilian research center: Hayton, *The South China Sea,* 81.

250 It "shows the Vietnamese force": Ibid., 83.

251 Similar construction has also been carried out: Victor Robert Lee, "China's New Military Installations in the Disputed Spratly Islands," March 16, 2015, https://medium.com/satellite-image-analysis/china-s-new-military -installations-in-the-spratly-islands-satellite-image-update-1169bacc 07f9.

251 In a sure indication of the importance: Bree Feng, "China's Naval Chief Visited Disputed Islands in the South China Sea, Taiwan Says," *New York Times,* October 16, 2014.

252 "There is a need for a base": David S. Cloud, "China's Man-Made Islands in Disputed Waters Raise Worries," *Los Angeles Times,* January 28, 2015.

255 "What China is doing right now": Alexander Vuving, IR.Asia, May 27, 2015, http://www.international-relations.asia/alexander-vuving-apcss/#_ftn1.

257 Much less widely noted than the infrastructure element: Martha Brill Olcott, "China's Unmatched Influence in Central Asia," Carnegie Endowment for International Peace, September 18, 2013.

257 By this, he meant: Jeremy Page, "China Sees Itself at Center of New Asian Order," *Wall Street Journal,* November 9, 2014.

258 By one estimate, China's new initiatives: Feng Zhang, "Beijing's Master Plan for the South China Sea: China Has Far Greater Ambitions for the Region Than Just Reclaiming Some Tiny Islands," *Foreign Policy,* June 23, 2015.

258 On the strength of such numbers: Page, "China Sees Itself at Center of New Asian Order."

258 "One Belt One Road is an attempt": These comments originally appeared in the Chinese-language website of the *Financial Times,* December 30, 2014. The English translation here is courtesy of David Cowhig, https://gaodawei.wordpress.com/2015/10/24/cass-scholar-xue-li-the-foreign-affairs-risks-for-china-of-the-silk-road-economic-belt-and-the-21st-century-maritime-silk-road/.

259 China initially refused to cooperate on such a code: "Stirring Up the South China Sea (III)," 26.

259 When China first filed notice with the UN: Ibid., 24.

260 The meeting focused in unusually detailed ways: "Xi Steps Up Efforts to Shape a China-Centered Regional Order," *China Brief* 13, issue 22, Jamestown Foundation, November 7, 2013.

260 Such results were not to be obtained: Ibid.

260 This was an incentive-based approach: Ibid.

261 "Xi Jinping would like to see": Ju Jiejin, "China Secures Veto Power as Members Sign Up to New Bank," Bloomberg, June 28, 2015.

261 At a news conference in Beijing: Page, "China Sees Itself at Center of New Asian Order."

261 But in the spring of 2015: "Remarks by President Obama and Prime Minister Abe of Japan in Joint Press Conference," White House, April 28, 2015, https://www.whitehouse.gov/the-press-office/2015/04/28/remarks-president-obama-and-prime-minister-abe-japan-joint-press-confere.

262 "The thing that upset us": Demetri Sevastopulo, "US Takes Stern Line on UK's Shift to China," *Financial Times,* October 20, 2015.

262 They had proclaimed into existence: Charles Clover and Lucy Hornby, "China's Great Game: Road to a New Empire," *Financial Times,* October 12, 2015.

262 "Military alliances are exclusive in nature": Fu Ying, "Answering Four Key Questions About China's Rise," *Huffington Post,* October 17, 2014.

262 On that occasion, Xi had spoken not only: Olcott, "China's Unmatched Influence in Central Asia."

264 "In both the eastern Ukraine and the South China Sea": David Brunnstrom, "U.S. Compares China's South China Sea Moves to Russia's in Ukraine," Reuters, June 26, 2015.

CONCLUSION

265 Commenting on the new radar stations: Karen de Young, "Beijing's Actions in South China Sea Aimed at 'Hegemony,' U.S. Admiral Says," *Washington Post,* February 23, 2016.

265 "have to believe in a flat Earth": David Axe, "China's Overhyped Submarine Threat," *The Diplomat,* October 20, 2011.

266 This turn of events was anticipated a half century ago: Wang Gungwu, "Early Ming Relations with Southeast Asia: A Background Essay," in *The Chinese World Order: Traditional China's Foreign Relations,* ed. John King Fairbank (Cambridge, MA: Harvard University Press, 1968).

267 Is it plausible to think: Stephen Brooks and William Wohlforth, "The Rise and Fall of the Great Powers in the Twenty-First Century: China's Rise and the Fate of America's Global Position," *International Security,* Winter 2015.

267 After a crisis with China over Taiwan in 1996: "Sea Power: Who Rules the Waves?," *Economist,* October 17, 2015.

268 "For both the United States and China": Michael D. Swaine, "Beyond American Predominance in the Western Pacific: The Need for a Stable U.S.-China Balance of Power," Carnegie Endowment for International Peace, April 20, 2015.

268 "Riders in a crowded elevator cabin": Edward Luttwak, *The Rise of China vs. the Logic of Strategy* (Cambridge, MA: Belknap Press of Harvard University Press, 2012), 7.

269 In April 2016, one of the largest destroyers: Yukio Mukai, "MSDF Vessels Call at South China Sea Ports," *Yomiuri Shimbun,* April 4, 2016.

271 "One of China's greatest strengths": Andrew S. Erickson, "China's Naval Modernization: The Implications of Seapower," *World Politics Review,* September 23, 2014.

272 This was in accordance with a major new military policy document: China's 2015 Defense White Paper, via Andrew Erickson.

272 Although China is the only conceivable potential challenger: Brooks and Wohlforth, "The Rise and Fall of the Great Powers in the Twenty-First Century."

273 "is still more suited to fighting": Stephen Brooks and William Wohlforth,

America Abroad: The United States' Role in the 21st Century (New York: Oxford, 2016), 49.

274 "[T]he premise of the denial strategy": Ibid.

275 The most salient U.S. goal: Howard W. French, "China's Dangerous Game," *Atlantic,* November 2014.

276 "China's immediate periphery": Andrew J. Nathan and Andrew Scobell, *China's Search for Security* (New York: Columbia University Press, 2012), 5.

276 "Although no country is immune": Ibid., 19.

278 "Beijing will run around": E-mail exchange with Michael Pettis, August 25, 2015.

278 "The Marshall Plan rebuilt": Xue Li, "The Foreign Affairs Risks for China of the 'Silk Road Economic Belt' and the '21st-Century Maritime Silk Road,'" December 30, 2014, translated from the *Financial Times* Chinese-language website by David Cowhig, https://gaodawei.wordpress.com/2015/10/24/cass-scholar-xue-li-the-foreign-affairs-risks-for-china-of-the-silk-road-economic-belt-and-the-21st-century-maritime-silk-road/.

278 "A very large economic entity": "Industry in China: The March of the Zombies," *Economist,* February 27, 2016.

279 As a German economist: Author's interview with an economist who requested that he not be identified by name.

279 A 2007 paper by Mark L. Haas: Mark L. Haas, "A Geriatric Peace: The Future of U.S. Power in a World of Aging Populations," *International Security* 32, no. 1 (Summer 2007).

280 According to the *South China Morning Post*: Jun Mai, "Time to End China's One-Child Policy Urgently: Government Advisers Warn of Demographic Crisis Ahead," *South China Morning Post,* October 21, 2015.

280 "The government recognizes": Author's interview with Zheng Zhenzhen.

280 The number of young males in the country: Nicholas Eberstadt, "Asia-Pacific Demographics in 2010-2040: Implications for Strategic Balance," in *Asia's Rising Power and America's Continued Purpose,* ed. Ashley J. Tellis, Andrew Marble, and Travis Tanner (Seattle: National Bureau of Asian Research, 2010), 243.

281 "People say we can be two to three times the size": Didi Kirsten Tatlow, "Yi Fuxian, Critic of China's Birth Policy, Returns as an Invited Guest," *New York Times,* March 23, 2016.

281 What is worse, China's retirees: "China's Achilles Heel: A Comparison with America Reveals a Deep Flaw in China's Model of Growth," *Economist,* April 21, 2012.

281 In December 2015, Du Yang: Author's interview.

281 China's "median age": Mark L. Haas, "America's Golden Years?: U.S. Security in an Aging World," in *Political Demography: How Population Changes*

Are Reshaping International Security and National Politics, ed. Jack A. Goldstone, Eric P. Kaufmann, and Monica Duffy Toft (Oxford: Oxford University Press, 2012), 57.

282 Presently, nine million Chinese: "State of Minds: China Is Ill Prepared for a Consequence of Aging: Lots of People with Dementia," *Economist,* February 20, 2016.

282 Another recent study has found that 11.6 percent: Yu Xu, Limin Wang et al., "Prevalence and Control of Diabetes in Chinese Adults," *Journal of the American Medical Association,* September 4, 2013.

284 The liberal international order: John G. Ikenberry, "The Future of the Liberal World Order: Internationalism After America," *Foreign Affairs,* May–June 2011.

284 As even Yan Xuetong: Yan Xuetong, *Ancient Chinese Thought, Modern Chinese Power* (Princeton, NJ: Princeton University Press, 2011), 13.

Index

Page numbers in *italics* refer to illustrations.

Crescent Group, 170
Cuarteron Reef, 250, 251
Cuba, 66, 176, 269
Cultural Revolution, 152, 153, 165, 175,
    190, 205
Cultural Revolution Small Leading
    Group, 154
Czechoslovakia, Soviet invasion of, 158

Dadu (Beiping), *see* Beijing
da Gama, Vasco, 90–1, 92, 94, 108, 109
Đại Việt, *see* Vietnam
Defense Department, U.S., 188, 231, 264
de Koning, Philippe, 225
Democratic Party of Japan (DPJ), 207,
    208, 209, 210, 213, 221, 223
Deng Xiaoping, 154–5, 164, 179–80, 187,
    190, 202, 204, 205, 218, 248, 249, 251,
    282
Diaoyu, *see* Senkaku Islands
Diaoyutai State Guest House, 235
Dien Bien Phu, 152
Diffie, Bailey W., 91, 108
Diplomatic Documents of Qing, 70
Djibouti, 275
Dongfeng-21, 272
Dongfeng-26, 272
Dongguan, 122
Dong Nai Province, 240
Dong Quan, 138
*Dragon Defiant, A: A Short History of
    Vietnam* (Buttinger), 137
Dreyer, Edward L., 96, 97, 104
Dreyer, June Teufel, 112*n*
Dupuy, Florian, 58
Dupuy, Pierre-Marie, 58
Dutch, East Asian colonialism of, 45, 95,
    111, 178
Duterte, Rodrigo R., 84, 85, 86
Du Yang, 281

East Africa, 91, 109, 257
East Asia, 10–11, 15, 32, 50, 63, 71, 92, 94,
    110, 119, 178, 197, 199, 243, 244, 267
  China's reassertion of power in, 9–11,
    15–16, 27, 28–30, 53, 54, 72–3, 172,
    177, 180–1, 230, 238, 265–6, 267–8,
    276–7
  as Chinese hegemon, 4–8, 9
  financial crisis of 1997–98 in, 181
  international system and, 9
  interstate alliances in, 269, 275
  nadir of Chinese power in, 8–9
  Spanish trading in, 110
  Western imperialism in, 9, 71, 102; *see
    also specific countries*
East Asia, U.S. power in, 14, 65–8, 97–8,
    178–9, 185, 187–8, 231, 267–8, 275
  supplanting of, as Chinese goal, 11–12,
    30, 53, 172, 179–80, 208, 236, 253–4,
    256, 260, 264, 265, 275–6
East China Sea, 34, 211, 213, 221, 231,
    266*n*
  China-Japan relations in, 199–200,
    204–5
  China's reassertion of power in, 18,
    230
  Chinese territorial claims in, 205, 207,
    212
  gas fields in, 20
  Japanese claims in, 212
  proposed Chinese-Japanese oil and gas
    exploration in, 204–5, 206–7, 209, 211,
    233
  Ryukyu Islands in, *see* Ryukyu Islands
  Senkaku Islands in, *see* Senkaku Islands
East China Sea Agreement, 209
Eastern Europe, 201
East Europe, fall of Communism in, 201
Economist, 28, 278–9, 281
economy, Chinese
  aging population and, 277, 279–82
  Asian financial crisis and, 181
  in Cultural Revolution, 175
  excess production in, 278–9
  Hong Kong and, 121–3
  Japanese investments in, 182, 190–1,
    194, 199, 202
  Japanese trade and, 213
  Japan surpassed by, 16, 187
  as manufacturing powerhouse, 181, 182,
    273

ILLUSTRATION CREDITS

Shuri Castle, Okinawa, built ca. 1500: Howard W. French

The Philippine navy's BRP *Sierra Madre*: *Washington Post*

Shakedown cruise of China's first aircraft carrier, the *Liaoning*:
Associated Press

Edwin Seracarpio: Howard W. French

Statue of Saint Francis Xavier, St. Paul's Church, Malacca: Howard W. French

Traffic roundabout with large-scale model of a treasure ship: Howard W.
French

Chinese cemetery from its war with Vietnam: Howard W. French

Okinawa cemetery from World War II: Howard W. French

Xi-Abe meeting in Beijing: Associated Press

Anti-Japanese demonstration in Shanghai: Howard W. French

Dredging operations and island building in the South China Sea, Mischief
Reef: Victor Robert Lee

Subic Bay, Philippines: Reuters/Erik De Castro

Confrontation with Vietnam over Chinese deep-sea oil rig deployment:
AP Photo/Vietnam Coast Guard

Obama-Xi summit at Sunnylands, California: White House Photo, Pete Souza

Printed in the United States
by Baker & Taylor Publisher Services